Mastering
Shakespeare

Mastering Shakespeare

An
ACTING CLASS
in
Seven Scenes

Scott Kaiser

ALLWORTH PRESS
NEW YORK

07 06 05 04 03   5 4 3 2 1

Published by Allworth Press
An imprint of Allworth Communications, Inc.
10 East 23rd Street, New York, NY 10010

Cover design by Derek Bacchus
Interior layout and design by Sharp Des!gns, Inc.

Cover photo: Dan Donohue as Henry V, at the Oregon Shakespeare Festival.
Photo by Andrée Lanthier.
Cover photo of book and page by Igor Dravinsky.

ISBN: 1-58115-308-2

Library of Congress Cataloging-in-Publication Data
Kaiser, Scott.
Mastering Shakespeare: an acting class in seven scenes / Scott Kaiser.
p. cm.
Includes index.
ISBN 1-58115-308-2 (pbk.)
1. Shakespeare, William, 1564–1616—Dramatic production—Drama.
2. Method (Acting)—Drama. 3. Acting—Drama. I. Title.
PS3611.A67M37 2003
812'.6—dc22
2003018218

Printed in Canada

To
Nanabel,
Mom,
Cathy,
&
Rachel

Contents

Acknowledgements / *ix*
Index of Speeches and Exercises / *xi*
Introduction / *xiii*
Persons of the Play / *xvii*

SCENE 1: THE ART OF ORCHESTRATION / *1*
Speech Measures
Punctuation
Operative Words

SCENE 2: FOCAL POINTS / *33*
Scene Partners
Audience
Audience and Self
Multiple Focal Points

SCENE 3: IMAGES / *69*
Image to Image, with a Single Focal Point
Image to Image, with Multiple Focal Points
Image and Partner
Image and Audience

SCENE 4: SPOKEN SUBTEXT / *97*
Head, Heart, Guts, and Groin
Secret Fears
Secret Hopes and Dreams
Secret Intentions
Realizations
Decisions

SCENE 5: ACTIONS / _139_
Purely Physical Actions
Opposing Actions
Laban Effort Actions
Psycho-physical Verbs
Psycho-physical Verbs with Multiple Focal Points
Qualities to Actions

SCENE 6: COMPLEX ORCHESTRATION / _183_
The Actor's Toolkit
The Right Tool
Spontaneity
Emotion

SCENE 7: TOWARDS PERFORMANCE / _223_
Previsualization
Scene Objectives
Act Objectives
Play Objectives
Super-objectives
Questions and Answers

Index / _261_

Acknowledgments

I'd like to thank Robert L. Hobbs, upon whose work and teaching practices this book is based; Barry Kraft, Oregon Shakespeare Festival dramaturg, actor, and gadfly, for his extraordinary knowledge, passion, and generosity, as well as his invaluable feedback on the manuscript; John Sipes, OSF Movement and Fight Director, for years of unwavering support and friendship; Rebecca Clark, for her insightful notes on the manuscript; Linda Alper, for her advice and counsel; Elizabeth Norment, for her feedback and support; Libby Appel, Artistic Director of the Oregon Shakespeare Festival; Kenneth Washington, Director of Company Development at the Guthrie Theater; David Dreyfoos, OSF Producing Director; Nicole Potter at Allworth Press; Hilary Tate; Jennifer Reiley; Amy Richard; Kit Leary; Sheila Leary; the actors at the Oregon Shakespeare Festival, past, present, and future; the students of the Guthrie Experience for Actors in Training, past, present, and future; and finally, the master teachers upon whose writings this work is based: Constantin Stanislavsky, Richard Boleslavsky, Robert Lewis, and Rudolf Laban.

A Note About the Text

The Shakespearean texts used in this book are based upon production scripts performed at the Oregon Shakespeare Festival over the last two decades, and represent the experience, creativity, and hard work of many directors, dramaturgs, voice and text directors, actors, stage managers, assistant stage managers, production stage managers, and interns. I thank them all, too numerous to name, for their dedication to the language of the plays and to the most demanding and ephemeral of all art forms, the live theater.

Index of Speeches & Exercises

All's Well that Ends Well
Helena (1.3)
"Then I confess"
Secret Fears, p.105

Antony and Cleopatra
Cleopatra (1.3)
"But here comes Antony"
Secret Intentions, p.117

As You Like It
Phoebe (3.5)
"Think not I love him"
Opposing Actions, p.145

Coriolanus
Coriolanus (4.4)
"A goodly city is this Antium"
Scene Objectives, p.225

Cymbeline
Imogen (3.6)
"I see a man's life"
The Actor's Toolkit, p.183

Hamlet
Gertrude (5.1)
"One woe doth tread upon another"
Image to Image with a Single Focal Point, p.66

Henry the Fifth
Chorus (4.1)
"Now entertain conjecture"
Image and Audience, p.88

Henry the Fourth, Part Two
Lady Percy (2.3)
"O, yet, for God's sake"
Emotion, p.213

Henry the Sixth, Part One
Joan la Pucelle (1.2)
"Dauphin, I am by birth"
Qualities to Actions, p.175

Henry the Sixth, Part Three
King Henry (2.5)
"Oh God! methinks it were a happy life"
Speech Measures, p.2

Julius Caesar
Brutus (2.1)
"It must be by his death"
Operative Words, p.20

King John
Lewis (5.2)
"Your grace shall pardon me"
Psycho-physical Verbs, p.160

King Lear
Edgar (2.3)
"I heard myself proclaimed"
Decisions, p.131

Love's Labor's Lost
Berowne (4.3)
"Have at you then, affection's men-at-arms"
Scene Partners, p.33

Macbeth
Macbeth (2.1)
"Is this a dagger?"
The Right Tool, p.192

Measure for Measure
Angelo (2.2)
"What's this?"
Head, Heart, Guts, and
Groin, p.97

Merchant of Venice, The
Portia (3.2)
"I pray you tarry"
Secret Hopes and Dreams,
p.111

Midsummer Night's Dream, A
Oberon (2.1)
"My gentle Puck, come hither"
Image and Partner, p.81

Much Ado about Nothing
Benedick (2.3)
"This can be no trick"
Audience and Self, p.49

Othello
Iago (2.3)
"And what's he then?"
Audience, p.42

Pericles
Pericles (2.1)
"An armor, friends?"
Super-objectives, p.244

Richard the Second
King Richard (3.3)
"We are amaz'd"
Laban Effort Actions, p.152

Richard the Third
Lady Anne (1.2)
"Foul devil"
Multiple Focal Points, p.55

Romeo and Juliet
Juliet (3.2)
"Gallop apace"
Image to Image with
Multiple Focal Points, p.73

Tempest, The
Trinculo (2.2)
"Here's neither bush nor
shrub"
Spontaneity, p.205

Titus Andronicus
Tamora (1.1)
"My worthy lord"
Act Objectives, p.231

Troilus and Cressida
Cressida (3.2)
"Boldness comes to me now"
Purely Physical Actions,
p.139

Twelfth Night
Viola (2.2)
"I left no ring with her"
Realizations, p.124

Two Gentlemen of Verona, The
Julia (1.2)
"O hateful hands!"
Psycho-physical Verbs, with
Multiple Focal Points, p.169

Two Noble Kinsmen, The
Arcite (2.3)
"Banish'd the kingdom?"
Play Objectives, p.237

Winter's Tale, The
Hermione (2.2)
"Sir, spare your threats"
Punctuation, p.10

Introduction

When it comes to advice on how to act Shakespeare, the English have recently acquired a virtual monopoly. Nearly all of the books written in the last quarter-century about how to act Shakespeare are written by English authors, like John Barton, Cicely Berry, and Patsy Rodenburg.

Mind you, these are wonderful, groundbreaking books, full of insights into Shakespeare's plays, his characters, and his language—how to analyze them, how to physicalize them, and how to speak them.

American actors have developed an appetite for these books because they provide the kind of practical, craft-based, no-nonsense advice about Shakespeare that they sorely need. But more than that, American actors have an affinity for these books because they seem to offer a set of clues to the secret, the secret which English actors seem to know from birth—the secret to mastering Shakespeare.

Shakespeare-based movies of the past two decades serve to highlight this notion—that Shakespeare is mother's milk to the English actor, and ipecac to the American actor. Talented American actors like Claire Danes, Leo DiCaprio, Michael Keaton, Jack Lemmon, Jessica Lange, and Alicia Silverstone seem to blur when sharing the silver screen with classically trained English actors like Anthony Hopkins, Kenneth Branagh, Derek Jacobi, Paul Scofield, Emma Thompson, and Judi Dench in film versions of *Romeo and Juliet*, *Much Ado about Nothing*, *Hamlet*, *Love's Labors Lost*, and *Titus Andronicus*.

Never mind that these American actors were cast in their roles not for their proficiency in speaking four-hundred-year-old verse, but for their box-office appeal on our side of the pond. When it comes to Shakespeare, the Brits just seem to have "it" and we don't.

It would be easy to say that the reason is training. That the American actor simply does not receive the extensive training in voice, speech, dramatic verse, and classical texts that the English actor does. But this is simply not true.

Since the Thatcher government pulled the plug on aid to arts organizations in the eighties, actor training has been in a steady decline in Britain, with overcrowded classes, aging facilities, and overworked teachers.

American conservatory training, on the other hand, during the same period, has become robust, with hundreds of actor training programs across the nation offering master's degrees in some of the finest performing arts facilities in the world.

In addition, the number of regional Shakespeare festivals in the United States has positively exploded, offering places for young actors to ply their craft in nearly every state in the union.

So, why isn't the American actor better at acting Shakespeare?

To understand the reason, one must travel back in time to June 8, 1931. That was the day when twenty-eight actors and three directors—Lee Strasberg, Cheryl Crawford, and Harold Clurman—left New York City to begin a great experiment.

Arriving at Brookfield Center in Connecticut that day, the Group Theatre began its quest to develop a single unified approach to acting based upon the teachings of Constantin Stanislavsky.

In doing so, they would create a style of acting based on psychological realism which would forever change the face of American theater, and exert a profound influence on movies and television.

Today, 99 percent of American actors are trained in the tradition of Stanislavsky. It is the universal language spoken in all American drama classes, from junior high school to master's programs. It is the *modus operandi* used in rehearsal rooms from Bellingham to Broadway.

This is both a blessing and a curse.

It's a blessing because Stanislavsky-based training produces what is perhaps the greatest strength of the American actor: a muscular, passionate, can-do presence, which perfectly suits the mythology of the American national character.

It's a way of working which begat Elia Kazan and Stella Adler, who begat Marlon Brando and Julie Harris, who begat Paul Newman and Geraldine Page, who begat Jack Nicholson and Jane Fonda, who begat Meryl Streep and Kevin Kline, who begat Tom Hanks and Julia Roberts, who begat Matt Damon and Gwyneth Paltrow, who begat—who knows who will emerge from American conservatories in the next ten years?

But it's also a curse, because it has diminished our ability to act in language-based plays, period plays, and plays of style, like those of Sophocles, Moliere, Ibsen, and of course, Shakespeare.

Stanislavsky usually gets the blame for our weakness in the classics—for all the mumbling, slouching, scratching, and sniffing that often passes for American acting. But he doesn't deserve it.

He doesn't deserve it because back in the thirties, at Brookfield Center, what Lee Strasberg (and later his disciples) were teaching as Stanislavsky's "system" was only a *portion* of Stanislavsky's work.

When Stanislavsky's book *An Actor Prepares* was published in 1936, it focused primarily on the *internal* workings of an actor—on techniques regarding a sense of truth, imagination, concentration, communion, objectives, actions, emotional memory, and sense memory.

Stanislavsky never intended *An Actor Prepares* to fully represent his way of working. It was always planned as the first of a *pair* of books about the craft of acting.

Thirteen years later, in 1949, when Stanislavsky's *Building a Character* was published, he focused on the *external* workings of the actor, on the use of body and voice to meet the demands of language, period, and style plays—that is, the skills needed to act Shakespeare.

But the delay of thirteen years made all the difference in this country. Because by 1949, it was already too late. The roots of American psychological realism were firmly embedded in the soil of the American stage. The Group Theatre had already come and gone. The Actor's Studio had already been founded. Marlon Brando had already appeared on Broadway in *A Streetcar Named Desire*. And "the classics" were doomed.

To this day, our uniquely American interpretation of a portion of Stanislavsky's work keeps the American theater on a short leash and a choker collar, robbing it of poetry and possibility.

And while *An Actor Prepares* is still required reading for most Intro to Acting classes in the United States, *Building a Character* is still sorely neglected.

This is an enormous shame, because *Building a Character* contains the secret that so many American actors are searching for in those books by the British—that is, a way of rehearsing the classics, especially Shakespeare, that is completely compatible with what he or she already knows and does well.

For it is in this book that Stanislavsky reveals how deeply he cares about movement, voice, diction, words, phrasing, intonation, rhythm, tempo, accentuation, pausing, intelligibility, volume, tone, punctuation, vowels, consonants, standard speech, verse, scansion, rhetoric—all of the same things that Barton, Berry, and Rodenburg talk about in their books.

But inexplicably, though there have been dozens of books written about the Stanislavsky system—how to learn it, how to teach it, and how to use it to rehearse a role—no books exist about how to apply a Stanislavsky-based approach to the challenges of acting Shakespeare.

This, then, is the aim of the volume you now hold in your hands—to help the American actor bring what he already knows and does well to the plays of Shakespeare. To apply *all* of Stanislavsky's work, including those long-neglected ideas about body and voice, to the lifelong pursuit of mastering Shakespeare.

To accomplish this aim, this book builds upon a form devised by Richard Boleslavsky in his book *Acting: The First Six Lessons*. A member of Moscow Art Company, Boleslavsky fled the Russian revolution in 1919, arrived in America in 1922, and helped to found the American Laboratory Theater in 1923, where he taught acting techniques learned from Stanislavsky. (It was at the Lab, in 1924, in a class being taught by Boleslavsky, that Strasberg first encountered the Stanislavsky system and began to dream of changing the American theater.)

In *Six Lessons*, Boleslavsky imagines a dialogue between a Master Teacher and a young student endeavoring to master the craft of acting. Their conversation takes place over six scenes, as the student struggles, over time, with different aspects of her craft.

The brilliance of Boleslavsky's book is that it recognizes that one cannot learn acting from a book. Since the Greeks, the craft of acting has been handed down through an oral tradition—by watching other actors work, and by working with other actors; by learning from generous teachers; and by generously teaching what you have learned.

That is why *Mastering Shakespeare* is also written in dialogue form—as a play—to reflect how the craft of acting is actually learned in this country. Not through the solitary study of exercise books, but by working with great teachers who have engaged in a lifelong endeavor to master Shakespeare in their own professional practice.

The action of the play takes place in an acting studio, where a master teacher and his sixteen students grapple with the challenges of acting Shakespeare. The play unfolds in seven scenes—seven master classes which present a logical progression of acting skills, from the most fundamental to the most complex.

Each scene contains several of Shakespeare's speeches, which present specific acting challenges. Specific techniques are offered to meet those challenges. Each speech is discussed in terms of "given circumstances," that is, the students are asked—Where are you? Who are you talking to? What do you want? What's preventing you from getting it?

The dialogue of the play uses terms heard every day in American classrooms and rehearsal rooms—familiar terms from the Stanislavsky system, like "action," "objective," and "obstacle."

Rather than using footnotes at the bottom of each page, difficult words and phrases in the speeches are illuminated for the reader by the students themselves, who put these passages into their own words. The discussion of meaning is incorporated into the dialogue because a complete comprehension of the text is vital before an actor can begin to do anything else. That point cannot be overstated.

The book should first be read from cover to cover in a linear fashion in order to fully understand how each technique relates to all the others in the book. Following that, *Mastering Shakespeare* can be used as a workbook, allowing the reader to employ specific techniques in a nonlinear fashion as the need arises.

One warning to the reader: although each scene takes place in a single class period in a single day, one should not expect to acquire any of these skills overnight. The techniques presented in this book will take a great deal of time—years, rather than days—to master. So be patient, and keep working.

Finally, please keep in mind that this book is not presented to the reader as "The Way." It is simply "a way." And if it doesn't work for you, by all means, seek advice elsewhere.

Even if it means looking across the pond.

Persons of the Play

The Master Teacher:
Mr. Kay

The Women:
Claire
Elena
Gabriella
Madison
Rachel
Sarah
Tayo
Trinity

The Men:
Avi
Dante
Jake
Jesse
Luke
Noah
Sam
Tim

The Art of Orchestration

The Acting Studio. Monday.

A windowless, gray, florescent-lit room. At the front of the space rises a small stage area, cluttered with battered rehearsal furniture and framed by dingy beige curtains.

A dozen acting students sit in their customary desk-chairs, facing the stage, notebooks open and pens ready. Many of them have dog-eared editions of The Complete Works of William Shakespeare *at their feet. Most of them wear their coats and scarves to fight off the chill of the barely heated room.*

On each wall of the room, and on the ceiling, someone has affixed a small "x" in black tape. On the wall by the door hang a clock, a bulletin board on which a variety of assignments and articles are posted, and an enormous sign, a relic salvaged from a forgotten production, which asks in bold letters: "HOW LONG CAN THEY LAST?"

At the back of the room, the Master Teacher, whom the students call "Mr. Kay," rises.

MR. KAY: Ladies and gentlemen, this is a very dangerous time for you all. You've reached a stage in your training which is very precarious indeed.

Over the past two years, you've worked hard, very hard, to acquire tools—in this acting class, in voice class, in speech class, in movement, in dance, fencing, singing, dialects. You've been mastering the tools of the classical actor.

For the past two years, you've been breathing into your ribs, perfecting the *punto reverso,* and waltzing in three-quarter time.

You can speak with a Russian accent. You can cold-read an audition monologue. You can juggle three pins in the air.

You know a spondee from a pyrrhic, you know an action from an activity, and, when the wind is southerly, you know a hawk from a handsaw.

(The class laughs.)

For the past two years, you've been striving to acquire technique, to gain full control of body and voice for the stage. You've been striving to master the *craft* of acting.

That is why this is a dangerous time for you. You have all these tools, but you do not yet fully understand how to *use* them. How to make artistic *choices* based on an understanding of a play. How to *shape* these choices, moment by moment, into a performance. How to create a role.

What I'm talking about is the *art* of acting.

And the art of acting, the thing that distinguishes the most extraordinary actors from merely capable actors is the art of *orchestration.*

(The students write "the art of orchestration" in their notebooks.)

By orchestration, I mean the artistic process of selecting, arranging, and heightening each moment of a role.

I'll say that again. Orchestration is the artistic process of *selecting, arranging,* and *heightening* your choices for each moment of your time onstage.

(The students write "selecting, arranging, and heightening" in their notebooks.)

That's what we'll be striving to understand, and to *master,* for the rest of your time with us in training.

And we'll begin that work today by looking at those Shakespearean speeches I asked you to prepare. Does everybody have those ready to go?

(The class shifts nervously.)

Who would like to begin?

✺ SPEECH MEASURES ✺

AVI: I will!

MR. KAY: Good, Avi, good, thank you.

(Avi goes up onto the stage.)

And what are you going to show us today?

AVI: King Henry, from *Henry the Sixth, Part Three.*

MR. KAY: All right. And if you would place yourself in your scene, please, so I can ask you a few questions.

(Avi sits on the floor of the stage, and gazes outward, quietly.)

Where are you, King Henry?

AVI: Sitting on a molehill, on a battlefield.

MR. KAY: Where is this battlefield?

AVI: In Yorkshire.

MR. KAY: And who are you fighting?

AVI: We're fighting the York family for the crown of England.

MR. KAY: So why are you just sitting there? Why aren't you fighting?

AVI: I've been told by Queen Margaret and The Earl of Warwick to stay out of the way so they can fight.

MR. KAY: I see. And who are you talking to?

AVI: Myself.

MR. KAY: Why? What do you hope to accomplish by talking to yourself?

AVI: I want to prove to myself that the life of a shepherd would have been better than the life of a king.

MR. KAY: And what's the obstacle? What's keeping you from proving that to yourself?

AVI: It's impossible to prove because I'm the king, and will never be a shepherd.

MR. KAY: Good, and begin, please.

KING HENRY: Oh God! methinks it were a happy life
To be no better than a homely swain;
To sit upon a hill, as I do now,
To carve out dials quaintly, point by point,
Thereby to see the minutes how they run:
How many makes the hour full complete,
How many hours brings about the day,
How many days will finish up the year,
How many years a mortal man may live;
When this is known, then to divide the times:
So many hours must I tend my flock,
So many hours must I take my rest,
So many hours must I contemplate,
So many hours must I sport myself,
So many days my ewes have been with young,
So many weeks ere the poor fools will ean,
So many years ere I shall sheer the fleece.
So minutes, hours, days, months, and years,
Pass'd over to the end they were created,
Would bring white hairs unto a quiet grave.
Ah, what a life were this! how sweet! how lovely!

Gives not the hawthorn-bush a sweeter shade,
To shepherds looking on their silly sheep,
Than doth a rich embroider'd canopy,
To kings that fear their subjects' treachery?
O yes, it doth! a thousand-fold it doth!
And to conclude, the shepherd's homely curds,
His cold thin drink out of his leather bottle,
His wonted sleep under a fresh tree's shade,
All which secure and sweetly he enjoys,
Is far beyond a prince's delicates,
His viands sparkling in a golden cup,
His body couchèd in a curious bed,
When care, mistrust, and treason waits on him.

MR. KAY: Good, Avi, that's a good start on that. Now, before we look at this speech again, let's make sure we understand everything King Henry is saying.

(To the class) Avi, of course, being the intelligent, well-trained, and highly-prepared actor that he is, has already done a great deal of text work on the speech.

He's already scanned the verse, analyzing the meter of every line and noting any irregularities that might inform his choices.

He knows how to pronounce every word in the speech, because he's looked in his *Webster's Dictionary*, as well as a variety of Shakespearean pronouncing dictionaries.

And he's read the footnotes from several different editions of the play, double-checking difficult words in his *Schmidt's Lexicon*, so he can tell us the exact meaning of every word and phrase in the speech.

(To Avi) Right, Avi?

AVI: Um . . . sure, absolutely.

MR. KAY: So, let me ask you this, Avi: what's "a homely swain"?

AVI: Um . . . a simple shepherd.

MR. KAY: Yes. And what do you mean by "carve out dials quaintly"?

AVI: That means . . . "to make beautifully carved sundials."

MR. KAY: I see. And what do you mean by "brings about the day"?

AVI: Completes the day.

MR. KAY: Good. And what do you mean when you say "the poor fools will ean"?

AVI: The sheep will give birth to lambs.

MR. KAY: I see. And what do you mean by "silly sheep"?

AVI: My helpless sheep.

MR. KAY: Yes. What do you mean by "his wonted sleep"?

AVI: His customary nap.

MR. KAY: Good. And what do mean by "secure"?

AVI: Without a care in the world.

MR. KAY: And what are "a prince's delicates"?

AVI: Royal delicacies.

MR. KAY: And what are viands?

AVI: Food.

MR. KAY: And what's a "curious bed"?

AVI: A fancy, decorated bed.

MR. KAY: Good, Avi, thank you. And thank you also for choosing this particular speech, because it's the perfect place for us to begin exploring the art of orchestration.

And the best way to begin that exploration is to look at the most basic building blocks of any orchestration, which are called *speech measures.*

(The students write "speech measures" in their notebooks.)

(To the class) A speech measure is a *parcel of text* which contains a single acting choice.

It's a *unit of sense* through which the actor can play a single thought, or image, or action.

It's a *vessel of language* into which an actor can pour a single moment of human behavior.

A speech measure can appear in a variety of lengths. It can be a single sound, like: "O!"

Or one word, like: "Banishment?"

Or a phrase, like: "A damnèd saint."

Or an entire line, like: "He jests at scars that never felt a wound."

Or more than a line, like:

"How art thou out of breath when thou hast breath
To say to me that thou art out of breath?"

Whatever can be understood by the audience as a single moment of human behavior, and spoken by the actor on a single breath.

Now, if you look at this Henry speech on the page, you can see that Shakespeare has rather brilliantly written the text in a very regular, measured form to illuminate the idea of dividing a person's life into measures.

And just as King Henry talks about dividing up his life into measures of *time*—into minutes, hours, days, weeks, and years—the first thing we need to do to orchestrate this speech, or any speech for that matter, is to divide it up into *speech measures*—into sounds, words, phrases, and lines.

For example, Henry's lines about "So many hours." Would you say those lines again for us, please, Avi?

AVI: Um . . . sure.

(Avi thinks for a moment.)

So many hours must I tend my flock,
So many hours must I take my rest,
So many hours must I contemplate,
So many hours must I sport myself,
So many days my ewes have been with young,
So many weeks ere the poor fools will ean,
So many years ere I shall sheer the fleece.

MR. KAY: Yes. And do you hear how each one of those verse lines stands on its own as a single thought or idea? Each line can be spoken on a single breath, and understood by the audience as a single *unit of sense*. There's no need to break them up into smaller units. Each one forms a *perfect speech measure*.

AVI: Yes, I see.

MR. KAY: Good. Now let's take another example. Let's go back and look at the very first line of the speech, Avi.

AVI: "Oh God! methinks it were a happy life"?

MR. KAY: Yes. Let's see what happens if you take that line of verse and divide it into *two* speech measures.

AVI: All right.

MR. KAY: And allow me to count, if you would.

AVI: Count?

MR. KAY: Yes. I'll assign a *number* to each speech measure before you speak it. I'll say "ONE," then you'll speak the first speech measure, then "TWO," and you'll speak the second speech measure, and so on. Got that?

AVI: Uh-huh, I think so.

MR. KAY: Good. Ready? *(Avi thinks for a moment.)* ONE.

AVI: Oh God!

MR. KAY: TWO.

AVI: methinks it were a happy life

MR. KAY: Good, Avi. Now we have two distinct speech measures, which define two distinct moments of behavior. In the first speech measure, Henry connects with god, and in the second, he dreams about a happier life. Did you all see that?

(Affirmative nods from the class.)

Good. Let's look at another example. Let's take the line "Ah, what a life were this" and divide that up into three separate speech measures. Would you give that a try, Avi?

AVI: Okay.

(Avi thinks for a moment.)

MR. KAY: ONE.

AVI: Ah, what a life were this!

MR. KAY: TWO.

AVI: how sweet!

MR. KAY: THREE.

AVI: how lovely!

MR. KAY: Yes, good. So now we have three distinct speech measures, three moments in which King Henry responds to three different images of the shepherd's life he sees in his mind's eye.

Let's take another example. Would you please say the last line of the speech, Avi?

AVI: "When care, mistrust and treason"?

MR. KAY: Yes. Let's see what happens if you divide that line into *four* speech measures.

(Avi thinks for a moment.)

MR. KAY: ONE.

AVI: When care,

MR. KAY: TWO.

AVI: mistrust,

MR. KAY: THREE.

AVI: and treason

MR. KAY: FOUR.

AVI: waits on him.

MR. KAY: Yes, good, that's *four* distinct speech measures. First King Henry *personifies* in his imagination the three abstract ideas of care, mistrust, and treason, then he sees them as his own *servants* waiting upon him.

Let's look at another example. Let's take the line "So minutes" and divide that up into *five* speech measures. If you would, please, Avi.

(Avi thinks for a moment.)

MR. KAY: ONE.

AVI: So minutes,

MR. KAY: TWO.

AVI: hours.

MR. KAY: THREE.

AVI: days,

MR. KAY: FOUR.

AVI: months,

MR. KAY: FIVE.

AVI: and years,

MR. KAY: Yes, good. That's *five* distinct speech measures, five moments in which King Henry contemplates a unit of time, each one telescoping larger than the last.

And when *you* take the time, Avi, to create a personal image for each measure of time, it's no longer a laundry list, but a sequence in which we see a man's time on the planet pass before his eyes.

Well done, Avi, thank you.

(Avi comes down off the stage.)

(To the class) Do you see how the text comes alive by dividing it up into units, and presenting it to the audience in distinct speech measures?

By *parceling* out the text in this manner, not only does Avi have the time he needs to be specific about the *next* idea, but the audience has the time it needs to comprehend the *last* idea.

You'll hear this technique handled exquisitely if you listen to recordings of the great speakers of the twentieth century, such as Franklin D. Roosevelt, John F. Kennedy, and Martin Luther King, Jr. They all presented their speeches to an audience in easily digestible bits. They gave an audience a single thought or image or action, waited for the audience to absorb that idea, and then offered up the next. One unit of sense at a time, one speech measure at a time. As public speakers, they perfected a shared cycle of talking and listening in which the spaces *between* the words were as important as the text itself.

What I'm talking about, when I talk about the spaces in between speech measures, is the *logical pause.* And choosing where to take your logical pauses is the first step in the art of orchestration.

(Madison raises her hand.)

Yes, Madison?

MADISON: But, how do you know where to put the logical pauses? I mean, how do you know how big a speech measure should be?

MR. KAY: You don't when you begin—you can only make educated guesses. But then, as you begin to make acting choices, your speech measures will shift and change as you discover new possibilities through trial and error.

Your speech measures will constantly expand and contract as you select, arrange, and heighten your choices towards a fully orchestrated performance.

That's called rehearsal, by the way.

(The class laughs. Claire raises her hand.)

Yes, Claire?

CLAIRE: Okay, I'm like, totally confused, because I thought we weren't supposed to chop up the verse in the middle of a line!

MR. KAY: Yes, that's true. As I've told you many times, some of you have a tendency to *contemporize* a text by chopping up a line of verse, like this:

(Mr. Kay demonstrates.)

Oh God! Methinks . . . *(pause)* . . . it were a happy life
To be . . . *(pause)* . . . no better than a . . . *(pause)* . . . homely swain;
To . . . *(pause)* . . . sit upon a hill, as . . . *(pause)* . . . I do now
(The class laughs.)

The reason this sounds so ridiculous is that these are not *logical* pauses. These are *illogical pauses.* Illogical pauses chop up the words into random groups, into units of *nonsense*, obliterating the speech measures, and turning the verse into, like, y'know, totally meaningless drivel.

Do you . . . like . . . *(pause)* . . . follow me, Claire?

CLAIRE: I'm, like . . . *(pause)* . . . totally with you.

(The class laughs.)

SAM: *(Jumping in)* But I thought we were supposed to arc through the big thoughts—do them all in one breath—so it's easier for the audience to understand?

MR. KAY: The length of a speech measure has nothing to do with the actor's breath capacity, and everything to do with the ability of the average audience member to hear and understand. And the ability of the average person to hear and understand complicated text is *shrinking* all the time!

We've all been trained by modern technology to absorb *visual* information faster and faster. Our ability to process rapid sequences of *visual* images only split seconds in duration is steadily increasing. But at the same time, our ability to absorb complex *aural* information is steadily declining.

That means that you, as actors, have no choice but to present smaller units of sense to an audience than previous generations.

JAKE: But won't the speech plod if we break up the text so much?

MR. KAY: No more than breaking a dance down into individual steps will prevent you from dancing. At first, as you're learning, it seems impossible that you'll ever be able to put the steps together. But with practice, the parts flow together, the work becomes invisible, and you simply dance.

(A pause while the class considers that idea.)

Let's look at another speech and see if we can come to a better understanding about speech measures.

Who wants to go next?

❧ PUNCTUATION ❧

CLAIRE: I will!

(Claire goes up unto the stage.)

MR. KAY: What are you going to show us today, Claire?

CLAIRE: Queen Hermione, from *The Winter's Tale.*

MR. KAY: All right. If you would place yourself in your scene, please, so I can ask you a few questions.

(Claire stands weakly at center stage and gazes outward.)

Where are you, Queen Hermione?

CLAIRE: In a royal court of justice.

MR. KAY: And who are you talking to?

CLAIRE: King Leontes—my husband, and the father of my children.

MR. KAY: Who else is present in the court? Are you talking to anyone else?

CLAIRE: The court is full of lords who are here to judge my case. And I do talk to them a little. But mostly I'm talking to my husband.

MR. KAY: Why are you here in this court of justice? What have you been accused of?

CLAIRE: My husband has accused me of sleeping with his friend, King Polixenes, and having a child by him.

MR. KAY: I see. So what's your objective? What do you hope to accomplish?

CLAIRE: I want to prove my innocence.

MR. KAY: Yes. And what are the obstacles to that? What makes it difficult for you to prove your innocence?

CLAIRE: Well, I just gave birth, so I'm exhausted. My children have been taken away from me, including my newborn baby girl, so I'm very upset. Leontes won't listen to reason, and no one here dares to speak in my defense. I have no proof of my innocence, so I have to rely on Apollo to reveal the truth.

MR. KAY: Good, and begin, please.

HERMIONE: Sir, spare your threats.
The bug which you would fright me with, I seek.
To me can life be no commodity;
The crown and comfort of my life, your favor,
I do give lost, for I do feel it gone,
But know not how it went. My second joy,
And first fruits of my body, from his presence
I'm barr'd, like one infectious. My third comfort
(Starr'd most unluckily) is from my breast
(The innocent milk in its most innocent mouth)
Hal'd out to murder; myself on every post
Proclaim'd a strumpet; with immodest hatred
The childbed privilege deny'd, which 'longs
To women of all fashion; Lastly, hurry'd
Here, to this place, i' th' open air, before
I have got strength of limit. Now, my liege,
Tell me what blessings I have here alive,
That I should fear to die? Therefore, proceed.
But yet hear this: mistake me not: for life,
I prize it not a straw, but for mine honor,
Which I would free: If I shall be condemn'd
Upon surmises (all proofs sleeping else,
But what your jealousies awake) I tell you
'Tis rigor, and not law. Your honors all,
I do refer me to the oracle:
Apollo be my judge.

MR. KAY: Good, Claire. I noticed you made a small word change in the text.

CLAIRE: Did I? *(Thinking)* Oh, yes, I did. I changed "no life, I prize it not a straw" to "*for* life, I prize it not a straw."

MR. KAY: Why did you do that?

CLAIRE: Well, I thought it would be clearer if it sounded more like "as for my life." So I changed it.

(A concerned pause.)

Is that, like, totally appalling?

MR. KAY: Actually, I'm not the least bit appalled, Claire. I think it was an intelligent and acceptable change. It makes the structure of Hermione's argument much clearer, and does no harm to the meter. So why not?

(The class is stunned.)

(To the class) You'll find, ladies and gentlemen, that in the theater it's common, very common, in fact, for directors to make all kinds of emendations to the text in rehearsal. That's a major difference between *academic* study of the plays, and actual *theater* practice.

Academics can write books and articles and dissertations with endless footnotes to illuminate their ideas about impenetrable passages in Shakespeare's plays. But theater practitioners don't have that luxury. They have to make Shakespeare's four-hundred-year-old texts accessible to a modern audience using primarily the actor's *body* and *voice*. And if a director feels she has to change a word, or rearrange a few lines, or eliminate a passage, or cut an entire scene to make something clearer, usually, in the professional theater, she goes right ahead and does it.

So I have no problem with Claire making that one-word change in Hermione's text. As long as the change is well-considered and not arbitrary.

I do have one caveat, however. It may take you an entire lifetime of working with Shakespeare to truly know the difference between what is well-considered and what is arbitrary.

(The class laughs.)

So, Claire, let's talk about the text for a moment, and let's be sure we understand every word of the speech before we look at it again.

What do you mean by "the bug"?

CLAIRE: The bugbear.

MR. KAY: Bugbear? What's a bugbear?

CLAIRE: Um . . . it's an imaginary thing that scares people, like a ghost, or a goblin.

MR. KAY: I see. And what do you mean by "life can be no commodity"?

CLAIRE: I don't think my life is worth living any more.

MR. KAY: And what do you mean by "I do give lost"?

CLAIRE: I give up for lost.

MR. KAY: And what do you mean by "Starr'd most unluckily"?

CLAIRE: That means "born under an unlucky star."

MR. KAY: And what do you mean by "Hal'd out"?

CLAIRE: Dragged away.

MR. KAY: What do you mean by "with immodest hatred"?

CLAIRE: Um . . . that means "with extreme malice."

MR. KAY: And what do you mean by "which 'longs to women of all fashion"?

CLAIRE: Which belongs to women of every rank.

MR. KAY: What do you mean by "before I have got strength of limit"?

CLAIRE: Before I've regained a limited amount of strength.

MR. KAY: What do you mean by "which I would free"?

CLAIRE: Which I would clear of wrongdoing.

MR. KAY: Which is your objective, right? To prove your innocence? It's stated right there in the text, isn't it?

CLAIRE: Yes, I guess it is.

MR. KAY: I just wanted to be sure you were clear about that.

CLAIRE: Yes.

MR. KAY: What do you mean by "'tis rigor, and not law"?

CLAIRE: It's tyranny, not justice.

MR. KAY: What do you mean by "I do refer me to the oracle"?

CLAIRE: I put my case into the hands of the Apollo.

MR. KAY: Good, Claire, you've done some good work on that.

Now, let's look at this speech again, and see how we might divide it up into speech measures.

You'll remember that when we looked at the King Henry speech with Jake, we saw that Henry's thoughts were very ordered, and very regular. His thoughts most often came to him at the end of each line of verse.

So, let me ask you this, Claire, when you look at this speech as it's printed on the page, where does *Hermione* tend to get her next idea or thought?

CLAIRE: Um . . . I think, mostly in the middle of the lines, at punctuation marks.

MR. KAY: Yes, I agree, she tends to get her thoughts mid-line, at punctuation marks. Her thoughts are very disordered, very irregular, because, as you said before, she's exhausted and she's very upset.

So, what I'd like to do now, Claire, is look at how this speech can be divided into speech measures by honoring those punctuation marks.

(The students write "punctuation" in their notebooks.)

(To the class) Could someone with a *Complete Works* please find this speech and follow along in the text?

RACHEL: I've got it!

MR. KAY: Thanks, Rachel. Now, Claire, let's go through the speech again. But this time through, I'd like you to let Rachel help you to divide the text into speech measures.

Rachel, whenever she gets to a punctuation mark in the text, I'd like you to say aloud what it is—"COMMA," "SEMICOLON," "COLON," "PERIOD," "EXCLAMATION POINT," or "QUESTION MARK." All right?

RACHEL: Okay.

MR. KAY: Claire, please listen to Rachel, and stop at each punctuation mark. Take some time to think about the next measure. Then inhale, and speak only as much text as will take you to the next punctuation mark. All right?

CLAIRE: Yes.

MR. KAY: So, if you would restore your scene in your imagination, please.

(Claire does so.)

And remind us, please, what's the objective?

CLAIRE: To prove my innocence.

MR. KAY: Yes, and first speech measure?

CLAIRE: Sir,

RACHEL: COMMA.

CLAIRE: spare your threats.

RACHEL: PERIOD.

CLAIRE: The bug which you would fright me with,

RACHEL: COMMA.

CLAIRE: I seek.

RACHEL: PERIOD.

CLAIRE: To me can life be no commodity;

RACHEL: SEMICOLON.

CLAIRE: The crown and comfort of my life,

RACHEL: COMMA.

CLAIRE: your favor,

RACHEL: COMMA.

CLAIRE: I do give lost,

RACHEL: COMMA.

CLAIRE: for I do feel it gone,

RACHEL: COMMA.

CLAIRE: But know not how it went.

RACHEL: PERIOD.

CLAIRE: My second joy,

RACHEL: COMMA.

CLAIRE: And first fruits of my body,

RACHEL: COMMA.

CLAIRE: from his presence
I'm barr'd,

RACHEL: COMMA.

CLAIRE: like one infectious.

RACHEL: PERIOD.

CLAIRE: My third comfort

RACHEL: PARENTHESIS.

CLAIRE: (Starr'd most unluckily)

RACHEL: PARENTHESIS.

CLAIRE: is from my breast

RACHEL: PARENTHESIS.

CLAIRE: (The innocent milk in its most innocent mouth)

RACHEL: PARENTHESIS.

CLAIRE: Hal'd out to murder;

RACHEL: SEMICOLON.

CLAIRE: myself on every post
Proclaim'd a strumpet;

RACHEL: SEMICOLON.

CLAIRE: with immodest hatred
The childbed privilege deny'd,

RACHEL: COMMA.

CLAIRE: which 'longs
To women of all fashion;

RACHEL: SEMICOLON.

CLAIRE: Lastly,

RACHEL: COMMA.

CLAIRE: hurry'd
Here,

RACHEL: COMMA.

CLAIRE: to this place,

RACHEL: COMMA.

CLAIRE: i' th' open air,

RACHEL: COMMA.

CLAIRE: before
I have got strength of limit.

RACHEL: PERIOD.

CLAIRE: Now,

RACHEL: COMMA.

CLAIRE: my liege,

RACHEL: COMMA.

CLAIRE: Tell me what blessings I have here alive,

RACHEL: COMMA.

CLAIRE: That I should fear to die?

RACHEL: QUESTION MARK.

CLAIRE: Therefore,

RACHEL: COMMA.

CLAIRE: proceed.

RACHEL: PERIOD.

CLAIRE: But yet hear this:

RACHEL: COLON.

CLAIRE: mistake me not:

RACHEL: COLON.

CLAIRE: for life,

RACHEL: COMMA.

CLAIRE: I prize it not a straw,

RACHEL: COMMA.

CLAIRE: but for mine honor,

RACHEL: COMMA.

CLAIRE: Which I would free:

RACHEL: COLON.

CLAIRE: If I shall be condemn'd
    Upon surmises

RACHEL: PARENTHESIS.

CLAIRE: (all proofs sleeping else,

RACHEL: COMMA.

CLAIRE: But what your jealousies awake)

RACHEL: PARENTHESIS.

CLAIRE: I tell you
    'Tis rigor,

RACHEL: COMMA.

CLAIRE: and not law.

RACHEL: PERIOD.

CLAIRE: Your honors all,

RACHEL: COMMA.

CLAIRE: I do refer me to the oracle:

RACHEL: COLON.

CLAIRE: Apollo be my judge.

RACHEL: PERIOD.

MR. KAY: Very good, Claire, thank you.

(Claire comes down off the stage.)

(To the class) Now, did you all see and hear how using the punctuation to divide the text into speech measures significantly changed Claire's rendering of the speech? What did you notice? Anybody?

MADISON: She's not so emotional!

MR. KAY: Yes, exactly, she's not as emotional. It's no longer all weeping and sobbing, so we can actually hear the text, we can actually understand what Hermione is trying to tell the court.

And this is a key point. Because Hermione's objective isn't to show the court how emotionally exhausted she is. Her emotional exhaustion, as Claire told us, is an obstacle. Hermione's objective is to *prove her innocence.*

And dividing the speech into speech measures gives Claire the time she needs to breathe in the next thought, to get the next image, to play the next action in order to prove her innocence *despite her emotions.*

So now, instead of trying to ride a wave of emotion, which has to be continually forced in order to be sustained, Claire is riding a wave of structured reasoning. She's using the language to make her appeal, rather than emotion. She's letting the words prove her innocence, rather than her feelings.

More importantly, She's no longer *chasing the text*—inhaling, speaking, and then hoping the act of saying the words will make something happen for her. Instead, her thoughts are ahead of the text, the way human beings actually communicate.

This is the way humans have used language since our first grunts in the caves—we get an idea we want to share, we inhale to speak, then we articulate the words which represent our idea.

It's only when we *memorize* text that this cycle is subverted. It's only in memorized text that we inhale, speak, and then get the idea!

By using the punctuation to parcel the text out into manageable bits—into speech measures—Claire knows exactly when each idea comes to her, exactly when she must inhale, and exactly how much oxygen she'll need to share just that thought.

SAM: *(Interrupting)* But, wait a minute, wait a minute. I'm still confused, because my punctuation is totally different!

MR. KAY: Different? What do you mean different?

SAM: Well, for one thing, most of those colons, I have as dashes.

MR. KAY: I see.

TAYO: *(Cutting in)* My script doesn't have any of those parentheticals the way hers does.

MR. KAY: Hmm.

GABRIELLA: *(Adding her two cents)* And I have commas in places where she doesn't.

MR. KAY: Really?

TIM: *(His two cents)* And I have an exclamation point at the end of "Apollo be my judge!"

MR. KAY: Wait! Do you mean to tell me that the punctuation in all of your editions of the play is different? How could that possibly be? I mean, Shakespeare is Shakespeare, right?

(A perplexed pause.)

Wrong.

You folks must understand, you're looking at Shakespeare through a looking glass, through a filter, put there by an editor who has made choices for you, very often without even telling you.

Or, if he does tell you, he hides it in the little "strip of terror" at the bottom of the page, which no actor ever reads. Or he buries it in tiny print at the end of the play, where no actor ever dares venture.

This scholar has usually spent a lifetime studying Shakespeare in libraries, and has made his punctuation choices based on what he thinks is most *readable*.

You, on the other hand, entrusted with the privilege of bringing Shakespeare's words to life on the stage, must choose what is most *actable*.

So you're going to have to become adept at resolving these punctuation differences for yourselves.

One way you might do this is to go out and buy up every edition of the play you can get your hands on—the Penguin, the Pelican, the Oxford, the Cambridge, the Arden, the Riverside, the Signet, the Folger—then compare and contrast what you see on the page, and choose for yourself which punctuation you think works best.

Or? What else? Other ideas?

SAM: Go to the Folio!

MR. KAY: Yes, Sam, go to the Folio, and see for yourself how the lines have been punctuated there. But, be sure to keep in mind that the Folio may not represent Shakespeare's original punctuation either.

SAM: What? How can that be?

MR. KAY: A good question. How can that be? Anyone?

(A pause.) When was the first Folio printed?

LUKE: 1623.

MR. KAY: Yes, Luke. And when did Shakespeare die?

LUKE: Um . . . 1616?

MR. KAY: Yes, 1616. Remember, two of the actors from his company, John Heminge and Henry Condell, put the Folio together seven years *after he died.* So we know that Shakespeare himself never got to proofread the Folio before it was printed. So the punctuation you see in the Folio is also questionable.

Was it copied from a manuscript in Shakespeare's handwriting? Was it copied from an earlier printing of the play—a Quarto? Was the Quarto accurate or corrupt? Was it assembled from actor's sides? Did it include memorial reconstructions from actors in the company? Did an editor make changes? Did the typesetter make mistakes? Who knows? It's impossible to know. But many people have made careers fretting over it.

Ultimately, my friends, you're going to have to study the options in front of you, and make your own informed choices. But because you are *actors*, not scholars, you must never forget that your careers will not be made by fretting over commas and semicolons, but by *selecting*, *arranging*, and *heightening* strong, bold, theatrical choices for every moment of your time on the stage.

(The class is silent, digesting the last few thoughts.)

Okay then, who's next?

ᕈᕈ OPERATIVE WORDS ᕈᕈ

DANTE: I am!

(Dante goes up onto the stage.)

MR. KAY: All right, Dante. What are you going to show us today?

DANTE: Brutus from *Julius Caesar.*

MR. KAY: All right. If you would place yourself in your scene, please, so I can ask you a few questions.

(Dante stands center stage, arms folded, gazing downward.)

Where are you, Brutus?

DANTE: I'm at home, in my garden.

MR. KAY: And who are you talking to?

DANTE: Myself.

MR. KAY: Why are you talking to yourself? What do you hope to accomplish?

DANTE: I want to convince myself that murdering Caesar is right and necessary.

MR. KAY: I see. And why are you having trouble convincing yourself of that? What are the obstacles?

DANTE: Well, I like the man, and he's never wronged me personally. And he hasn't crowned himself King yet, although it seems very likely he will. And if we kill him now, before he's done anything, how will we explain his death to the people of Rome, who love him? So, I'm not completely convinced murdering him is the right thing to do, and my conscience is bothering me.

MR. KAY: Good, and begin, please.

BRUTUS: It must be by his death; and for my part,
 I know no personal cause to spurn at him,
 But for the general. He would be crown'd.
 How that might change his nature, there's the question.
 It is the bright day that brings forth the adder,
 And that craves wary walking. Crown him that,
 And then I grant we put a sting in him
 That at his will he may do danger with.
 The abuse of greatness is, when it disjoins
 Remorse from power. And to speak truth of Caesar,
 I have not known when his affections sway'd
 More than his reason. But 'tis a common proof
 That lowliness is young ambition's ladder,
 Whereto the climber upward turns his face;
 But when he once attains the upmost round,
 He then unto the ladder turns his back,
 Looks in the clouds, scorning the base degrees
 By which he did ascend. So Caesar may.
 Then lest he may, prevent. And since the quarrel

Will bear no color for the thing he is,
Fashion it thus: that what he is, augmented,
Would run to these and these extremities;
And therefore think him as a serpent's egg,
Which hatch'd, would as his kind grow mischievous,
And kill him in the shell.

MR. KAY: Good, Dante, that's a good beginning. Now, before we look at this speech again, let's make sure we understand every word of the text. What do you mean, Dante, by "to spurn at him"?

DANTE: Well, it literally means "to kick Caesar," but I'm really talking about killing him.

MR. KAY: Interesting that you don't say the word "kill" here, though. When do you say that word?

DANTE: Not until the last line.

MR. KAY: A good clue.

DANTE: Yes.

MR. KAY: What do you mean when you say "for the general"?

DANTE: For the public good.

MR. KAY: I see. And what do you mean by "craves wary walking"?

DANTE: That means . . . um . . . "demands proceeding cautiously."

MR. KAY: And what do you mean by "Crown him that"?

DANTE: Crown Caesar emperor of Rome.

MR. KAY: Yes, and did you notice here that Brutus won't say the word "emperor." That's an interesting clue.

DANTE: Yes, it is.

MR. KAY: What do you mean by "when it disjoins remorse from power"?

DANTE: Um . . . when absolute power shows no compassion.

MR. KAY: And what do you mean by "when his affections sway'd more than his reason"?

DANTE: When his passions overruled his judgment.

MR. KAY: And what do you mean by "But 'tis a common proof"?

DANTE: But everybody knows.

MR. KAY: What do you mean by "lowliness"?

DANTE: That means "pretending to be humble."

MR. KAY: And what do you mean by "the upmost round"?

DANTE: The top rung of the ladder.

MR. KAY: What do you mean by "the base degrees"?

DANTE: The lowest rungs on the ladder, and the people on those rungs.

MR. KAY: What do you mean when you say "the quarrel will bear no color for the thing he is"?

DANTE: His murder will seem unjust based on his conduct so far.

MR. KAY: Yes, and notice how Brutus cannot bring himself to say the word "murder." Another interesting clue.

DANTE: Yes.

MR. KAY: What do you mean by "Fashion it thus"?

DANTE: Present it like this.

MR. KAY: What do you mean by "these and these extremities"?

DANTE: Extremely tyrannous acts.

MR. KAY: What do you mean by "grow mischievous"?

DANTE: Become dangerous.

MR. KAY: Excellent, Dante. Now, I want to look once again at the process of dividing a speech into speech measures.

We've looked at speech measures as determined by line endings, and by punctuation. Now let's look at how choosing *operative words* can determine speech measures.

(The students write "operative words" in their notebooks.)

By operative word, I mean the word in a speech measure that gets the *primary stress*, through the use of pitch, duration, or volume.

So, let's work on this Brutus speech from operative word to operative word, Dante.

Before each speech measure, I'd like you to tell us *aloud* which word you intend to make the *operative* word in the measure. Keep in mind that you can create only *one* operative word per speech measure.

DANTE: But what if there's more than one word that's important?

MR. KAY: In that case, you're going to have to make a choice. You're going to have to decide which is the *primary* word to stress, and let the others become *secondary*, or *tertiary*. Or, if you can't choose one word to be your operative, you must break the measure into smaller units of sense, and choose operative words for each of the new measures. Got it?

DANTE: I think so.

MR. KAY: Good, then let's try it. If you would, please restore your scene in your imagination.

(Dante does so.)

And remind us, please, what's the objective?

DANTE: To convince myself that murdering Caesar is right and necessary.

MR. KAY: Operative word for the first speech measure?

DANTE: DEATH.

MR. KAY: Good, and text?

DANTE: It must be by his *death*;

MR. KAY: Good, and just for the sake of argument, try *must* as the operative word.

(Dante goes back to the top.)

DANTE: It *must* be by his death;

(Dante pauses.)

MR. KAY: Which choice did you like better?

DANTE: Well, I still think *death* is better.

MR. KAY: Why, Dante? Why is "death" the stronger choice for an operative in that measure?

DANTE: I'm not sure.

MR. KAY: What did the line mean when you stressed "must"?

DANTE: Um . . . Caesar *has* to die.

MR. KAY: So in that reading, you've been considering whether to kill Caesar, or to let him live?

DANTE: Yes.

MR. KAY: And what did the line mean when you stressed "death"?

DANTE: Um . . . the only solution to the problem is to kill Caesar.

MR. KAY: So in that reading, you've been considering *other* possible solutions—exile or imprisonment, for example?

DANTE: Yes.

MR. KAY: And which choice is more like Brutus—choosing between two options, or considering every possible option?

DANTE: I think Brutus would consider every possible option.

MR. KAY: I agree. Which is why I agree with you that "death" is the stronger operative word. But now we're sure of it because we actually *tested* it.

(To the class) Do you all see how the choice of operative shifts the meaning of the measure? It's crucial that you understand that when you work on these speeches, or on any speech. You must always strive to make choices which illuminate the meaning of each speech measure to an audience.

(To Dante) Let's continue, please. Operative word for the second speech measure?

DANTE: Um . . . MY.

MR. KAY: And text?

DANTE: and for *my* part,

MR. KAY: Now, I'm sure that stressing "my" feels natural and familiar to your twenty-first century ears, Dante. But I'm not so sure that I'd suggest "my" as the strongest possible operative word in that speech measure. More importantly, I don't think that Shakespeare is suggesting "my" as the operative word in that measure either.

(To the class) How do I know that? Anybody?

TAYO: From the scansion?

MR. KAY: Yes, Tayo, from the scansion—by analyzing the meter of the line.

(To Dante) Let me ask you this, Dante—how does the line scan? Beat it out for us, would you, please?

(Dante beats out the meter of the line with his fist in the air.)

DANTE: It MUST be BY his DEATH, and FOR my PART.

MR. KAY: Ah. So it's an iambic pentameter line?

DANTE: Yes.

MR. KAY: With *my* in an unstressed syllable?

DANTE: Um . . . yes.

MR. KAY: And that's how we know that Shakespeare doesn't want you to make the word "my" the *operative*. Because if he wanted you to make "my" the operative word, he would have placed it in a *stressed* syllable in the meter.

Remember, folks, that scansion is a strong indicator of how Shakespeare wants you to speak the line, where he wants you to place your primary emphasis. That's why you must always scan the line before you choose an operative word. So, Dante, let's try another possible choice.

DANTE: What about *part*?

MR. KAY: Try it.

DANTE: *(Going back)* PART.
And for my *part*,
(Pause.)
That's better.

MR. KAY: Yes, I think so too. But now I think now we understand *why* it's better. Continue, please. Next operative word?

DANTE: Uh . . . PERSONAL.
I know no *personal* cause to spurn at him,

MR. KAY: That's a possibility. Although I'd suggest contracting that word from three syllables to *two* in order to honor the scansion.

DANTE: Do you mean, like, *pers'nal*?

MR. KAY: Yes, exactly, Dante, *pers'nal.* Try it again.

DANTE: Uh . . . PERS'NAL.
I know no *pers'nal* cause to spurn at him,

MR. KAY: Good, Dante. What about *cause*? Try that as the operative word in that measure.

DANTE: Uh . . . CAUSE.
I know no pers'nal *cause* to spurn at him,

MR. KAY: That's another possibility. What about *spurn*? Try *spurn.*

DANTE: SPURN.
I know no pers'nal cause to *spurn* at him,

MR. KAY: Which do you think is best, Dante?
(Dante silently ponders his choices.)
All three of those words are reasonable possibilities for the operative word. All three words are meaningful in context. All three words are in stressed syllables in the meter. How on earth are we going to decide which is best?
(Dante mutters the three different readings under his breath.)
(To the class) Perhaps there are some other clues in the line that would help us to choose the operative word? Anyone?
(Gabriella raises her hand.)

MR. KAY: Yes, Gabriella?

GABRIELLA: Parts of speech?

MR. KAY: Parts of speech? What do you mean by *parts of speech*?

GABRIELLA: Well, I mean, pers'nal is an *adjective* . . .

MR. KAY: Yes.

GABRIELLA: And cause is a *noun* . . .

MR. KAY: Yes.

GABRIELLA: And spurn is *verb* . . .

MR. KAY: Yes. So?

GABRIELLA: So, some parts of speech have more *juice* than others.

MR. KAY: *(Amused)* Yes, Gabriella, thank you—some parts of speech have more *juice* than others. More muscle. More beef. Which means we can sometimes choose an operative word by identifying the parts of speech in the measure and choosing the word with the most to offer.

Mind you, there are no hard-and-fast rules for selecting an operative word based on parts of speech, because it depends so much on context. But I can tell you that generally *verbs* tend to be operatives more often than *nouns,* and *nouns* more often than *adverbs, adverbs* more often than *adjectives, adjectives* more often than *prepositions, prepositions* more often than *conjunctions, conjunctions* more often than *pronouns, pronouns* more often than *interjections,* and *interjections* more often than *negatives.*

(The students write the parts of speech and their rankings in their notebooks.)

So, Dante, having said all that, which word do you think is the *juiciest* word in the measure?

DANTE: Definitely *spurn.*

MR. KAY: Yes, I agree, the verb *spurn* is the richest and most striking word in the measure. So let's go back and try that as the operative, please.

DANTE: *(Going back)* SPURN.

I know no pers'nal cause to *spurn* at him,

(Pause.)

Yes, that's good, that's nice and juicy.

(The class laughs.)

MR. KAY: Yes, I think so too.

Let's go on to the next measure, please. Operative word?

DANTE: GENERAL.

But for the *general*.

CROWNED.

He would be *crown'd*.

CHANGE.

How that might *change* his nature, there's the question.

MR. KAY: And what if "there's the question" were a separate speech measure?

DANTE: Um . . . let me try that.

(Going back) CHANGE.

How that might *change* his nature,

QUESTION.

there's the *question*.

MR. KAY: That's a possibility to consider. And continue, please.

DANTE: ADDER.

It is the bright day that brings forth the *adder*,

WARY.

And that craves *wary* walking.

THAT.

Crown him *that,*

STING.

And then I grant we put a *sting* in him

DANGER.

That at his will he may do *danger* with.

GREATNESS.

The abuse of *greatness* is,

MR. KAY: Yes, I think *greatness* is a possibility, but what about *abuse*? The point you're making is about the *abuse* of power, right?

DANTE: Let me try that.

(Going back) ABUSE.

The *abuse* of greatness is,

MR. KAY: I think that's clearer.

DANTE: I do, too.

MR. KAY: Just be sure to keep *greatness* as a strong *secondary* stress. Continue, please.

DANTE: POWER.

> when it disjoins
> Remorse from *power*.

MR. KAY: And let's see what happens if you break that into two speech measures, and make *remorse* an operative word inside a speech measure of its own.

DANTE: REMORSE.

> When it disjoins
> *remorse*

POWER.

> from *power*.

MR. KAY: Good. That may not be necessary, but it certainly does make the text crystal clear by giving us time to hear and absorb those two big abstract concepts. Continue, please.

DANTE: CAESAR.

> And to speak truth of *Caesar,*

AFFECTIONS.

> I have not known when his *affections* sway'd
> More than his reason.

MR. KAY: And again, let's see what happens if you break that into two measures, and make *reason* the operative word inside a measure of its own.

DANTE: AFFECTIONS.

> I have not known when his *affections*

REASON.

> sway'd
> More than his *reason.*

MR. KAY: Good. *(To the class)* And did you all hear how the operatives in those two measures related to one another? By balancing those two opposing concepts—*affections* and *reason*—as operative words, Dante illuminated a *figure of speech* in the text—an *antithesis*.

(To Dante) Excellent. Continue, please.

DANTE: PROOF.

> But 'tis a common *proof*

LADDER.

> That lowliness is young ambition's *ladder,*

UPWARD.

Whereto the climber *upward* turns his face;

ATTAINS.

But when he once *attains* the upmost round,

BACK.

He then unto the ladder turns his *back,*

CLOUDS.

Looks in the *clouds,*

SCORNING.

scorning the base degrees
By which he did ascend.

CAESAR.

So *Caesar* may.

LEST.

Then *lest* he may,

PREVENT.

prevent.

COLOR.

And since the quarrel
Will bear no *color* for the thing he is,

FASHION.

Fashion it thus:

MR. KAY: Yes, that's good, *fashion* is a good choice. But be sure you don't throw away the word *thus.*

(To the class) You understand, folks, that *fashion* may be the operative word, but *thus* still needs a strong *secondary* stress, so the audience can hear the colon, and the idea which follows it.

(To Dante) So would you try that measure again, please, with *fashion* as the operative word, and the word *thus* as a secondary stress?

DANTE: FASHION.

Fashion it *thus*:

MR. KAY: Excellent. That's very clear now. Continue, please.

DANTE: IS.

that what he *is,*

AUGMENTED.

augmented,

EXTREMITIES.

Would run to these and these *extremities*;

THEREFORE.

And *therefore*

EGG.

think him as a serpent's *egg,*

HATCHED.

Which *hatched,*

MISCHIEVIOUS.

would as his kind grow *mischievous,*

KILL.

And *kill* him in the shell.

MR. KAY: Yes, and what if "in the shell" were a separate speech measure?

DANTE: *(Going back)* KILL.

And *kill* him

SHELL

In the *shell.*

MR. KAY: Good, Dante, I think that's another possibility to consider. Giving *shell* an operative stress completes the image set up by the words *egg* and *hatched* in previous speech measures.

We'll need much more rehearsal before we can make final decisions about any of these operative words, of course.

But something you may find useful at this point is the idea that keeping track of these operative words—actually making a list of them in your mind—is a great way to begin orchestrating this speech.

Just to prove my point, Dante, let's see if you can run through the speech again, using only the operative words. Think you can do that?

DANTE: I'll give it a try.

MR. KAY: Okay.

DANTE: *(Going back in his mind)* So let's see now . . .

Death . . . part . . . spurn . . . general . . . crown'd . . . change . . . question . . . adder . . . wary . . . that . . . sting . . . danger . . . abuse . . . remorse . . . power . . . Caesar . . . affections . . . reason . . . proof . . . ladder . . . upward . . . attains . . . back . . . clouds . . . scorning . . . Caesar . . . lest . . . prevent . . . color . . . fashion . . . is . . . augmented . . . extremities . . . therefore . . . egg . . . mischievous . . . hatched . . . kill . . . shell.

MR. KAY: Very good, Dante, thank you.

(Dante comes down off the stage.)

(To the class) This is an excellent exercise, folks, because instead of intellectually recalling your text by rote until the words are as dry and brittle as old toast, as many of you do, this exercise asks you to summon up the main thrust of each speech measure, to invoke the sequence of words that do all the heavy lifting in your speech.

(Mr. Kay looks up at the clock.)

It looks like we're out of time for today.

Keep working on these speeches, folks. Be sure to incorporate the work we did today on speech measures, punctuation, and operative words.

I'll see you all back here tomorrow.

BLACKOUT.

SCENE 2

Focal
Points

The Acting Studio. Tuesday.

MR. KAY: Good morning, folks. Yesterday we were talking about dividing the text up into speech measures. Today we're going to look at *focal points*.

(The students write "focal points" in their notebooks.)

A *focal point* is a spot in the room where you can focus your eyes and make a specific connection. It's a visual target from which you can inhale, towards which you can send your energies, onto which you can project an image, and at which you can direct an action.

(The students scramble to write all that down.)

Today we'll look at various ways to use focal points to help us orchestrate these speeches.

Who would like to begin?

∾ SCENE PARTNERS ∾

JESSE: I'm ready!

(Jesse goes up onto the stage.)

MR. KAY: Good, Jesse, thank you. And what are you going to show us today?

JESSE: Berowne, from *Love's Labors Lost.*

MR. KAY: All right. And if you would place yourself in your scene, please, so I can ask you a few questions.

(Jesse stands center stage, and gazes outward.)

Where are you, Berowne?

JESSE: In the King's palace in Navarre.

MR. KAY: And what are you doing in the King's palace in Navarre?

JESSE: Funny you should ask that!

(The class laughs.)

You see, four of us—the King, myself, Longaville and Dumaine—have taken an oath to study for three years, and to see no women during that time.

MR. KAY: I see. And how's that been going?

JESSE: Not very well, actually. We all broke our oaths right away, when the Princess of France showed up with her three beautiful attendants.

MR. KAY: Ah, I see. And who are you talking to now?

JESSE: The King, Longaville, and Dumaine.

MR. KAY: And why are you talking to them? What do you hope to accomplish?

JESSE: They've asked me to prove that we haven't broken our oaths by wooing these women.

MR. KAY: And what's the obstacle? What makes it difficult to prove that?

JESSE: Well, I can't really prove that each of us didn't make the oath. We did. We all signed our names to it. But I *can* try to prove that the oath itself was unlawful, because it violated the laws of nature.

MR. KAY: Yes, good, then let's hear you try to prove that. Begin, please.

BEROWNE: Have at you then, affection's men-at-arms:
Consider what you first did swear unto,
To fast, to study, and to see no woman;
Flat treason 'gainst the kingly state of youth.
Say, can you fast? your stomachs are too young,
And abstinence engenders maladies.
O! we have made a vow to study, lords,
And in that vow we have forsworn our books:
For when would you, my liege, or you, or you,
Have found the ground of study's excellence
Without the beauty of a woman's face?
Why, universal plodding poisons up
The nimble spirits in the arteries,
Other slow arts entirely keep the brain,
But love, first learnèd in a lady's eyes,
Doth give to every pow'r a double power
Above their functions and their offices:
A lover's eyes will gaze an eagle blind;

A lover's ear will hear the lowest sound;
Love's feeling is more soft and sensible
Than are the tender horns of cockl'd snails.
For valor, is not Love a Hercules?
And when Love speaks, the voice of all the gods
Make heaven drowsy with the harmony.
From women's eyes this doctrine I derive:
They are the books, the arts, the academes,
That show, contain, and nourish all the world.
Then fools you were these women to forswear,
Or keeping what is sworn, you will prove fools.
For wisdom's sake, a word that all men love,
Or for love's sake, a word that loves all men,
Or for women's sake, by whom we men are men,
Let us once lose our oaths to find ourselves,
Or else we lose ourselves to keep our oaths.

MR. KAY: Thanks, Jesse, and may I say that's a clever bit of cutting you've done on that speech.

JESSE: *(Feigning humility)* Well . . . thank you.

MR. KAY: I think we should talk about your cutting a little bit later. But first, let's make sure we understand every word of what you're saying before we look at this speech again.

What do you mean by "affection's men-at-arms"?

JESSE: *(Posing absurdly)* Love's warriors.

(The class laughs.)

MR. KAY: Yes, I see. And what do you mean by "abstinence engenders maladies"?

JESSE: Um . . . that fasting can make you sick.

MR. KAY: Yes. And what do you mean by "the ground of study's excellence"?

JESSE: It means . . . um . . . "the most basic benefits of learning."

MR. KAY: Good. And what do you mean by "Other slow arts entirely keep the brain"?

JESSE: Um . . . learning useless information can numb your gray matter.

(The class laughs.)

MR. KAY: Yes, or, more literally . . . some knowledge stays in your head.

JESSE: Yes. I knew that, I just couldn't think of it.

(The class laughs.)

MR. KAY: And what do you mean by "above their functions and their offices"?

JESSE: Over and above what they can normally do.

MR. KAY: Yes. And what do you mean by "the academes"?

JESSE: The schools.

MR. KAY: Yes. What do you mean by "sensible"?

JESSE: That means "sensitive."

MR. KAY: Yes. And what do you mean by "cockl'd snails"?

JESSE: That means "snails in their shells."

MR. KAY: Good. What do you mean by "these women to forswear"?

JESSE: To renounce women.

MR. KAY: And what do you mean by "a word that loves all men"?

JESSE: A word that inspires all men.

MR. KAY: Yes. And what do you mean by "let us once lose our oaths"?

JESSE: Just this once, let's break our word.

MR. KAY: Good, Jesse. Now let's talk about this speech for a moment.

I think one of the biggest challenges of doing this speech is that it requires you to manage *three* imagined scene partners, rather than just one.

Of course, if you were in a production of this play, you'd have three flesh-and-blood actors to connect with.

But right now, because you're attempting to connect with three imaginary scene partners at once, you're not very specific about who you're talking to at any given moment.

And because you're not specific about who you're talking to, your eyes keep wandering back and forth across the room.

And because your eyes are wandering, your physical energies are not focused.

And because your physical energies are not focused, you have no breath support.

And because you have no breath support, your voice lacks resonance.

And because your voice lacks resonance, the speech lacks vocal variety.

And because the speech lacks vocal variety, it seems to be all one long, generalized action.

And because the speech seems long and generalized, we stop listening to you.

JAKE: But besides that, Mrs. Lincoln, how did you like the play?

(The class laughs.)

MR. KAY: *(To the class)* Seriously though, folks, do you see how one craft problem dominoes into another until you've lost the audience altogether?

(To Jesse) The way to solve this problem, Jesse, is to orchestrate exactly who you're talking to from speech measure to speech measure. You must make sure that you're always connecting with *one person at a time,* rather than three imagined partners at once.

To do this, you'll need to set three *focal points*—three places in the space where you can focus your eyes, three "spots" onto which you can project an image of each of the men.

To help you to do that, let's use those three "x"s that I put up on the walls many eons ago.

(Pointing to the walls) Let's say that this "x" in the center of the house—the one behind me—is the King. And this one at house left is Dumaine. And this one at house right is Longaville.

JESSE: But those are so far away! Won't people be able to tell that I'm not looking at something close to me?

MR. KAY: No. It's impossible for an audience to tell whether your focus is short or long. We're simply creating the illusion that your friends are close to you, even though the spots are far off. And besides, even if you wanted to, it isn't possible to focus on a spot in midair!

JESSE: I suppose not.

MR. KAY: So, show me where your friends are.

JESSE: *(Pointing to center)* The King

(Pointing to house left) Dumaine

(Pointing to house right) Longaville.

MR. KAY: Good, you've got it.

Now, let's go through the speech again, Jesse, and this time, let's orchestrate the speech so that you're always directing *specific speech measures* to *specific scene partners.*

(The students write "directing specific speech measures to specific scene partners" in their notebooks.)

In other words, I'd like you to tell us aloud who you're connecting with— "KING," "DUMAINE," or "LONGAVILLE"—*before* you speak each speech measure.

So you'll connect with a focal point, name the person, and speak the entire speech measure. Then you'll shift to another focal point, connect, name, and speak. Got it?

JESSE: *(Drilling it)* Connect. Name. Speak. Got it.

MR. KAY: Yes. So, if you would, please restore the scene in your imagination. *(Jesse does so.)*

And remind us, please, what's the objective?

JESSE: To prove that we haven't broken our oaths.

MR. KAY: And who was the last person to speak to you?

JESSE: Um . . . DUMAINE, I think.

MR. KAY: So is he the first focal point?

JESSE: Yes.

MR. KAY: So begin with him, please. And go.

JESSE: *(Focusing on the house left "x")* DUMAINE.

MR. KAY: And text?

JESSE: Have at you then, affection's men-at-arms:

MR. KAY: Good, and continue, please. New focal point

JESSE: *(Focusing on the house right "x")* LONGAVILLE.
   Consider what you first did swear unto,

MR. KAY: Good. New focal point?

JESSE: *(Focusing on the center "x")* KING.
   To fast,

MR. KAY: New focal point?

JESSE: DUMAINE.
   to study,
   LONGAVILLE.
   and to see no woman;
   KING.
   Flat treason 'gainst the kingly state of youth.

MR. KAY: Excellent! *(To the class)* That moment works well to the *King*, doesn't it, because of the phrase "kingly state."
   (Back to Jesse) Continue, please, Berowne, on your own.

JESSE: DUMAINE.
   Say, can you fast? your stomachs are too young,
   And abstinence engenders maladies.
   LONGAVILLE.

O! we have made a vow to study, lords,
And in that vow we have forsworn our books:

KING.

For when would you, my liege,

DUMAINE.

or you,

LONGAVILLE.

or you,

KING.

Have found the ground of study's excellence
Without the beauty of a woman's face?

LONGAVILLE.

Why, universal plodding poisons up
The nimble spirits in the arteries,

DUMAINE.

Other slow arts entirely keep the brain,

KING.

But love, first learnèd in a lady's eyes,
Doth give to every pow'r a double power
Above their functions and their offices:

DUMAINE.

A lover's eyes will gaze an eagle blind;

LONGAVILLE.

A lover's ear will hear the lowest sound;

KING.

Love's feeling is more soft and sensible
Than are the tender horns of cockl'd snails.

LONGAVILLE.

For valor, is not Love a Hercules?

DUMAINE.

And when Love speaks, the voice of all the gods
Make heaven drowsy with the harmony.

KING.

From women's eyes this doctrine I derive:

DUMAINE.

They are the books,

KING.

the arts,

LONGAVILLE.

the academes,

KING.

That show, contain, and nourish all the world.

DUMAINE.

Then fools you were these women to forswear,

KING.

Or keeping what is sworn, you will prove fools.

LONGAVILLE.

For wisdom's sake, a word that all men love,

DUMAINE.

Or for love's sake, a word that loves all men,

KING.

Or for women's sake, by whom we men are men,

LONGAVILLE.

Let us once lose our oaths to find ourselves,

KING.

Or else we lose ourselves to keep our oaths.

MR. KAY: Well done, Jesse. There's a whole world of improvement in this speech now, simply because you're making specific connections—directing specific speech measures to specific scene partners.

And because you always know who you're talking to and what you want to say, your physical energies are focused.

And because your physical energies are focused, your voice is functioning naturally and resonating well.

And because your voice is resonating well, we hear much greater vocal variety.

And because you have vocal variety, the text is clearer.

You're even beginning to develop different relationships with each of the three men!

Wow! All this from such a simple adjustment. Make sense?

JESSE: Yes!

MR. KAY: *(To the class)* Any thoughts, comments, questions?

RACHEL: Yes! I'm looking at this speech in my *Complete Works,* and it looks totally different!

MR. KAY: Ah! *(To the class)* Check your editions, folks, because many of you will have different versions of this speech. Some of you may even have twenty-three *fewer* lines of verse in this speech.

(The students open their Complete Works *to find the speech.)*

RACHEL: But how is that possible?

MR. KAY: It's possible because some editors are so convinced that these twenty-three lines belong to an earlier draft of the speech that they delete them altogether. Or sometimes they're printed, but placed in brackets to call your attention to them. Or sometimes they're printed with no brackets at all. So you have to be alert.

Now, Jesse has done exactly what most directors of the play have to do when they grapple with this speech—that is, figure out whether to include the lines, or to delete the lines, or to *conflate* the lines.

GABRIELLA: What do you mean by *conflate?*

MR. KAY: What do I mean by conflate? Anyone?

TIM: Isn't that when you combine two different versions of a text together into one?

MR. KAY: Yes, exactly, Tim. And Jesse has done just that—he's cut some of the more difficult lines from the speech, and replaced them with lines from inside the bracketed passage which seem clearer to him. In other words, he's *conflated* two different drafts of this speech to make his own version of the speech.

RACHEL: But is it okay to do that?

MR. KAY: As I've said before, Rachel, I think there are a lot of Shakespeare scholars who might object to this kind of rescripting. But, the fact is, the way Jesse has customized this speech is common theater practice. Because in the theater, *clarity* is what matters most. So, in this instance, I think Jesse is absolutely right to assume that if it's clear, and if it's theatrical, then it's okay.

JESSE: Those were my thoughts exactly.

(The class laughs.)

MR. KAY: Thank you, Jesse. You can come down now.

(Jesse takes a little bow, and comes down off the stage.)

Who would like to go next?

Ᏸ⁊ AUDIENCE Ᏸ⁊

JAKE: I'm ready!

(Jake goes up onto the stage.)

MR. KAY: What are you going to show us today, Jake?

JAKE: Iago, from *Othello.*

MR. KAY: Good, and if you would place yourself in your scene, please, so I can ask you a few questions.

(Jake stands center stage and gazes outward.)

Where are you, Iago?

JAKE: On a street in Cyprus, outside Othello's quarters.

MR. KAY: And what's just happened, the moment before this speech?

JAKE: Well, I've just been talking to Othello's lieutenant, Cassio.

MR. KAY: Yes? What about?

JAKE: He's upset because he just lost his position.

MR. KAY: And why did Cassio lose his position?

JAKE: Because I got him drunk, and he started a brawl.

MR. KAY: I see. So what did you advise him to do?

JAKE: I advised him to ask Desdemona to help him get his position back.

MR. KAY: And who is Desdemona?

JAKE: Othello's wife.

MR. KAY: And you think Desdemona would be willing to talk to her husband on Cassio's behalf?

JAKE: *(With a grin)* Oh yes, definitely.

MR. KAY: I see. And who are you talking to now?

JAKE: The audience.

MR. KAY: And why are you talking to the audience? What do you hope to accomplish?

JAKE: I want to win their support and admiration for my plot to undo Othello.

MR. KAY: I see. And what's the obstacle to that?

JAKE: For some reason, they don't approve of my scheming, and lying, and treachery. Well, most of them anyway.

(The class laughs.)

MR. KAY: All right then, let's see if you can win the rest of them over. And begin, please.

IAGO: And what's he then that says I play the villain
When this advice is free I give, and honest,
Probal to thinking, and indeed the course
To win the Moor again? For 'tis most easy
Th' inclining Desdemona to subdue
In any honest suit; she's fram'd as fruitful
As the free elements. And then for her
To win the Moor, were't to renounce his baptism,
All seals and symbols of redeemèd sin,
His soul is so enfetter'd to her love,
That she may make, unmake, do as she list,
Even as her appetite shall play the god
With his weak function. How am I then a villain
To counsel Cassio to this parallel course,
Directly to his good? Divinity of hell!
When devils will the blackest sins put on,
They do suggest at first with heavenly shows,
As I do now. For whiles this honest fool
Plies Desdemona to repair his fortune
And she for him pleads strongly to the Moor,
I'll pour this pestilence into his ear,
That she repeals him for her body's lust;
And by how much she strives to do him good,
She shall undo her credit with the Moor.
So will I turn her virtue into pitch,
And out of her own goodness make the net
That shall enmesh them all.

MR. KAY: Good, Jake. Now, before we look at this speech again, let's make sure we understand every word of the text. What do you mean by "probal to thinking"?

JAKE: Something logical, or reasonable to assume.

MR. KAY: What do you mean by "Th' inclining Desdemona"?

JAKE: She's inclined to help people when she can.

MR. KAY: What do you mean by "to subdue"?

JAKE: To persuade.

MR. KAY: What do you mean by "fruitful"?

JAKE: Generous.

MR. KAY: What do you mean by "the free elements"?

JAKE: Earth, air, fire, and water.

MR. KAY: What do you mean by "All seals and symbols of redeemèd sin"?

JAKE: Sacraments in the church that show that man can be redeemed from sin.

MR. KAY: What do you mean by "do what she list"?

JAKE: Do whatever she likes.

MR. KAY: What do you mean by "her appetite"?

JAKE: Her will.

MR. KAY: What do you mean by "his weak function"?

JAKE: His dulled ability to act.

MR. KAY: What do you mean by "this parallel course"?

JAKE: This corresponding plan.

MR. KAY: What do you mean by "Divinity of hell"?

JAKE: An argument the devil might admire.

MR. KAY: What do you mean by "the blackest sins put on"?

JAKE: Urge evil acts.

MR. KAY: What do you mean by "Suggest"?

JAKE: Tempt.

MR. KAY: What do you mean by "plies"?

JAKE: Begs repeatedly.

MR. KAY: What do you mean by "pestilence"?

JAKE: Poison.

MR. KAY: What do you mean by "Repeals him"?

JAKE: Tries to get him reinstated.

MR. KAY: Good, Jake. Now, let's talk about this speech for a few minutes.

This is one of several speeches in Othello where Iago talks directly to the audience.

And this, of course, is one of the reasons people love this character so much, why they find him so fascinating. Because—like Richard the Third, Edmund in *Lear,* and Aaron in *Titus*—you tell us exactly what you're planning to do, and then we watch in horror and delight as you do it.

(To the class) Direct address is a convention that Shakespeare uses in

most of his plays, so it's important that we talk about effective ways to speak directly to the audience.

(The students write "direct address" in their notebooks.)

Although it seems a very simple thing to do, direct address can actually be very tricky to pull off successfully.

If you try to talk to *everyone in the audience* at once— which is what you're attempting, Jake, by panning and scanning your eyes around the room—we feel as though you're talking to no one in particular.

On the other hand, if you try to talk to *one person at a time* by pinpointing selected individuals, those people feel terribly self-conscious, and everyone else feels left out.

To solve this problem, I'd like to suggest a third approach.

(To Jake) I'd like to suggest, Jake, that you direct *specific speech measures* to *specific focal points* around the room.

(The students write "direct specific speech measures to specific focal points" in their notebooks.)

Let's have another look at this speech, and I'll show you what I mean by that.

And this time through, let's imagine that you're in a proscenium theater of about six hundred seats. And for now, I'm going to limit you to three, and *only* three, points of focus: one in the *center* the house, one at house *left,* and one at house *right.*

Of course, in a real theater, you could use the exit signs, or the aisle lights, or a light in the booth to find focal points during a performance. But in here, I want you to use those same three "x"s on the walls that we used for Berowne's friends a few minutes ago.

(Pointing to the walls) I'd like you to look at *one,* and *only* one, of those three points as you speak, and nowhere else.

Also, I'd like you to tell us *aloud* which of those three focal points you're connecting with as you work from measure to measure through the speech—by saying either "RIGHT," "LEFT," or "CENTER."

All right?

JAKE: Okay.

MR. KAY: And remind us, please, what's your objective, Iago?

JAKE: To win their support and admiration for my plot.

MR. KAY: And begin, please—first focal point?

JAKE: *(Focusing on an "x")* CENTER.

And what's he then that says I play the villain

(Focusing on another "x") RIGHT.

When this advice is free I give, and honest,

MR. KAY: And let me stop you there, because I want to ask you to do one more thing, Jake. I want you to take the time to *inhale* from your focal point before you speak each speech measure.

In other words, you must avoid saying "Center and what's he then" or "Right when this advice is free I give."

You must give yourself the time you need to establish a connection, to get the thought you wish to communicate in your mind, and to inhale that thought *before* you speak.

So, this is the sequence: you *connect* to the point of focus, you *name* it aloud, you *inhale* from your point of focus, you *speak* the speech measure.

Connect. Name. Inhale. Speak.

Got it?

JAKE: *(Drilling it)* Connect, name, inhale, speak.

Got it.

MR. KAY: Good, and go back to the top again, please.

JAKE: *(Connecting to a focal point, and naming it)* CENTER.

(He inhales the focal point, and speaks:)

And what's he then that says I play the villain

MR. KAY: Good, and continue . . .

JAKE: *(He connects, and names . . .)*

RIGHT.

(He inhales, and speaks . . .)

When this advice is free I give, and honest,

(He connects, and names . . .)

LEFT.

(He inhales, and speaks . . .)

Probal to thinking,

(He connects, and names . . .)

CENTER.

(He inhales, and speaks . . .)

and indeed the course
To win the Moor again?

MR. KAY: Excellent!

(To the class) And do you all *hear* the difference in his voice when he takes the time to *inhale* from his focal point?

When he inhales from a specific point in the theater, his body responds with the *support* necessary to reach that point with his voice.

When he speaks to that specific focal point, his tonal quality is resonant and clear and unforced, so it is much easier to *hear* and *understand* him.

(Back to Jake) And continue, please, Iago, from where you stopped.

JAKE: RIGHT.

For 'tis most easy
Th' inclining Desdemona to subdue
In any honest suit;

CENTER.

she's fram'd as fruitful
As the free elements.

LEFT.

And then for her
To win the Moor,

CENTER.

were't to renounce his baptism,

RIGHT.

All seals and symbols of redeemèd sin,

CENTER.

His soul is so enfetter'd to her love,
That she may make, unmake, do as she list,

LEFT.

Even as her appetite shall play the god
With his weak function.

CENTER.

How am I then a villain
To counsel Cassio to this parallel course,
Directly to his good?

MR. KAY: *(To the class)* And do you all see how much stronger his connection to the audience is?

His eyes are no longer panning and scanning around the theater, so his face is now *available* to the audience.

And because he's presenting one speech measure, containing one moment of human behavior, directed at one focal point at a time, it's much easier for the audience to *read* his performance.

(To Jake) Excellent, Jake.

Now, let's assume that you're in a theater of about 1200 seats. There's a *balcony* in this theater. So, let's add one more point of focus for the folks up there. Would you please use that "x" on the ceiling above me as the balcony? And continue from where you left off.

JAKE: *(Focusing on the "x" on the ceiling)* BALCONY.

Divinity of hell!

MR. KAY: *(To the class)* And do you hear how choosing the balcony as the focal point for that moment and *inhaling* from that focal point allows him to fill the space vocally with great power and ease? Excellent!

(To Jake) Continue, please, Iago.

JAKE: CENTER.

When devils will the blackest sins put on,

RIGHT.

They do suggest at first with heavenly shows,

LEFT.

As I do now.

CENTER.

For whiles this honest fool
Plies Desdemona to repair his fortune

BALCONY.

And she for him pleads strongly to the Moor,

LEFT.

I'll pour this pestilence into his ear,

RIGHT.

That she repeals him for her body's lust;

MR. KAY: *(To the class)* And do you all hear how he's using a quiet, conversational tone to left and right, a more resonant tone to center, and his strongest, most resonant tone to the balcony?

Choosing specific focal points inside the theater can help you to orchestrate a speech for *dynamic variety,* creating changes in *volume,* from soft to loud and all points in between, which keeps the audience listening.

(To Jake) Continue, please, Iago.

JAKE: CENTER.

And by how much she strives to do him good,

BALCONY.

She shall undo her credit with the Moor.

LEFT.

So will I turn her virtue into pitch,

RIGHT.

And out of her own goodness make the net

CENTER.

That shall enmesh them all.

MR. KAY: Thank you, Jake. Well done.

(Jake comes down off the stage.)

(To the class) I want to remind you, folks, that the use of focal points is nothing new to you. You've been using them all along in dance class, in tai chi, in fencing, in yoga.

Using focal points in your *acting* helps you to bring all that training to bear by focusing your breath and your physical energies on a single point in time and space, just as it does in those other disciplines.

(The students reflect upon that idea for a moment.)

Let's look at another speech. Who wants to work?

✦ AUDIENCE AND SELF ✦

NOAH: I'll go!

(Noah goes up onto the stage.)

MR. KAY: What are you going to show us today, Noah?

NOAH: Benedick, from *Much Ado About Nothing.*

MR. KAY: All right. If you would place yourself in your scene, please, so I can ask you a few questions.

(Noah hides in front of the curtain at stage left.)

Where are you, Benedick?

NOAH: I'm in the garden of Governor Leonato's house, in Messina.

MR. KAY: And what are you doing there in the garden?

NOAH: Well, I've been eavesdropping on a conversation between my friends.

MR. KAY: I see. Did you hear anything interesting?

NOAH: Yes. I just found out that the woman who has driven me crazy for many years is actually in love with me.

MR. KAY: Who is that?

NOAH: Beatrice.

MR. KAY: I see. And are you alone now?

NOAH: Yes.

MR. KAY: So who are you talking to?

NOAH: Myself, and the audience.

MR. KAY: Why? What do you hope to accomplish by talking to yourself and the audience?

NOAH: I need to decide whether to fall in love with Beatrice.

MR. KAY: And what are the obstacles to that? Why wouldn't you fall in love with her?

NOAH: Well, I'd look like a fool to fall in love with this woman after squabbling with her for all these years. And I've always mocked love and lovers, and swore I'd never get married. Besides, this might just be a trick my friends are playing on me.

MR. KAY: All right, then, let's hear how you make your decision. Begin, please.

BENEDICK: This can be no trick. The conference was sadly borne; they have the truth of this from Hero; they seem to pity the lady. It seems her affections have their full bent. Love me? Why, it must be requited. I hear how I am censured. They say I will bear myself proudly if I perceive the love come from her. They say too that she will rather die than give any sign of affection. I did never think to marry. I must not seem proud. Happy are they that hear their detractions and can put them to mending. They say the lady is fair—'tis a truth, I can bear them witness; and virtuous—'tis so, I cannot reprove it; and wise—but for loving me; by my troth, it is no addition to her wit, nor no great argument of her folly, for I will be horribly in love with her. I may chance have some odd quirks and remnants of wit broken on me because I have railed so long against marriage. But doth not the appetite alter? A man loves the meat in his youth that he cannot endure in his age. Shall quips and sentences and these paper bullets of the brain awe a man from the career of his humor? No, the world must be peopled. When I said I would die a bachelor, I did not think I should live till I were married. Here comes Beatrice. By this day, she's a fair lady. I do spy some marks of love in her.

MR. KAY: Good, Noah. Before we look at this speech again, let's make sure we understand every word of the text.

What do you mean by "The conference was sadly borne"?

NOAH: Their discussion was serious.

MR. KAY: What do you mean by "her affections have their full bent"?

NOAH: Her love is stretched to the limit.

MR. KAY: What do you mean by "their detractions"?

NOAH: Criticism of my faults.

MR. KAY: What do you mean by "I cannot reprove it"?

NOAH: I can't argue with that.

MR. KAY: What do you mean by "some odd quirks and remnants of wit"?

NOAH: Some old, stale pranks, and leftover jokes.

MR. KAY: What do you mean by "quips and sentences and these paper bullets of the brain"?

NOAH: Jokes and anecdotes and meaningless hot air.

MR. KAY: What do you mean by "awe a man from the career of his humor"?

NOAH: Frighten a man from pursuing his heart's desire.

MR. KAY: Good, Noah. Let's look at this speech again.

(To the class) Now, it's possible, folks, to perform this speech talking entirely to *yourself*, and never including the audience. But since this is a *comedy*, that doesn't seem at all like a fun approach.

It's also possible to speak this speech entirely to the *audience*, and never talk to yourself. But I think you'd miss some fun moments of self-reflection with that approach, too.

It's clear from watching this that Noah has decided that he wants to talk both to *himself* and the *audience*, and I think that's a smart choice.

But it's the *execution* of that approach that I want to look at now.

(To Noah) Because sometimes, Noah, we can't tell where you intend to place your focus. Your eyes wander so much within the speech measures that we can't tell who you're talking to—yourself, or us.

The other problem I think we need to address is your tendency to look down to get new ideas. I know that feels natural to you, but it makes you completely unavailable to the audience.

So, this time through, from speech measure to speech measure, I'm going to ask you to tell us exactly where you intend to place your focus, by saying aloud either "SELF" or "AUDIENCE."

(The students write "self" and "audience" in their notebooks.)

For AUDIENCE, please use those same three "x"s taped on the walls for focal points.

For SELF, would you please use that "x" on the ceiling as a focal point *above* the audience. Not *in* the audience, but clearly *above* us, so we know you're not talking to *us*, but to *yourself*. All right?

NOAH: Got it.

MR. KAY: So you *connect* with the focal point, you say AUDIENCE or SELF, you *inhale* from the point of focus, and you *speak* your text.

Connect. Name. Inhale. Speak.

Got it?

NOAH: Yes.

MR. KAY: So, if you would restore your scene in your imagination, please, Noah.

(Noah does so.)

And remind us, please, what's your objective?

NOAH: To decide whether to fall in love with Beatrice.

MR. KAY: Good, and first focal point? Self or audience?

NOAH: *(Focused on the house right "x")* AUDIENCE.

MR. KAY: And text?

NOAH: This can be no trick.

MR. KAY: Good, and continue, please—self or audience?

NOAH: *(Focused on the "x" on the ceiling)* SELF.

The conference was sadly borne;

(Focused on the house left "x") AUDIENCE.

they have the truth of this from Hero;

(Focused on the "x" on the ceiling) SELF.

they seem to pity the lady.

(Focused on the center "x") AUDIENCE.

It seems her affections have their full bent.

MR. KAY: *(To the class)* And do you all see how placing the focal point for SELF just above the audience makes his face *available* to everyone in the house? We paid good money to see his *face* as these revelations come to him, not the top of his head!

(To Noah) Continue, please, Benedick—next focal point?

NOAH: *(To the balcony)* SELF.

Love me?

(To house right) AUDIENCE.

Why, it must be requited.

MR. KAY: Good, Noah. Now, let's get even more specific with this.

Would you please tell us, when you choose AUDIENCE, exactly *who* you're talking to—that is, *describe* the person in the audience you're connecting with.

(The students write "describe the person in the audience" in their notebooks.)

And here's a hint, Noah—whenever you can, choose people who will *inspire* the next speech measure. You follow me?

NOAH: *(Getting the idea)* Yes, I think so.

MR. KAY: And don't forget to keep focusing on just those four spots. Continue, please. Who are you talking to, Berowne?

NOAH: Um . . . AN OLD WOMAN.

I hear how I am censured.

MR. KAY: Good, continue.

NOAH: A SOLDIER IN UNIFORM.

They say I will bear myself proudly if I perceive the love come from her.

A NURSE.

They say too that she will rather die than give any sign of affection.

A MARRIED MAN.

I did never think to marry.

SELF.

I must not seem proud.

A FAT GUY.

Happy are they that hear their detractions and can put them to mending.

A BEAUTIFUL BLONDE.

They say the lady is fair—

SELF.

'tis a truth, I can bear them witness;

A NUN.

and virtuous—

SELF.

'tis so, I cannot reprove it;

A PROFESSOR.

and wise—

SELF.

but for loving me;

A JUDGE.

by my troth, it is no addition to her wit,
nor no great argument of her folly,

SELF.

for I will be horribly in love with her.

A REDNECK.

I may chance have some odd quirks and remnants of wit broken on me
because I have railed so long against marriage.

A COOK.

But doth not the appetite alter?

A TEENAGER.

A man loves the meat in his youth
that he cannot endure in his age.

A LAWYER.

Shall quips and sentences and these paper bullets of the brain awe a man
from the career of his humor?

SELF.

No,

A PRIEST.

the world must be peopled.

A BACHELOR.

When I said I would die a bachelor,

A DOCTOR.

I did not think I should live till I were married.

MR. KAY: Good, and now let's add Beatrice as a focal point. Where is she coming from?

NOAH: From the house.

MR. KAY: Which is where?

NOAH: *(Pointing upstage)* Up there.

MR. KAY: All right, then. Please connect with a focal point upstage, and continue, Benedick.

NOAH: *(Focusing upstage)* BEATRICE.

Here comes Beatrice.

(Focusing house center) A LITTLE GIRL.

By this day, she's a fair lady.

BEATRICE.

I do spy some marks of love in her.

MR. KAY: Excellent, Noah. Thank you.

(Noah comes down off the stage.)

(To the class) Did you all see and hear how projecting an *imaginary person* onto each focal point informed his choice of *operative words,* and inspired new *actions* for each speech measure? That's another effective way to orchestrate a speech in direct address.

Any questions, comments, or thoughts about any of this?

(Tayo raises her hand.)

Tayo?

TAYO: But it seems so artificial to do it this way! I mean, why can't he just wait until he gets an audience, and then talk to *real* people?

MR. KAY: That's a great question, Tayo.

There are at least *two* reasons why it's better to orchestrate your connections ahead of time with *imaginary* people than to wait for an *actual* audience.

The first reason is that you probably won't be able to *see* who's in the audience past the first few rows anyway, because the lights will be in your eyes.

The second reason is that even if you *could* see individuals clearly, it's very *unlikely* that the people you connect with from night to night will inspire you to play a sequence of actions as strong and as varied as what we just saw Noah play.

So why leave things up to chance? Orchestrate your connections ahead of time, and create the *illusion* that you're talking to specific people in the spur of the moment! It's the magic of theater.

Let's look at another speech. Who'd like to go next?

〰 MULTIPLE FOCAL POINTS 〰

ELENA: My turn!

(Elena goes up onto the stage, carrying a white sheet.)

MR. KAY: What will you be showing us today, Elena?

ELENA: Lady Anne, from *Richard the Third.*

(She spreads the sheet out onto the ground.)

MR. KAY: All right, then. And if you would place yourself in your scene, please, while I ask you some questions.

(Elena stands over the sheet, and gazes outward.)

First of all, may I ask you your full name?

ELENA: Yes, you may. My name is Anne Neville. I'm the daughter of Richard Neville, the Earl of Warwick.

MR. KAY: I see. And where are you now, Anne Neville?

ELENA: In the streets of London.

MR. KAY: And what are you doing?

ELENA: I'm taking the body of King Henry to Chertsey, where he'll be buried.

MR. KAY: Which King Henry?

ELENA: King Henry the Sixth.

MR. KAY: I see. And why are you taking the body of King Henry the Sixth to Chertsey?

ELENA: I'm the chief mourner.

MR. KAY: So, were you related to the King?

ELENA: I was married to his son Edward, before he was killed.

MR. KAY: And who killed your husband, Edward?

ELENA: Richard, Duke of Gloucester.

MR. KAY: And who killed King Henry the Sixth?

ELENA: Richard, Duke of Gloucester.

MR. KAY: And who are you talking to now?

ELENA: Richard, Duke of Gloucester.

MR. KAY: I see. Is anyone else there with you?

ELENA: Yes, there are guards, and pallbearers with me, but mostly I'm cursing out Richard.

MR. KAY: Why? What's your objective?

ELENA: I want revenge for the death of King Henry.

MR. KAY: And how are you going to get your revenge in this moment?

ELENA: I'm going to ask God to strike him down with a thunderbolt, and I'm going to ask the earth to open up and swallow him alive.

MR. KAY: And what's the obstacle? What's preventing you from getting that revenge in this moment?

ELENA: I'm absolutely powerless to make those things happen.

MR. KAY: Good, and begin, please.

ANNE: Foul devil, for God's sake hence and trouble us not,
For thou hast made the happy earth thy hell,
Fill'd it with cursing cries and deep exclaims.
If thou delight to view thy heinous deeds,
Behold this pattern of thy butcheries.
O gentlemen, see, see! Dead Henry's wounds
Open their congealèd mouths and bleed afresh.
Blush, blush, thou lump of foul deformity,
For 'tis thy presence that exhales this blood
From cold and empty veins where no blood dwells.
Thy deed, inhuman and unnatural,
Provokes this deluge most unnatural.
O God, which this blood made'st, revenge his death.
O earth, which this blood drink'st, revenge his death.
Either heav'n with lightning strike the murderer dead,
Or earth gape open wide and eat him quick
As thou dost swallow up this good king's blood,
Which his hell-govern'd arm hath butcherèd.

MR. KAY: Very good, Elena. Before we do the speech again, let's make sure we have a complete understanding of the text.

What do you mean when you say "for God's sake hence"?

ELENA: For Christ's sake, go away!

MR. KAY: What do you mean by "deep exclaims"?

ELENA: Sorrowful moaning.

MR. KAY: What do you mean by "this pattern of thy butcheries"?

ELENA: This bloody example of your handiwork.

MR. KAY: What do you mean by "exhales this blood"?

ELENA: Draws the blood out from his dead body.

MR. KAY: What do you mean by "bleed afresh"?

ELENA: Well . . . people used to think that a murdered man would bleed again in the presence of his murderer.

MR. KAY: I see. And what do you mean by "eat him quick"?

ELENA: Eat him alive.

MR. KAY: Good, Elena. Now, let's talk about this speech for a moment or two.

This is a scene that you might see in the news on any given day: a distraught woman grieving over the body of a murdered loved one, and crying for vengeance from heaven.

And this is one of the challenges of playing Lady Anne—the play has barely begun, and she's dealing with a tragedy which, in any other play, might occur at the *end* of the evening, rather than the beginning.

Then Shakespeare has the audacity to bring the murderer himself into the scene! And what does the ogre want? He wants to marry you!

Now, I think you're doing a good job, Elena, of finding the despair and the venom that motivates her desire for vengeance in this speech.

But I think there's so much more opportunity for *clarity* and *variety* here, if you would simply orchestrate your focal points.

The problem is that your focus is all over the place. You're trying to talk in so many directions all at the same time—to Richard, to the guards, to the heavens—that we're not sure who you're talking to at any given moment. And so the speech goes by in a blur.

(To the class) Of course, in life people do this all the time—they shift rapidly between several points of focus. They *multitask.*

A human being will drive his car, talk on the phone, smoke a cigarette, fiddle with the radio, watch a bird, and eat a burrito all at the same time.

And when you're acting for the camera with contemporary text it's all right to do this—to shift rapidly and randomly between several points of focus.

But in the live theater, and especially in *Shakespeare,* if you do this, you get mud.

You get mud because a theater audience needs you to do just *one thing at a time* in linear sequence in order to *read* your performance—to know your objective, to see your images, to discern your actions.

So, you must learn to manage *multiple focal points* by connecting with one, and *only* one, focal point at a time.

(The students write "multiple focal points" in their notebooks.)

(To Elena) So let's go through this again, Elena, and I'd like to suggest that we orchestrate the speech by choosing one, and *only* one, focal point for each speech measure.

First, let's list all the possible focal points.

Would you please tell us, Elena, *everyone* and *everything* you connect with during this speech?

ELENA: Well, as you said, I connect with *Richard,* of course, and the *guards* . . .

MR. KAY: Yes.

ELENA: And I talk to *God,* and to the *earth*, and, uh . . .

MR. KAY: Do you connect with Henry's *body*?

ELENA: Yes.

MR. KAY: Do you connect with Henry's *wounds*?

ELENA: Yes.

MR. KAY: Anything else?

ELENA: Not that I can think of.

MR. KAY: All right, then, let's assign *focal points* in the room for all of those things you listed.

First of all, show us your focal point for *Richard.*

ELENA: *(Indicating house left)* That "x" over there.

MR. KAY: All right, and your focal point for the *guards*?

ELENA: *(Indicating house right)* That "x".

MR. KAY: And where is your focal point for *God*?

ELENA: *(Pointing up)* The "x" on the ceiling.

MR. KAY: Good. And your focal point for the *earth*?

ELENA: *(Pointing down)* The floor.

MR. KAY: Can you be more specific? Where on the floor?

ELENA: Um, this piece of green tape.

MR. KAY: Good. And your focal point for *Henry's body*?

ELENA: This sheet.

MR. KAY: And your focal point for the *wounds*?

ELENA: *(Pointing down)* Um, well, there's a blob of red paint here on the floor.

MR. KAY: That's certainly convenient!

(The class laughs.)

Now, let's go through the speech again, and I'd like you to tell us each new focal point *aloud* by saying "RICHARD" or "THE GUARDS" or whatever it is you're connecting with.

So, once again, as we've done before, this is the sequence: you *connect* with the new focal point, you *name* the focal point, you *inhale* from your point of focus, and you *speak* your text.

ELENA: Connect, name, inhale, speak.

MR. KAY: You've got it. So let's go back to the top, please.

(Elena restores the scene.)

And remind us, please—what's your objective, Anne?

ELENA: To avenge the death of King Henry.

MR. KAY: First focal point?

ELENA: RICHARD.

MR. KAY: And text?

ELENA: Foul devil, for God's sake hence and trouble us not,
For thou hast made the happy earth thy hell,
Fill'd it with cursing cries and deep exclaims.
If thou delight to view thy heinous deeds,
Behold this pattern of thy butcheries.

MR. KAY: *(Interrupting)* And let me stop you there, please, Elena, because you shifted your focus just now without telling us about it.

ELENA: I did?

MR. KAY: Yes, you stopped looking at Richard and moved on to a new focal point. What are you focused on now?

ELENA: Um, the body, I guess?

MR. KAY: Yes, I think so. So, let's go back to the top, please, and this time, tell us *aloud* when you shift your focus to the body. Okay?

ELENA: Okay.

(She goes back to the beginning of her speech.)

RICHARD.

Foul devil, for God's sake hence and trouble us not,
For thou hast made the happy earth thy hell,
Fill'd it with cursing cries and deep exclaims.
If thou delight to view thy heinous deeds,

(Focusing down on the sheet) HENRY'S BODY.
Behold this pattern of thy butcheries.

MR. KAY: Good, good, continue, please.

(Elena drops to her knees and throws off the sheet.)

ELENA: THE WOUNDS.

O gentlemen, see, see! Dead Henry's wounds
Open their congealèd mouths and bleed afresh.

MR. KAY: *(Interrupting)* And let me stop you again, please, Elena—where is your focus now?

ELENA: Um, on the *wounds.*

MR. KAY: On the wounds?

ELENA: Yes.

MR. KAY: But, you looked up at the *guards* several times during that last speech measure.

ELENA: I did?

MR. KAY: Yes. And because you're shifting your eyes rapidly back and forth between two points of focus—between the *guards* and the *wounds*—the scene is now mush.

(The students laugh.)

(To Elena) So, let's go back to "O gentlemen" and decide whether you're going to connect with the *guards,* or the *wounds.*

ELENA: Well, I'm confused, because I say, "O gentlemen," so I'm talking to the *guards,* but I'm *looking* at the wounds.

MR. KAY: So, you're looking at the *wounds* on "O gentlemen"?

ELENA: Yes.

MR. KAY: All right then. For now, let's say that the first focal point will be the *wounds.* Begin there. Then, when you're ready, tell us when you shift to the *guards.* All right?

ELENA: Okay.

MR. KAY: So restore to that moment, please.

(She spreads the sheet out again, and gazes down at it.)

Uncover the body.

(She does so.)

Focal point?

ELENA: THE WOUNDS.

MR. KAY: And text?

ELENA: O gentlemen, see, see!

MR. KAY: Next focal point?

ELENA: *(Looking up)* THE GUARDS.

MR. KAY: And text?

ELENA: Dead Henry's wounds
Open their congealèd mouths and bleed afresh.

MR. KAY: Good. Very good, Elena. That's very clear now.

So, that's one possible approach. Let's try another. This time, shift to the guards for only the second "see." Then shift back to the wounds.

Any idea why am I asking you to do that?

ELENA: Um . . . no.

MR. KAY: *(To the class)* Anybody?

TRINITY: So that the two "see"s will be different?

MR. KAY: Precisely. Since the word "see" is repeated, why play it the same way twice? It's an opportunity to orchestrate two different moments using the same word.

(To Elena) So restore to that same moment, again, please, Elena.

(She does so.)

Uncover the body.

(She does so.)

Focal point?

ELENA: THE WOUNDS.

MR. KAY: Text?

ELENA: O gentlemen, see,

MR. KAY: Now to the guards!

ELENA: *(Looking up)* THE GUARDS.

see!

MR. KAY: And back to the wounds.

ELENA: *(Looking down)* THE WOUNDS.

Dead Henry's wounds
Open their congealèd mouths and bleed afresh.

MR. KAY: Excellent, Elena. So that's another possible way to handle that moment. There are probably two dozen more. And once you've explored them all through *trial and error,* you'll know which one is the best. This is what is known as *rehearsal.*

(The class laughs.)

So, let's continue. From "blush," please.

(Elena focuses on the house left "x".)

ELENA: RICHARD.

Blush, blush, thou lump of foul deformity,
For 'tis thy presence that exhales this blood

THE WOUNDS.

From cold and empty veins where no blood dwells.

RICHARD.

Thy deed, inhuman and unnatural,
Provokes this deluge most unnatural.

GOD.

O God, which this blood made'st, revenge his death.

EARTH.

O earth, which this blood drink'st, revenge his death.

HEAVEN.

Either heav'n with lightning strike the murderer dead,

EARTH.

Or earth gape open wide and eat him quick

HENRY.

As thou dost swallow up this good king's blood,

RICHARD.

Which his hell-govern'd arm hath butcherèd.

MR. KAY: Excellent! That's very *clear,* Elena.

Now we can read your performance in a linear sequence—uncover the body, see the wounds, talk to the guards, curse out Richard, plead to God, smite the earth—one focal point a time.

And now that you're clear about your *focus* from moment to moment, there's much more physical and vocal *variety* in the speech as well.

(To the class) Remember, folks, the art of orchestration is about creating a linear sequence of connections, a sequence which is artistically *selected, arranged,* and *heightened* based on the text, a sequence which can be read by the audience from moment to moment in order to follow your character's journey through the play.

(To Elena) Now, just to prove my point, Elena, let's review our orchestration of this scene so far.

I'd like you to go through the speech again, but this time *without text,* moving through space and saying only the *focal points* in sequence as we've rehearsed them. All right?

ELENA: Okay.

MR. KAY: So, would you restore to the top of the scene, please.

(Elena resets the sheet and stands up again, gazing outward.)

MR. KAY: Ready? And begin.

ELENA: *(Focusing right)* RICHARD.

(Focusing down) HENRY.

(Removing the sheet, focusing down) WOUNDS.

(Focusing left) GUARDS.

(Focusing down) WOUNDS.

(Focusing right) RICHARD.

(Focusing down) WOUNDS.

(Focusing right) RICHARD.

(Focusing up) GOD.

(Focusing down) EARTH.

(Focusing up) HEAVEN.

(Focusing down) EARTH.

(Focusing down) HENRY.

(Focusing right) RICHARD.

MR. KAY: Excellent, Elena. Thank you.

(Elena comes down off the stage.)

(To the class) This is a great way to work, folks, because you're memorizing the sequence of connections that *inspire* text, rather than the text itself. This will ensure that your performance is always alive and fresh and spontaneous, rather than lifeless and cold, like King Henry's corpse.

(The class laughs.)

(Mr. Kay looks up at the clock.)

It looks like our time is up for today.

Keep working on these speeches, folks, incorporating the work we've begun. See you tomorrow.

BLACKOUT.

SCENE 3

Images

The Acting Studio. Wednesday.

MR. KAY: Good morning, folks. Yesterday we talked about how to work with focal points. Today we're going to look at images.

(The students write "images" in their notebooks.)

What do I mean by an image? Anyone?

ELENA: *(Wagering a guess)* Something you see in your imagination?

MR. KAY: Yes, definitely, Elena, an image is something you see in your imagination, something you see with the mind's eye.

But for an actor, an image can be more than that.

It can also be something you *hear* with your mind's *ear.*

Or something you *taste* with the mind's *tongue.*

Or *touch* with the mind's *skin.*

Or *smell* with the mind's *nose.*

So, with that in mind, let's do a little experiment.

I'd like you to all to sit quietly for a moment, with your eyes open, and focus on a point somewhere in the room.

(The students find focal points around the room.)

Good. And now, I'd like you to think for a moment about the house you grew up in.

Picture a specific detail about that house in your mind's eye. What do you *see*?

(A pause.)

Now you can *hear* something in that house. It's a very specific sound you can hear in your mind's ear. What is it? What do you *hear*?

(A pause.)

Now, you can *taste* something from inside the house. Be specific. What do you *taste* on your mind's tongue?

(A pause.)

And now imagine that you can *touch* something in the house. Be specific. What is it? What does it *feel* like on your skin?

(A pause.)

And imagine you can *smell* something from that house. Be specific. What does it *smell* like in your nose?

(A pause.)

Good. And now gently bring yourselves back into this room, please. And relax.

(The students relax.)

Thank you.

Now, I'm sure, because you are all imaginative people—that's why you've chosen to become actors—that conjuring up those details from the house you grew up in was not a difficult task.

And I'm sure you understand now that when I talk about *image,* I'm talking about all five senses—anything that you can *see, hear, taste, touch,* or *smell* in your imagination.

So as we work today on your speeches, I want you to be as *specific* and *detailed* and *personal* about the images you use in Shakespeare as you are about the houses you grew up in.

So, who wants to work?

ᕯᕯᕯ IMAGE TO IMAGE WITH ᕯᕯᕯ
A SINGLE FOCAL POINT

GABRIELLA: I'll go first!

(Gabriella goes up onto the stage.)

MR. KAY: Thank you, Gabriella. What are you going to show us?

GABRIELLA: Queen Gertrude, from *Hamlet.*

MR. KAY: Okay, and if you would place yourself in your scene, please, I'll ask you a few questions.

(Gabriella stands upstage center, and gazes outward.)

Where are you, Queen Gertrude?

GABRIELLA: In the Castle at Elsinore.

MR. KAY: Are you in particular room?

GABRIELLA: In a drawing room.

MR. KAY: And who's there with you?

GABRIELLA: Laertes, Ophelia's brother.

MR. KAY: And who else?

GABRIELLA: The King, my husband.

MR. KAY: And what's just happened?

GABRIELLA: I just told Laertes that his sister is dead.

MR. KAY: How did she die?

GABRIELLA: She drowned in the brook.

MR. KAY: I see. Did you actually *watch* her drown?

GABRIELLA: Yes.

MR. KAY: Why didn't you do something to stop her?

GABRIELLA: I saw her from a window in the castle. But by the time I understood what was happening, it was too late.

MR. KAY: I see. So who are you talking to now? Laertes?

GABRIELLA: No, it's too painful to look him in the eyes. I'm not looking at him at all. I'm looking away from him.

MR. KAY: You're talking to yourself?

GABRIELLA: Yes.

MR. KAY: Why? What do you hope to accomplish?

GABRIELLA: I'm trying to find some meaning in Ophelia's death.

MR. KAY: And what's the obstacle to that?

GABRIELLA: I'm in shock. I can't find a reason these things are happening.

MR. KAY: Good, and begin, please.

GERTRUDE: There is a willow grows aslant the brook
  That shows his hoar leaves in the glassy stream.
  Therewith fantastic garlands did she make
  Of crowflow'rs, nettles, daisies, and long purples,
  That lib'ral shepherds give a grosser name,
  But our cold maids do "dead men's fingers" call them.
  There on the pendant boughs her crownet weeds
  Clamb'ring to hang, an envious sliver broke,

When down the weedy trophies and herself
Fell into the weeping brook. Her clothes spread wide,
And mermaid-like awhile they bore her up,
Which time she chanted snatches of old tunes,
As one incapable of her own distress,
Or like a creature native and endu'd
Unto that element. But long it could not be
Till that her garments, heavy with their drink,
Pull'd the poor wretch from her melodious lay
To muddy death.

MR. KAY: Very good, Gabriella. Now, let me ask you about some of the language in this speech before we continue.

What do you mean by "aslant the brook"?

GABRIELLA: The branches of the willow tree reach over the brook.

MR. KAY: What do you mean by "hoar leaves"?

GABRIELLA: The leaves of the tree are silver-white.

MR. KAY: What do you mean by "long purples"?

GABRIELLA: Those are orchids.

MR. KAY: What do you mean by "lib'ral shepherds"?

GABRIELLA: Foul-mouthed shepherds.

MR. KAY: What do you mean by "cold maids"?

GABRIELLA: Young virgins.

MR. KAY: What do you mean by "the pendant boughs"?

GABRIELLA: The overhanging branches.

MR. KAY: What do you mean by "her crownet weeds"?

GABRIELLA: The garland that Ophelia made from her flowers.

MR. KAY: What do you mean by "an envious sliver"?

GABRIELLA: A spiteful little branch.

MR. KAY: What do you mean by "incapable of her own distress"?

GABRIELLA: Not understanding the danger she was in.

MR. KAY: What do you mean by "endu'd unto that element"?

GABRIELLA: Well-suited to the water.

MR. KAY: What's a "melodious lay"?

GABRIELLA: A pretty song.

MR. KAY: Good, Gabriella. Now, let's talk about this speech for a minute or two.

I agree with you, Gabriella, that Queen Gertrude is in shock in this scene.

She's learned that King Hamlet, her first husband, was murdered. She's seen Polonius stabbed to death in her own chamber. She's watched her son Hamlet exiled to England. And finally she's seen Ophelia go mad, and drown. She's witnessed the lives of all the people she once loved completely destroyed.

So, yes, Gertrude is deeply traumatized by this point in the play.

The problem is, Gabriella, that you're allowing her *shock* to overwhelm every other value in the speech. You're playing the *emotion* of the speech, rather than the *specifics* of the *text*.

Gertrude's description of how Ophelia drowned, for example, is minutely detailed, right down to the color of the leaves on the tree, the kind of flowers in her garlands, and how her clothes floated on the water.

But as we watch you, we don't see you *see* the things you describe. We get the emotion, we get the shock, but that's all we get. Because you haven't done the work of making the images in each speech measure *specific* and *detailed* in your own imagination.

So let's orchestrate a specific sequence of images for the speech. That is, let's decide exactly what you see-hear-taste-touch-smell in your imagination from speech measure to speech measure. All right?

GABRIELLA: Okay.

MR. KAY: So, the first thing we need to do is choose a single focal point onto which you can project those images.

Why don't we use that "x" in the center of the house, the one behind me, as your focal point?

GABRIELLA: All right.

MR. KAY: And let's work through the text again, Gabriella, from speech measure to speech measure, always connecting with that single focal point to find each image.

(The students write "image to image using a single focal point" in their notebooks.)

And I'm going to ask you to work in a very specific way. Here's how we'll do this:

First you'll project an *image*—whatever it is you see, hear, taste, touch, or smell in your imagination—onto the focal point.

Then you'll *name* the image aloud in your *own* words.

Then you'll *inhale* that image.

Then you'll *speak* one speech measure from Gertrude's text.

Then you'll repeat the whole process.

Image. Name. Inhale. Speak.

Got it?

GABRIELLA: *(Drilling it)* Image. Name. Inhale. Speak.

Got it.

MR. KAY: Good. So, would you please restore the scene in your imagination?

(Gabriella connects with her focal point.)

And remind us, please—what's your objective?

GABRIELLA: To find meaning in Ophelia's death.

MR. KAY: First image? What do you see-hear-taste-touch-smell?

GABRIELLA: I SEE THE WILLOW.

MR. KAY: Good, and make sure to be *specific* and *detailed* about that willow tree!

How old is the tree? How big? What color? What shape? What does the bark feel like? Does it have a smell?

Do you have all those details in your mind?

(Gabriella nods.)

Good, and say it again, please—image, Gertrude?

GABRIELLA: I SEE THE WILLOW.

MR. KAY: Good, and now *inhale* from that image, please—and *text*?

(She inhales, and speaks.)

GABRIELLA: There is a willow grows aslant the brook

MR. KAY: Good! Next image? What do you see-hear-taste-touch-smell?

GABRIELLA: I SEE REFLECTIONS.

MR. KAY: Yes, and be sure to be *specific* and *detailed* about those reflections.

What color is the water? How deep? How cold? What color are the leaves? What shape? What size?

Do you have all those details in your mind?

(Gabriella nods.)

And say it again, please—image, Gertrude

GABRIELLA: I SEE REFLECTIONS.

MR. KAY: Yes—inhale, and text?

(She inhales, and speaks.)

GABRIELLA: That shows his hoar leaves in the glassy stream.

MR. KAY: Good, and next image, please, Gertrude?

GABRIELLA: I SEE GARLANDS.

MR. KAY: Yes, and be *specific* and *detailed* about those garlands.

Is Ophelia wearing them? Did she hang them on the tree? How long are the garlands? What colors? What do they smell like? How fragile are they in your hands?

Do you have all those details in your mind?

(Gabriella nods.)

And say it again, please—image, Gertrude?

GABRIELLA: I SEE GARLANDS.

MR. KAY: Yes—inhale, and text?

GABRIELLA: Therewith fantastic garlands did she make

MR. KAY: Excellent—and continue on your own, please, Gertrude.

GABRIELLA: I SEE CROWFLOWERS.

Of crowflow'rs,

I SEE NETTLES.

nettles,

I SEE DAISIES.

daisies,

I SEE ORCHIDS.

And long purples,

I SEE SHEPHERDS.

That lib'ral shepherds give a grosser name,

I SEE A LITTLE GIRL.

But our cold maids do "dead men's fingers" call them.

I SEE BRANCHES.

There on the pendant boughs

I SEE OPHELIA REACHING.

her crownet weeds
Clamb'ring to hang,

I HEAR A SNAP.

an envious sliver broke,

I HEAR A SPLASH.

When down the weedy trophies and herself
Fell into the weeping brook.

I SEE OPHELIA FLOATING.

Her clothes spread wide,

I SEE A MERMAID.

And mermaid-like

I SEE A BUBBLE.

awhile they bore her up,

I HEAR A CHILD'S TUNE.

Which time she chanted snatches of old tunes,

I SEE A BABY.

As one incapable of her own distress,

I SEE A DOPLHIN.

Or like a creature native and endu'd
Unto that element.

I SEE OPHELIA'S DRESS.

But long it could not be
Till that her garments,

I FEEL A SPONGE.

heavy with their drink,

I SEE OPHELIA SINKING.

Pull'd the poor wretch

I HEAR OPHELIA SINGING.

from her melodious lay

I FEEL THE MUD.

To muddy death.

MR. KAY: Excellent, Gabriella. Thank you.

(Gabriella comes down off the stage.)

(To the class) Do you see how this process is like making a *movie in your head*?

Like a cinematographer, you're *selecting* "shots" from your imagination which you project onto your focal point.

Like a film editor, you're *arranging* those images from your mind into a sequence which can be replayed at any time.

Like a film director, you're *heightening* this sequence until the movie becomes exactly what you want it to be.

Let's look at another speech. Who's ready to go?

IMAGE TO IMAGE WITH MULTIPLE FOCAL POINTS

MADISON: I'm next!

(Madison goes up onto the stage.)

MR. KAY: All right, Madison, what are you going to show us?

MADISON: Juliet, from *Romeo and Juliet.*

MR. KAY: Fine, let's have a look at that. If you would place yourself in your scene, please, so I can ask you a few questions.

(Madison sets down a chair facing upstage, puts her knees up on the seat, and grasps the back of it, as if it were a balcony railing. She looks up, as if scanning the sky.)

MR. KAY: Where are you, Juliet?

MADISON: In my bedroom, on the balcony.

MR. KAY: And what time of day is it?

MADISON: Late afternoon.

MR. KAY: Yes. And who are you talking to?

MADISON: I'm talking to the night.

MR. KAY: Why are you talking to the night? What do you hope to accomplish?

MADISON: I want to speed up the night, so it will arrive, and Romeo will come to me.

MR. KAY: I see. And what are the obstacles to that?

MADISON: It can't be done!

MR. KAY: Let's see if you can do it anyway. Begin, please.

JULIET: Gallop apace, you fiery-footed steeds,
Towards Phoebus' lodging. Such a waggoner
As Phaeton would whip you to the west
And bring in cloudy night immediately.
Spread thy close curtain, love-performing night,
That runaways' eyes may wink, and Romeo
Leap to these arms untalk'd of and unseen.
Lovers can see to do their am'rous rites
By their own beauties; or, if love be blind,
It best agrees with night. Come, civil night,
Thou sober suited matron all in black,

And learn me how to lose a winning match
Play'd for a pair of stainless maidenhoods.
Hood my unmann'd blood, bating in my cheeks,
With thy black mantle till strange love grown bold
Think true love acted simple modesty.
Come night, come Romeo; come, thou day in night,
For thou wilt lie upon the wings of night
Whiter than new snow on a raven's back.
Come, gentle night; come, loving, black-brow'd night,
Give me my Romeo, and when I shall die
Take him and cut him out in little stars,
And he will make the face of heaven so fine
That all the world will be in love with night
And pay no worship to the garish sun.
O, I have bought the mansion of a love
But not possess'd it, and though I am sold,
Not yet enjoy'd. So tedious is this day
As is the night before some festival
To an impatient child that hath new robes
And may not wear them.

MR. KAY: Thank you, Madison, that's a lovely start on that.

Now let's make sure we all understand everything Juliet says in this speech before we look at it again.

First of all, who is Phoebus?

MADISON: Phoebus is the sun god.

MR. KAY: Yes, and what are the "fiery-footed steeds"?

MADISON: The horses that pull his chariot.

MR. KAY: And what is "Phoebus' lodging"?

MADISON: Where the sun sets, in the west.

MR. KAY: And who is "Phaeton"?

MADISON: He's the sun god's *son,* who borrowed his father's chariot and went for a little joy ride.

MR. KAY: Yes, and what do you mean by "That runaways' eyes may wink"?

MADISON: I want the runaway horses to close their eyes so they won't see me and Romeo run off together.

MR. KAY: And what do you mean by "learn me how to lose a winning match"?

MADISON: Teach me how to win Romeo by giving myself to him.

MR. KAY: What do mean by "Play'd for a pair of stainless maidenhoods"?

MADISON: When the game is over, we'll both lose our virginity.

MR. KAY: What do you mean by "Hood my unmann'd blood, bating in my cheeks"?

MADISON: Well, this is all about falconry . . .

MR. KAY: Yes?

MADISON: You have to cover the head of an untamed hawk so it won't beat its wings and try to fly off . . .

MR. KAY: Yes?

MADISON: So, I'm asking night to cover the untamed blood flushing my cheeks.

MR. KAY: I see. And what do you mean by "till strange love grown bold"?

MADISON: Until love overcomes its shyness.

MR. KAY: Okay, and what do you mean by "true love acted"?

MADISON: Making love with someone you love.

MR. KAY: And what do you mean by "and when I shall die"?

MADISON: Well, it means when I have an orgasm . . . when I come.

MR. KAY: Yes, I agree. Although, did you know that a lot of editors change that "I" to "he"?

MADISON: "He"?

MR. KAY: Yes! In some editions, Juliet says, "and when *he* shall die.

(To the class) Check your editions, folks—how many have "he"? Raise your hands.

(Several hands go up.)

About half of you.

(Musing) So, even though the speech is positively oozing with the sexual fantasies of this young girl, there are editors who would rather choose an alternate reading from the fourth Quarto than face the raw sensuality of this moment.

(Making his point) Remember, folks, editors are *scholars,* not *actors,* and are not to be trusted with decisions like this. You must learn to do your own homework, and make your own decisions about the text. Go to your Folio. Go to your Quartos. Look at other editions. Otherwise you'll be stuck with "he," when "I" would have led you to much stronger acting choices.

Now, let's talk about this speech for a few minutes.

Juliet has one of the richest imaginations in all of Shakespeare—the imagination of an extremely bright and passionate thirteen-year-old girl.

And this presents enormous challenges for an actress, because you have to do so much hard work to keep up with her flights of fancy.

(To Madison) The problem is, Madison, that there are times in this speech when you're falling behind Juliet—speaking memorized text before you've connected with the image which *inspires* that text.

We can *see* that in your eyes, because they keep panning and scanning around the room, searching for the image that's coming out of your mouth.

And we can *hear* that in your voice, because you're spouting words about things which you simply do not see-hear-taste-touch-smell in your imagination.

Or, when you *do* connect with an image before you speak, often it isn't *specific* enough, *detailed* enough, or *personal* enough to affect you—to be revealed to the audience through body or through voice.

In order to solve this, you must do several things:

You must go back and orchestrate the speech from *image to image.*

You must choose a specific *focal point* for each image.

You must choose images that are *detailed* and *specific.*

You must choose images that affect you *personally.*

And most importantly, you must allow those images to *affect* you in the moment before you speak.

So let's go back to the top again, please, Madison, and with all this in mind, orchestrate the speech from image to image.

MADISON: All right.

(Madison sets herself back on the chair.)

MR. KAY: And, unlike the Gertrude speech, where every image was projected onto a *single* focal point, this speech requires that you project your images onto *multiple* focal points.

(The students write "image to image using multiple focal points" in their notebooks.)

So this time through, I'd like you to use *all* the focal points we've established in this room—house right, house left, house center, and the ceiling.

Would you please choose a focal point for your first image?

(Madison focuses intently on the "x" at center.)

MADISON: Center.

MR. KAY: Good. And remind us, please, Juliet—what's your objective?

MADISON: To speed up the night.

MR. KAY: Good, and, first image? What do you see-hear-taste-touch-smell?

MADISON: Uh . . . I SEE STEEDS.

MR. KAY: Steeds. Good, and make sure to be *specific* and *detailed* about those steeds.

How many steeds are there? How are they fiery-footed? How do they fly? How fast? How big?

Do you have all those details in your mind?

(Madison nods.)

Good, and say it again, please—image, Juliet?

MADISON: I SEE STEEDS.

MR. KAY: Good, and now *inhale* from that image, please—and *text*?

(She inhales, and speaks.)

MADISON: Gallop apace, you fiery-footed steeds,

(Shifting her focus right) Towards Phoebus' lodging.

MR. KAY: Now, wait a minute—in the middle of that phrase, you shifted your focus over to stage right. What's at stage right?

MADISON: That's where the sun sets.

MR. KAY: So when you say "Towards Phoebus' lodging" you're no longer seeing the steeds?

MADISON: No, I guess not.

MR. KAY: What, then? What's the new image?

MADISON: I SEE THE WEST.

MR. KAY: The west. All right, then, let's try those two images in sequence—first, the steeds, and then, the west.

So, from the top again, please. First image?

MADISON: *(Focusing center)* I SEE STEEDS.

Gallop apace, you fiery-footed steeds,

MR. KAY: Second image?

MADISON: *(Focusing right)* I SEE THE WEST.

Towards Phoebus' lodging.

MR. KAY: Good, very clear—and continue. Third image?

MADISON: *(Focusing center)* I SEE PHAETON.

MR. KAY: Good, and make sure to be *specific* and *detailed* about Phaeton.

What does he look like? How does he handle the chariot? How does he spur on the horses? Does he make any sound?

Do you have all those details in your mind?

(Madison nods.)

Good, and say it again, please—image, Juliet?

MADISON: I SEE PHAETON.

MR. KAY: Good, and now *inhale* from that image, please—and *text*?

(She inhales, and speaks.)

MADISON: Such a waggoner
As Phaeton would whip you to the west

MR. KAY: And let me stop you there, because you did another quick eye dart over to stage right when you said "west." Are you going back to your image of the west, or are you still seeing Phaeton?

MADISON: Um . . . I'm still seeing Phaeton.

MR. KAY: All right then, stick with Phaeton. Don't dart your eyes back to that old image of the west. That creates mud.

MADISON: Okay.

MR. KAY: Go from Phaeton, please.

MADISON: *(Focusing center)* I SEE PHAETON.

MR. KAY: Good, and text?

MADISON: Such a waggoner
As Phaeton would whip you to the west

MR. KAY: Good, that's very clear. Fourth image?

MADISON: *(Focusing up)* I SEE DARK CLOUDS.
And bring in cloudy night immediately.

MR. KAY: Good. Fifth image? What does Juliet see, hear, taste, touch, or smell before she inhales to speak?

MADISON: *(Focusing up)* I SEE A BED CURTAIN.

MR. KAY: Good. Text?

MADISON: Spread thy close curtain, love-performing night,

MR. KAY: Sixth image?

MADISON: *(Focusing center)* I SEE FLYING HORSES.
That runaways' eyes may wink,

MR. KAY: Good—continue, please.

MADISON: *(Focusing left)* I FEEL ROMEO LEAPING!

(She embraces herself.)
and Romeo
Leap to these arms

MR. KAY: Yes! Excellent! *(To the class)* Did you see and hear how strongly her body and voice responded to that powerful image? All of her images should affect her that strongly! The entire speech should be like that!

(To Madison) And continue, please—next image, Juliet?

MADISON: *(Focusing left)* I SEE A SECRET GARDEN.

untalk'd of and unseen.

MR. KAY: Yes. Next image?

MADISON: *(Focusing left)* Um . . . I SEE LOVERS!

MR. KAY: Yes, continue . . .

MADISON: Lovers can see to do their am'rous rites
By their own beauties;

(Focusing left) I TASTE A KISS.

or, if love be blind,
It best agrees with night.

MR. KAY: Yes. New image?

MADISON: *(Focusing up)* I SEE A MATRON.

Come, civil night,
Thou sober suited matron all in black

MR. KAY: New image?

(Madison's face flushes with blood. She hesitates.)

Yes, that one! *(To the class)* Do you see how strongly that image affects her? She chooses a powerful sexual image, and allows it to affect her in the moment. All of her images should be this strong. The entire speech should be just like this.

(To Madison) Next image, Juliet? What is it?

MADISON: *(Focusing center)* I FEEL ROMEO'S HANDS.

MR. KAY: Good, continue . . .

MADISON: And learn me how to lose a winning match

(Focusing center) I SMELL ROMEO'S SKIN.

Play'd for a pair of stainless maidenhoods.

(Focusing up) I FEEL MY HEART POUNDING.

Hood my unmann'd blood, bating in my cheeks,
With thy black mantle

(Focusing right) I FEEL ROMEO ON TOP OF ME.

till strange love grown bold

(Focusing right) I FEEL ROMEO INSIDE OF ME.

Think true love acted simple modesty.

(Focusing up) I SEE MOUNTAINS . . .

Come night, come Romeo . . .

MR. KAY: "Come Romeo" is still MOUNTAINS?

MADISON: Uh, no, no . . .

MR. KAY: What then? New image?

MADISON: *(Focusing left)* I SEE ROMEO'S FACE.

Come Romeo . . .

MR. KAY: Yes, of course! Next image?

MADISON: *(Focusing left)* I SEE VENUS.

come, thou day in night . . .

MR. KAY: Excellent! *(To the class)* Did you see how strong the progression is when she uses three different images for three different "comes"?

(To Madison) Next image?

MADISON: *(Focusing left)* I FEEL FEATHERS.

For thou wilt lie upon the wings of night

(Focusing left) I FEEL SNOW.

Whiter than new snow on a raven's back.

(Focusing up) I FEEL NIGHT'S HAND.

Come, gentle night . . .

(Focusing up) I SEE A BLACK WATERFALL.

come, loving, black-brow'd night . . .

(Focusing up) I FEEL MYSELF FLOATING.

Give me my Romeo, and when I shall die

(Focusing up) I SEE PAPER STARS.

Take him and cut him out in little stars,

(Focusing up) I SEE THE GALAXY.

And he will make the face of heaven so fine

(Focusing right) I HEAR MUSICIANS.

That all the world will be in love with night

(Focusing center) I SEE BRIGHT ORANGE.

And pay no worship to the garish sun.

(Focusing left) I SEE A LITTLE HOUSE.

O, I have bought the mansion of a love
But not possess'd it

(Focusing on her finger) I SEE A RING.

and though I am sold,
Not yet enjoy'd.

MR. KAY: *(To the class)* Notice that she's added a new focal point there—her ring finger—which works well.

(To Madison) Continue, please, Juliet.

MADISON: *(Focusing center)* I SEE CHRISTMAS EVE.

So tedious is this day
As is the night before some festival

(Focusing left) I SEE A CHILD.

To an impatient child that hath new robes
And may not wear them.

MR. KAY: Good, Madison, this is much improved. You're working from image to image, and every image has a specific focal point. You're choosing images that are detailed and specific. You're choosing images that can affect you personally. And more importantly, you're allowing those images to affect you in the moment before you speak—to flush your cheeks, to stir your loins, and to shake your soul.

And because of that, you're not having to worry about generating Juliet's passion, not having to dredge it up. Genuine passion came naturally as a *result* of working from image to image.

Thank you, Madison.

(Madison comes down off the stage.)

(To the class) As I said earlier, you're all very imaginative people, and you're all extremely good at conjuring up images in your mind. But using them as *tools* in your *work,* that's another matter. That requires more than just imagination. It also requires *discipline* and *technique.*

Let me say that again. The art of acting requires *discipline* and *technique.*

Let's look at another speech. Who wants to go next?

〜 IMAGE AND PARTNER 〜

SAM: I'm up!

(Sam goes up onto the stage.)

MR. KAY: What are you going to show us, Sam?

SAM: Oberon, from *A Midsummer Night's Dream.*

MR. KAY: All right, then. Put yourself in your scene, please.

(*Sam stands center stage and gazes outward.*)

And let me ask you, where are you, Oberon?

SAM: In the woods near Athens.

MR. KAY: And who are you talking to?

SAM: Puck.

MR. KAY: And who is Puck?

SAM: My number-one fairy.

MR. KAY: Yes, and what do you want from him?

SAM: I want him to fetch a magic flower.

MR. KAY: Yes, and what are the obstacles to getting that flower?

SAM: Well, there's not a lot of time, and it's not so easy to find one flower in the woods, and Puck can be pretty mischievous.

MR. KAY: Yes, good. And begin, please.

OBERON: My gentle Puck, come hither. Thou rememb'rest
Since once I sat upon a promontory
And heard a mermaid on a dolphin's back,
Utt'ring such dulcet and harmonious breath
That the rude sea grew civil at her song,
And certain stars shot madly from their spheres
To hear the sea-maid's music.
That very time I saw (but thou couldst not)
Flying between the cold moon and the earth
Cupid, all arm'd. A certain aim he took
At a fair vestal thronèd by the west,
And loos'd his love-shaft smartly from his bow,
As it should pierce a hundred thousand hearts.
But I might see young Cupid's fiery shaft
Quench'd in the chaste beams of the wat'ry moon,
And the imperial vot'ress passèd on,
In maiden meditation, fancy-free.
Yet mark'd I where the bolt of Cupid fell.
It fell upon a little western flow'r,
Before, milk-white, now purple with love's wound,
And maidens call it love-in-idleness.
Fetch me that flow'r; the herb I show'd thee once.
The juice of it, on sleeping eyelids laid,
Will make or man or woman madly dote

Upon the next live creature that it sees.
Fetch me this herb, and be thou here again
Ere the leviathan can swim a league.

MR. KAY: Good, Sam. Now, let's make sure we understand every word of the text. What do you mean by "dulcet and harmonious breath"?

SAM: Sweet and melodic songs.

MR. KAY: What do you mean by "the rude sea"?

SAM: The rough ocean.

MR. KAY: What do you mean by "Cupid, all arm'd"?

SAM: That Cupid has his bow and arrows with him.

MR. KAY: What do you mean by "A certain aim he took"?

SAM: Cupid aimed his shot carefully.

MR. KAY: What's "a fair vestal?"

SAM: A beautiful virgin.

MR. KAY: What do you mean by "loos'd his love-shaft"?

SAM: Cupid shot his arrow.

MR. KAY: What do you mean by "the imperial vot'ress"?

SAM: That same majestic virgin.

MR. KAY: What do you mean by "fancy-free"?

SAM: The maiden was free of Cupid's love spell.

MR. KAY: What's "the bolt of cupid"?

SAM: Cupid's arrow.

MR. KAY: What's "love-in-idleness"?

SAM: Pansies.

MR. KAY: What do you mean by "or man or woman"?

SAM: *Either* man or woman.

MR. KAY: What's a leviathan?

SAM: A whale.

MR. KAY: Good, Sam. Now let's talk about this speech for a minute or two.

Oberon is a magical inhabitant of the Athenian woods, and as such, his movements are always graceful, his voice mellifluous, his articulation crystalline.

The problem here, Sam, is that you're coming off like a clunky human being, more like Bottom and his cohorts than the King of the Fairy World.

And the reason is, like most foolish mortals, you're trying to do two things at once, and not doing either task particularly well.

You're trying to connect with an imagined partner, Puck, and run the movie in your head about where you saw that flower, both at the same time. And it's just not working.

It's not working because you keep turning your head back and forth between Puck and your images so often that both connections become a generic blur.

And because you don't know where to *focus* from moment to moment, your movement becomes awkward, your inhalations become shallow, your voice becomes unsupported, your tonal quality becomes breathy, your articulation becomes muddy, and your audience becomes exhausted trying to hear and understand you.

So, let's look at this speech again, Sam, and figure out how we're going to orchestrate a sequence of specific images while talking to an imagined partner.

(The students write "orchestrating images while talking to a partner" in their notebooks.)

To solve this problem, we need to orchestrate the speech so you know exactly which speech measures are directed towards *Puck,* and which speech measures are focused on an *image.*

So here's what I'd like to suggest, Sam. I'd like you to have a focal point that you use exclusively for *Puck*—let's say the one over there at *house left.*

And let's use the other three "x" marks in the room—center, right, and the ceiling—as focal points onto which you'll project your *images.*

I'd like you to tell us aloud, before each speech measure, when you're connecting with *Puck,* and when you're connecting with an *image.*

Each time you connect with an *image,* I'd like you to tell us aloud exactly what it is you see-hear-taste-touch-smell. Then you'll *inhale* that image, and speak.

Connect, image, inhale, speak.

Got it?

SAM: Yes, I think so.

MR. KAY: Okay then, let's restore your scene to the top.

(Sam does so.)

And remind us, please—what's your objective?

SAM: To get Puck to fetch a magic flower.

MR. KAY: First focal point?

(Sam focuses on the house left "x".)

SAM: PUCK.

MR. KAY: Good, and *inhale* from that image, please—and text?

SAM: My gentle Puck, come hither. *(Shifting)* Thou rememb'rest
Since once I sat upon a promontory

MR. KAY: Wait a minute, Sam, wait a minute—your focus changed!

SAM: It did?

MR. KAY: Yes. You bled over to another focal point in the middle of a speech
measure.

SAM: I did? I didn't mean to.

MR. KAY: No, I *know* you didn't. That's the power of *habit.* Are you still connecting with Puck?

SAM: Um, no. I'm seeing the view from the promontory.

MR. KAY: All right, then, let's go from the top again, and tell us exactly *when*
you shift your focus in order to see the view from the promontory in your
mind's eye.

(Sam restores the scene.)

SAM: *(Focusing house left)* PUCK.
My gentle Puck, come hither.
(Shifting focus to center) I SEE THE VIEW FROM THE PROMONTORY.
Thou rememb'rest
Since once I sat upon a promontory

MR. KAY: Good! That's very clear. Continue, please, Oberon.

SAM: *(Focusing center)* I SEE A MERMAID RIDING A DOLPHIN.
And heard a mermaid on a dolphin's back,

MR. KAY: Wait a minute now—did you actually *see* the mermaid, or did you
only *hear* her? What does the text say?

SAM: Uh . . . it says I *heard* her.

MR. KAY: All right then, so what exactly did you hear?

SAM: Laughing . . . the mermaid and the dolphin are both laughing.

MR. KAY: That's a wonderful detail. Now let's go back, and really *hear* those
laughs in your mind's ear.

SAM: *(Focusing up, and smiling)* I HEAR LAUGHING.

And heard a mermaid on a dolphin's back,

MR. KAY: Good! *(To the class)* And did you see how that very specific image infused that one speech measure? Now *we* can hear the mermaid and the dolphin because we believe that *he* hears it!

(To Sam) Continue, please, Oberon—next image?

SAM: *(Focusing up)* I HEAR THE MERMAID'S SONG.

MR. KAY: Good, and take the time to hear that song! And inhale it! And text?

SAM: Utt'ring such dulcet and harmonious breath

MR. KAY: Excellent! *(To the class)* *We* can hear the song, too, because *he* takes the time to hear it and allows it to affect him.

(To Sam) And continue on your own, please.

SAM: *(Focusing center)* I SEE CALM SEAS.

That the rude sea grew civil at her song,

(Focusing up) I SEE SHOOTING STARS.

And certain stars shot madly from their spheres

To hear the sea-maid's music.

(Focusing left) PUCK.

That very time I saw (but thou couldst not)

MR. KAY: And be careful not to look away from Puck before the speech measure is complete! You're *initiating* each connection well, Oberon, but be sure to also *terminate* properly! Don't try to slip away to the next focal point before you're finished with this one. That creates mud.

And continue, please.

SAM: *(Focusing up)* I SEE THE FULL MOON.

Flying between the cold moon and the earth

(Focusing right) I SEE CUPID.

Cupid,

(Focusing right) I SEE CUPID'S BOW AND ARROW.

all arm'd.

(Focusing left) PUCK.

A certain aim he took

(Focusing center) I SEE A MAIDEN, WALKING TO THE WEST.

At a fair vestal thronèd by the west,

(Focusing right) I HEAR THE ARROW WHISTLE.

And loos'd his love-shaft smartly from his bow,

(Focusing left) PUCK.

As it should pierce a hundred thousand hearts.

(Focusing up) I SEE THE GOLDEN ARROW, FLYING.

But I might see young Cupid's fiery shaft

(Focusing up) I SEE THE ARROW TANGLED IN MOONBEAMS.

Quench'd in the chaste beams of the wat'ry moon,

(Focusing center) I SEE THE MAIDEN, WALKING AWAY, UNTOUCHED.

And the imperial vot'ress passèd on,
In maiden meditation, fancy-free.

(Focusing left) PUCK.

Yet mark'd I where the bolt of Cupid fell.

(Focusing center) I SEE A PANSY.

It fell upon a little western flow'r,

(Focusing left) PUCK.

Before, milk-white,

(Focusing center) I SEE A PURPLE WOUND.

now purple with love's wound,

(Focusing center) I SEE A MAIDEN, PLUCKING A PANSY.

And maidens call it love-in-idleness.

(Focusing left) PUCK.

Fetch me that flow'r; the herb I show'd thee once.

(Focusing center) I SEE DROPS OF LOVE JUICE.

The juice of it,

(Focusing right) I SEE TITANIA, ASLEEP.

on sleeping eyelids laid,

(Focusing right) I SEE TITANIA, IN LOVE.

Will make or man or woman madly dote

(Focusing right) I SEE A MEDDLING MONKEY.

Upon the next live creature that it sees.

(Focusing left) PUCK.

Fetch me this herb, and be thou here again
Ere the leviathan can swim a league.

MR. KAY: Very good. Thank you, Sam.

(Sam comes down off the stage.)

(To the class) And did you all the see the improvement in his *body*?
How much more balanced, and centered, and grounded he was in his
movements?

The sequence of *connect, image, inhale, speak* allows you to bring all of your movement training to bear, so your body can reveal your choices to an audience.

And did you all hear the improvement in his *voice*? Did you hear the purity of his tone, and the clarity of his articulation, when he creates a specific image in his imagination, inhales it, and speaks?

The sequence of *connect, image, inhale, speak* allows you to bring all of your vocal training to bear, so your voice can reveal your choices to an audience.

More importantly, the sequence of *connect, image, inhale, speak* makes your orchestration *reliable* and *repeatable*. So there is never any need to hope and pray for *inspiration*. You can depend upon your orchestration to be there for you—whether it's an audition, the first run-through, opening night, or the eighty-fifth performance.

Let's look at another speech. Who's ready to go?

&~9 IMAGE AND AUDIENCE &~9

RACHEL: I'm ready!

(Rachel goes up onto the stage.)

MR. KAY: And what are you going to show us, Rachel?

RACHEL: The Chorus, from *Henry the Fifth.*

MR. KAY: Good, and if you would place yourself in your scene, I'll ask you a few questions.

(Rachel stands at center stage, gazing outward.)

Where are you?

RACHEL: In France, on a battlefield, at night.

MR. KAY: And what time is it exactly?

RACHEL: It's about three in the morning.

MR. KAY: And who are you talking to?

RACHEL: The audience.

MR. KAY: Why are you talking to us? What do you hope to accomplish?

RACHEL: I want to glorify the reign of Henry the Fifth.

MR. KAY: Yes, that's good, but that sounds to me like a *play* objective, something the Chorus hopes to accomplish by the time the *play* is over. What's the objective for this one *speech*?

RACHEL: Um . . . to set the scene for the Battle of Agincourt.

MR. KAY: Yes, and why is that important?

RACHEL: The audience needs to know that the night before King Henry's victory at Agincourt the English were exhausted and sick, knew the odds were against them, and thought they'd probably die the next morning.

MR. KAY: Good, and what are the obstacles to setting that scene for audience?

RACHEL: Well, I say the obstacles in the prologue of the play.

MR. KAY: In "O for a muse of fire"?

RACHEL: Yes.

MR. KAY: And what are they?

RACHEL: We have only a few actors to play thousands of soldiers, and only this small stage to represent the fields of France.

MR. KAY: Good, then let's hear how you set the scene for the battle. Begin, please.

CHORUS: Now entertain conjecture of a time
When creeping murmur and the poring dark
Fills the wide vessel of the universe.
From camp to camp, through the foul womb of night,
The hum of either army stilly sounds,
That the fix'd sentinels almost receive
The secret whispers of each other's watch.
Fire answers fire, and through their paly flames
Each battle sees the other's umber'd face.
Steed threatens steed, in high and boastful neighs
Piercing the night's dull ear; and from the tents,
The armorers, accomplishing the knights,
With busy hammers closing rivets up,
Give dreadful note of preparation.
The country cocks do crow, the clocks do toll,
And the third hour of drowsy morning name.
Proud of their numbers, and secure in soul,
The confident and over-lusty French
Do the low-rated English play at dice;
And chide the cripple tardy-gaited night,
Who, like a foul and ugly witch, doth limp
So tediously away. The poor condemnèd English,
Like sacrifices, by their watchful fires
Sit patiently, and inly ruminate
The morning's danger; and their gesture sad,

> Investing lank-lean cheeks, and war-worn coats,
> Presenteth them unto the gazing moon,
> So many horrid ghosts.

MR. KAY: Good, Rachel, thank you. Now, let's make sure we all understand every word in the speech.

What do you mean by "entertain conjecture"?

RACHEL: Imagine, if you will.

MR. KAY: And what do you mean by "creeping murmur"?

RACHEL: Barely audible voices.

MR. KAY: And what do you mean by "the poring dark"?

RACHEL: It's so dark you have to strain your eyes to see anything.

MR. KAY: What do you mean by "The hum of either army stilly sounds"?

RACHEL: You can hear the soft sounds of the armies on both sides of the field.

MR. KAY: What's an "umber'd face"?

RACHEL: The shadows on the soldiers' faces made by the campfires.

MR. KAY: What do you mean by "the over-lusty French"?

RACHEL: The French are overconfident and cheerful.

MR. KAY: What do you mean by "investing lank-lean cheeks and war-worn coats"?

RACHEL: The English have hollow cheeks and wear threadbare coats.

MR. KAY: Good, Rachel. Now let's talk about the challenges presented by this speech.

There are other chorus figures in Shakespeare, like the Chorus in *Romeo and Juliet,* Gower in *Pericles,* Rumor in *Henry the Fourth, Part Two,* and Time in *The Winter's Tale.*

But none of these figures asks the audience to do what this Chorus asks, that is, to use our imaginations to help the actors to tell the story.

Those other Shakespearean choruses provide the audience with exposition and plot points. This Chorus asks us to see-hear-taste-touch-smell in our imaginations all the details of Henry the Fifth's victory in France.

And that, of course, is the primary challenge of this speech. Because it's not enough to simply stand there as master of ceremonies and say "Sixteen years have passed" or "Pericles puts forth to sea."

You have to *go* there. You have to see-hear-taste-touch-smell all the details of the night before the Battle of Agincourt in your mind before you can impart those details to the audience through body and through voice.

The challenge of the speech is how to split your focus, so that half the time you're using your own imagination to conjure up those details, and the other half, you're asking the audience to use *their* imaginations to come along with you.

The problem, Rachel, is that you're trying to do *both* of these things at once. You're trying to connect with the *images* of the speech, and connect with the *audience*—at the same time. And it's just not working.

It's not working because your focus keeps sliding randomly back and forth between image and audience, never fully imagining what you're talking about, and never fully connecting with the audience.

And because you keep shifting focal points in the middle of your speech measures, the text begins to blur, and we can't understand what you're saying. We hear the words, but we can't grasp the images they represent.

So, let's look at this speech again, Rachel, and figure out how we're going to orchestrate a sequence of specific images while talking to the audience.

(The students write "orchestrating images while talking to the audience" in their notebooks.)

To solve this problem, we need to orchestrate the speech so that you *alternate* between image and audience, making one connection, and *only* one connection, per speech measure.

So here's what I'd like to suggest, Rachel. I'd like you to tell us aloud when you're connecting with the *audience,* and when you're connecting to the *image.*

When you connect with the *audience,* use only the focal point at house center.

When you connect with an *image,* use either house left, house right, or the balcony.

And of course, as we've done before, when you connect to an *image,* you'll tell us exactly what you see-hear-taste-touch-smell, then inhale that image, and speak. Got it?

RACHEL: Yes.

MR. KAY: Good. *(To the class)* Will somebody please write these down as we work?

LUKE: I will!

MR. KAY: Thanks, Luke.

(To Rachel) And if you would put yourself back into your scene, please, Rachel.

(Rachel does so.)

And remind us, please—what's your objective?

RACHEL: To set the scene for the Battle of Agincourt.

MR. KAY: First connection? Image or audience?

RACHEL: *(Focusing center)* AUDIENCE.

MR. KAY: Good, and text?

RACHEL: Now entertain conjecture of a time

MR. KAY: Good. Second connection—image or audience?

RACHEL: Image.

MR. KAY: Good, and what do you see-hear-taste-touch-smell?

RACHEL: *(Focusing right)* I HEAR VOICES.

MR. KAY: Text?

RACHEL: When creeping murmur

MR. KAY: Good, and third connection?

RACHEL: *(Focusing left)* I SEE THE DARKNESS.

MR. KAY: Text?

RACHEL: and the poring dark

MR. KAY: Good, and fourth connection?

RACHEL: *(Focusing up)* I SEE A STARRY SKY.

MR. KAY: Text?

RACHEL: Fills the wide vessel of the universe.

MR. KAY: Good, and continue, please, on your own.

RACHEL: *(Focusing right)* I SEE THE ENGLISH CAMP.
From camp
(Focusing left) I SEE THE FRENCH CAMP.
to camp,

MR. KAY: Good. *(To the class)* And now that she's established the French camp on one side, and the English camp on the other, she's going to have to make sure to keep those focal points *consistent* throughout the speech. Otherwise we're going to get very confused.
(To Rachel) Continue, please.

RACHEL: *(Focusing center)* AUDIENCE.
through the foul womb of night,
(Focusing up) I HEAR HUMMING.

The hum of either army stilly sounds,

(Focusing center) AUDIENCE.

That the fix'd sentinels almost receive

(Focusing up) I HEAR WHISPERING.

The secret whispers of each other's watch.

MR. KAY: Good. *(To the class)* And do you notice how she's focusing *up* in order to hear imagined sounds? That works well, and now that she's set up that convention, she should return to that focal point every time she hears a sound. Otherwise we're going to get very confused.

(To Rachel) Continue, please.

RACHEL: *(Focusing right)* I SEE AN ENGLISH CAMPFIRE.

Fire

(Focusing left) I SEE A FRENCH CAMPFIRE.

answers fire,

(Focusing center) AUDIENCE.

and through their paly flames

(Focusing right) I SEE AN ENGLISH SOLDIER'S FACE.

Each battle sees

(Focusing left) I SEE A FRENCH SOLDIER'S FACE.

the other's umber'd face.

(Focusing up) I HEAR THE SOUND OF HORSES.

Steed threatens steed, in high and boastful neighs

(Focusing center) AUDIENCE.

Piercing the night's dull ear;

(Focusing left) I SEE TENTS.

and from the tents,

(Focusing left) I SEE ARMORERS.

The armorers, accomplishing the knights,

(Focusing up) I HEAR THE SOUND OF HAMMERS.

With busy hammers closing rivets up,

(Focusing center) AUDIENCE.

Give dreadful note of preparation.

(Focusing up) I HEAR A ROOSTER CROW.

The country cocks do crow,

(Focusing up) I HEAR CHURCH BELLS RINGING.

the clocks do toll,

And the third hour of drowsy morning name.

(Focusing center) AUDIENCE.

Proud of their numbers, and secure in soul,

(Focusing left) I SEE THE DAUPHIN.

The confident and over-lusty French

(Focusing center) AUDIENCE.

Do the low-rated English play at dice;

(Focusing up) I SEE THE NIGHT.

And chide the cripple tardy-gaited night,

(Focusing center) AUDIENCE.

Who, like a foul and ugly witch, doth limp
So tediously away.

(Focusing right) I SEE ENGLISH SOLDIERS.

The poor condemnèd English,

(Focusing center) AUDIENCE.

Like sacrifices,

(Focusing right) I SEE AN ENGLISH CAMPFIRE.

by their watchful fires
Sit patiently,

(Focusing right) I SEE AN ENGLISH SOLDIER.

and inly ruminate
The morning's danger;

(Focusing right) I SEE SHOULDERS.

and their gesture sad,

(Focusing right) I SEE CHEEKS.

Investing lank-lean cheeks,

(Focusing right) I SEE COATS.

and war-worn coats,

(Focusing up) I SEE THE MOON.

Presenteth them unto the gazing moon,

(Focusing center) AUDIENCE.

So many horrid ghosts.

MR. KAY: Good, Rachel. Now let's look at this speech another way.

(To Luke) Would you give me what you've written down, Luke?

(Luke hands Mr. Kay a piece of paper.)

(To the class) What I have in my hand is Rachel's *score* for this speech.

A *score* is simply a *written* version of your orchestration.

(To Rachel) And now, if you would, please, Rachel, I'd like you to go through the speech again, image by image—not by speaking the *text* aloud, but by speaking your *score* aloud. Follow me?

RACHEL: Yes.

(The students write "speaking your score aloud" in their notebooks.)

MR. KAY: All right, then. If you would restore the scene, please, in your imagination.

(Rachel does so.)

And begin.

RACHEL: *(Focusing center)* AUDIENCE.

(Focusing right) VOICES.

(Focusing left) THE DARKNESS.

(Focusing up) A STARRY SKY.

(Focusing right) THE ENGLISH CAMP.

(Focusing left) THE FRENCH CAMP.

(Focusing center) AUDIENCE.

(Focusing up) HUMMING.

(Focusing center) AUDIENCE.

(Focusing up) WHISPERING.

(Focusing center) AUDIENCE.

(Focusing right) AN ENGLISH CAMPFIRE.

(Focusing left) A FRENCH CAMPFIRE.

(Focusing center) AUDIENCE.

(Focusing right) AN ENGLISH SOLDIER'S FACE.

(Focusing left) A FRENCH SOLDIER'S FACE.

(Focusing up) THE SOUND OF HORSES.

(Focusing center) AUDIENCE.

(Focusing left) TENTS.

(Focusing left) ARMORERS.

(Focusing up) THE SOUND OF HAMMERS.

(Focusing center) AUDIENCE.

(Focusing up) A ROOSTER CROWING.

(Focusing up) CHURCH BELLS RINGING.

(Focusing center) AUDIENCE.

(Focusing left) THE DAUPHIN.

(Focusing center) AUDIENCE.

(Focusing up) NIGHT.

(Focusing center) AUDIENCE.

(Focusing right) ENGLISH SOLDIERS.

(Focusing center) AUDIENCE.

(Focusing right) AN ENGLISH CAMPFIRE.

(Focusing right) AN ENGLISH SOLDIER.

(Focusing right) SHOULDERS.

(Focusing right) CHEEKS.

(Focusing right) COATS.

(Focusing up) THE MOON.

(Focusing center) AUDIENCE.

MR. KAY: Excellent, Rachel. Thank you.

(Rachel comes down off the stage.)

(To the class) Now, you see, she has a repeatable orchestration for the speech, and she can depend on it to be there for her whenever she needs it. She'll never have to pray to the theater gods for divine inspiration. She has her orchestration for the speech, recorded on paper as a written score.

From now on, I want all of you to rely on *orchestration,* rather than *inspiration.*

(Mr. Kay looks up at the clock.)

Well, I'm sorry to say we're out of time for today.

Please keep incorporating the work we've been doing these past few days on speech measures, focal points, and images into your speeches.

I'll see you tomorrow.

BLACKOUT.

SCENE 4

Spoken Subtext

The Acting Studio. Thursday.

MR. KAY: Good morning, folks. Yesterday we looked at how to use images to orchestrate a speech. Today we're going to look at *spoken subtext.*

(The students write "spoken subtext" in their notebooks.)

Spoken subtext is a way of making *public* the private thoughts and impulses of a character. It means speaking *aloud* the innermost secrets that inspire a character's text.

In other words, we're going to speak the character's *subtext* aloud in order to orchestrate the character's *text.*

(Scanning faces) So, who wants to work?

HEAD, HEART, GUTS, AND GROIN

TIM: I do!

(Tim goes up onto the stage.)

MR. KAY: Okay, Tim. And, what are you going to show us today?

TIM: Angelo, from *Measure for Measure.*

MR. KAY: Good, and if you would place yourself in your scene, please, I'll ask you a few questions.

(Tim stands center stage, gazing off to stage right.)

Where are you, Angelo?

TIM: I'm in my office.

MR. KAY: In your office. You hold a position of power?

TIM: Yes, I'm in charge of the city of Vienna while the Duke is away.

MR. KAY: I see. And who are you talking to?

TIM: Myself.

MR. KAY: Why? What's just happened?

TIM: Well, I've just been talking to Isabella, whose brother Claudio is condemned to die for getting his girlfriend pregnant.

MR. KAY: And what does Isabella want?

TIM: She's asked me to spare her brother's life.

MR. KAY: I see. And what answer did you give her?

TIM: I said I'd think about it, and told her to come back tomorrow.

MR. KAY: And why did you tell her that?

TIM: Because I'm smitten with her and want to see her again.

MR. KAY: I see. So what's the objective? What do you hope to accomplish by talking to yourself now?

TIM: I want to understand my feelings for this woman.

MR. KAY: You want to *understand* them, or *control* them?

TIM: Um . . . yes, maybe "control" is better.

MR. KAY: And how will you know that you've controlled those feelings?

TIM: When I know they have no affect on my judgment, on my decision about her brother.

MR. KAY: And what's the obstacle to getting control of your feelings?

TIM: Well, I'm completely overwhelmed by her beauty, and her intelligence, and her purity, and her sexuality. And I have no experience with women, so I don't know what to do with my lust for her.

MR. KAY: Good, then let's see if you can control those feelings. Begin, please.

ANGELO: What's this, what's this? Is this her fault or mine?
The tempter, or the tempted, who sins most, ha?
Not she, nor doth she tempt; but it is I
That, lying by the violet in the sun,
Do as the carrion does, not as the flower,
Corrupt with virtuous season. Can it be
That modesty may more betray our sense
Than woman's lightness? Having waste ground enough,

Shall we desire to raze the sanctuary
And pitch our evils there? O, fie, fie, fie!
What dost thou? Or what are thou, Angelo?
Dost thou desire her foully for those things
That make her good? O, let her brother live!
Thieves for their robbery have authority
When judges steal themselves. What, do I love her,
That I desire to hear her speak again,
And feast upon her eyes? What is't I dream on?
O cunning enemy, that to catch a saint,
With saints dost bait thy hook! Most dangerous
Is that temptation that doth goad us on
To sin in loving virtue. Never could the strumpet,
With all her double vigor, art and nature,
Once stir my temper; but this virtuous maid
Subdues me quite. Ever till now,
When men were fond, I smil'd and wondered how.

MR. KAY: Good, Tim. That's a good start on that. *Measure for Measure* is a difficult play, and this speech, like so much of Angelo's text, is very complex and dense. So let's be sure we understand the text completely before we look at it again.

First of all, will you explain what you mean in all those lines about "the violet in the sun"? What are they again?

TIM: But it is I
That, lying by the violet in the sun,
Do as the carrion does, not as the flower,
Corrupt with virtuous season.

MR. KAY: Yes, what does all that mean exactly?

TIM: Well, Isabella is the sun, which makes things either grow or decay. And I'm like a dead carcass rotting in the beams of her beauty, rather than growing, like a flower.

MR. KAY: I see. And what do you mean by "having waste ground enough . . ."? What's the rest of the line?

TIM: Having waste ground enough,
Shall we desire to raze the sanctuary
And pitch our evils there?

MR. KAY: Yes, what's all that mean?

TIM: Well, it means, um . . . with scorched earth all around me, why do I want to tear down the church to throw my sins there?

MR. KAY: And in that metaphor, the scorched earth is Vienna?

TIM: Yes.

MR. KAY: And Isabella is the church?

TIM: Yes.

MR. KAY: I see. And what do you mean when you say "Thieves for their robbery have authority, when judges steal themselves"?

TIM: Um, that means . . . "if judges break the law and steal, thieves will have the perfect excuse to do the same thing."

MR. KAY: And in that metaphor, you're the judge, and Claudio is the thief?

TIM: Yes.

MR. KAY: And what do you mean when you say, "O cunning enemy, that to catch a saint, with saints doth bait thy hook"?

TIM: The devil is one smart guy to send a gorgeous nun to tempt me to sin.

(The class laughs.)

MR. KAY: Yes, I see. And what do you mean when you say, "Never could the strumpet, with all her double vigor, art and nature, quite stir my temper"?

TIM: Um . . . it would be impossible for a prostitute, using both her skill and her sexuality, ever to shake me up like this.

MR. KAY: And what do you mean by "When men were fond"?

TIM: When *other* men were obsessed with women.

MR. KAY: Good, Tim, good. Now, let's talk about this speech a bit.

Angelo is an extremely conflicted character in this play, a character whose principles, emotions, and sexual desires violently oppose one another. In this speech, as in others, his intellect urges him to do one thing, his compassion another, his anger another, and his lust still another.

In other words, there's a war being fought between his *head,* his *heart,* his *guts,* and his *groin.*

(The class laughs.)

(To the class) Now, part of the problem, I think, is that Tim understands that Angelo is a conflicted character, but he's trying to reveal that conflict to the audience by playing "to be conflicted." That's a fine *literary* way to describe a character, but as an actor, it's simply impossible to play in any given moment!

Why? Because complexity and contradiction is something that an audience perceives in a character as a result of watching a carefully orchestrated performance.

To create complexity and contradiction in a character, you have to orchestrate a moment of yellow, followed by a moment of red, followed by a moment of blue. It's simply not possible to play red and blue and yellow all in the same moment. If you attempt that, you get mud.

So, let's look at this speech again, Tim, and see if we can't pull you out of that mud by using a spoken subtext exercise that I call *head, heart, guts, and groin.*

(The students write "head, heart, guts, and groin" in their notebooks.)

I'm going to ask you to tell us aloud, before each speech measure, whether the impulse to speak comes from your *head,* your *heart,* your *guts,* or your *groin.*

So, I'd like you to say aloud either "HEAD," or "HEART," or "GUTS," or "GROIN" before each speech measure. Got that?

TIM: Uh-huh, I think so.

MR. KAY: Good, then let's begin. Place yourself back in your scene, please.

(Tim restores the scene in his imagination.)

Isabella has just left your office. She's dazzled you! Head, heart, guts, or groin, Angelo?

TIM: GROIN.

MR. KAY: Yes, Tim, but it's not enough merely to *say* it. You must connect with the stirrings in your groin, and let them be the springboard to action!

So, again, please. Isabella is leaving your office. Got an image of that? Choose a personal image that affects you in the strongest possible way!

(Tim's face flushes.)

Yes, that one! Head, heart, guts, or groin, Angelo?

TIM: GROIN.

MR. KAY: Yes! And text?

TIM: What's this,

MR. KAY: Good! *(To the class)* And can you perceive how his connection to his *groin*—the engine of lust—infuses that one speech measure?

(To Tim) Next measure, please, Angelo. Head, heart, guts, or groin?

TIM: HEART.

what's this?

MR. KAY: Good! *(To the class)* And can you hear how his connection to his *heart*—the wellspring of love and compassion—softens his voice?

(To Tim) Next measure, please—head, heart, guts, or groin?

TIM: HEAD.

Is this her fault or mine?

MR. KAY: Yes! *(To the class)* And can you see how a connection to the *intellect*—the seat of analytical thought, philosophical ponderings, and ethical constructs—affects his body?

(To Tim) Next measure, please—head, heart, guts, or groin?

TIM: GUTS.

The tempter, or the tempted, who sins most, ha?

MR. KAY: *(To the class)* And can you see and hear how his connection to his *guts*—the hearth of violence, anger, selfishness, and raw ambition—springboards him into action?

And because he has shown us, in the first four measures, four vastly different ways of dealing with the same problem, we see a man who is hopelessly conflicted and at war with himself. Excellent!

(To Tim) And continue, please, Angelo.

TIM: HEART.

Not she, nor doth she tempt;

GROIN.

but it is I
That, lying by the violet in the sun,
Do as the carrion does, not as the flower,
Corrupt with virtuous season.

HEART.

Can it be
That modesty may more betray our sense
Than woman's lightness?

GUTS.

Having waste ground enough,
Shall we desire to raze the sanctuary
And pitch our evils there?

HEAD.

(Holding his head in his hands)

O, fie, fie, fie!

MR. KAY: Good, that "fie, fie fie" works well as *head*. But let's try a few other possibilities. Can you go back, please, and do "O, fie, fie" as *head*, and the third "fie" as *heart*?

TIM: HEAD.

(Holding his head in his hands)

O, fie, fie,

HEART.

(Dropping his hands and gazing upward)

fie!

MR. KAY: Good! That works, too.

(To the class) Do you see, folks, how, even when the *text* repeats itself, you need not repeat the same *choice* in your orchestration? In fact, you should begin to see *repetitions* in your text as *opportunities* to play something different each time.

(To Tim) Now how about *groin, heart, guts*?

TIM: GROIN.

(Closing his eyes)

O, fie,

HEART.

(Gazing upward)

fie,

GUTS.

(Shaking his fist)

fie!

MR. KAY: Excellent. What I like about that one is how we see you struggling to *control your feelings*—which is Angelo's objective, yes?

(To the class) So, that's three possible ways to orchestrate that moment. And there are many more. How will we know which way is the *best* way? We'll *select, arrange,* and *heighten* our choices for this speech through lots more *trial and error.*

(To Tim) Continue, please, Angelo. Next measure?

TIM: GUTS.

What dost thou?

GROIN.

Or what are thou, Angelo?

HEART.

Dost thou desire her foully for those things
That make her good?

GUTS.

O, let her brother live!

HEAD.

Thieves for their robbery have authority
When judges steal themselves.

HEART.

What, do I love her,
That I desire to hear her speak again,
And feast upon her eyes?

GROIN.

What is't I dream on?

HEAD.

O cunning enemy, that to catch a saint,
With saints dost bait thy hook!

GUTS.

Most dangerous
Is that temptation that doth goad us on
To sin in loving virtue.

HEAD.

Never could the strumpet,
With all her double vigor, art and nature,
Once stir my temper;

GROIN.

but this virtuous maid
Subdues me quite.

HEART.

Ever till now,
When men were fond, I smil'd and wondered how.

MR. KAY: Good, Tim. Well done. Thank you.

(Tim comes down off the stage.)

(To the class) This is very vulnerable work, folks. It's one thing to put your secret *thoughts* up on the stage, but an even more difficult thing to put your *heart,* your *guts,* and your *groin* out there as well.

But, of course, that's what we pay our money for in the theater—to see and hear the innermost thoughts and impulses of a character.

This is part of Shakespeare's genius: he puts it all into the text for you—the character's head, heart, guts and groin are right there on the page. But you have to have the courage as a performing artist to actually *play* what he's given you!

That's one spoken subtext exercise. Let's look at another one. Who wants to go next?

⚮ SECRET FEARS ⚮

SARAH: I'll go next.

(Sarah goes up onto the stage.)

MR. KAY: Thank you, Sarah. What are you going to show us?

SARAH: Helena, from *All's Well That Ends Well.*

MR. KAY: Good. And would you place yourself in your scene, please, so I can ask you a few questions before you begin.

(Sarah stands center stage, gazing outward.)

Where are you, Helena?

SARAH: I'm in the palace of my guardian, the Countess of Rousillion.

MR. KAY: And who are you talking to?

SARAH: The Countess.

MR. KAY: I see. And why are you talking to her? What's just happened?

SARAH: She's called me in to see her, and she's demanding that I tell her about my feelings for her son.

MR. KAY: Who's her son?

SARAH: Bertram.

MR. KAY: And what *are* your feelings about Bertram?

SARAH: I'm hopelessly in love with him, and desperately want to marry him.

MR. KAY: I see. So what's wrong with that?

SARAH: Well, he's above my station in life. I'm the daughter of a doctor, and he's the son of a Count . . .

MR. KAY: Yes?

SARAH: . . . and I'm afraid that the Countess will be angry at me, and will disown me, and kick me out of her house forever.

MR. KAY: I see. So what's your objective? What do you want from the Countess in this moment? What do you hope to accomplish?

SARAH: I want her to take pity on me.

MR. KAY: I see. Then, let me ask you this—how will you know when you *achieve* that objective? How will you know that you have her pity?

SARAH: She'll tell me that she understands, that she's not angry, that she still loves me.

MR. KAY: Yes, I see. Then let's see if you can get the Countess to say those things. Begin, please.

HELENA: Then I confess
Here on my knee, before high heaven and you,
That before you, and next unto high heaven,
I love your son.
My friends were poor, but honest, so's my love.
Be not offended, for it hurts not him
That he is lov'd of me; I follow him not
By any token of presumptuous suit,
Nor would I have him till I do deserve him,
Yet never know how that desert should be.
I know I love in vain, strive against hope;
Yet in this captious and intenible sieve,
I still pour in the waters of my love
And lack not to lose still. Thus Indian-like,
Religious in mine error, I adore
The sun, that looks upon his worshipper,
But knows of him no more. My dearest madam,
Let not your hate encounter with my love
For loving where you do; but if yourself,
Whose agèd honor cites a virtuous youth,
Did ever in so true a flame of liking
Wish chastely and love dearly, O then give pity
To her whose state is such that cannot choose
But lend and give where she is sure to lose;
That seeks not to find that her search implies,
But riddle-like, lives sweetly where she dies.

MR. KAY: Good, Sarah. Did you cut a little something in that?

SARAH: Yes, you caught me. I cut that bit about Dian.

MR. KAY: What was the line?

SARAH: Um . . . *(dredging her memory)* . . .
that your Dian
Was both herself and Love.

MR. KAY: And why did you cut that?

SARAH: I just felt that the mythology is, you know, lost on an audience.

MR. KAY: Ah, yes. I see. And, of course, that's precisely the kind of reasoning a director might use to justify a cut. So I suppose you should be able to use it as well.

(To the class) But beware, my friends, for this is a very slippery slope!

Shakespeare is full of references to mythology. Which ones should we cut? All the ones that we don't immediately understand? Or all the ones we assume an audience won't understand? Or should we just cut them all? Heck, why not cut every word we aren't familiar with? Why not cut every word we think an audience won't know? Why not paraphrase the entire script? Why not perform the *Cliff's Notes* instead?

(The class laughs.)

Seriously, folks, as I said before, I'm not opposed to making well-considered cuts and changes in a text. Just make sure that you don't toss something into the trash before you've worked with it for a little while. Make sure you're not cutting something wonderful out of a speech just because you don't immediately understand a word, or can't get your mouth around a phrase, or wish you didn't have to memorize a line.

Remember: the actor's process is about trial and error! So don't condemn anything in your text until you've given it a fair trial first. All right?

(To Sarah) Now, before we look at this again, let's make sure we all understand everything you're saying.

What do you mean by "my friends"?

SARAH: I mean my relatives, my family.

MR. KAY: Yes. And what's a "captious and intenible sieve"?

SARAH: Um . . . that's like using a strainer to hold water—it's deceptive because it *looks* like it will hold water, but it *can't.*

MR. KAY: And in that metaphor, the sieve is Bertram, and the water is your love, yes?

SARAH: Yes.

MR. KAY: All right. And, what do you mean by "lack not to lose still"?

SARAH: Well, I mean . . . I have such an infinite supply of love that I can keep pouring it down the drain forever.

MR. KAY: What do you mean by "Thus Indian-like, religious in mine error, I adore the sun"?

SARAH: Um, that means . . . "like a native that foolishly worships the sun as a god."

MR. KAY: Yes. And what do you mean by "Let not your hate encounter with my love"?

SARAH: There's no need to hate me for loving Bertram.

MR. KAY: What do you mean by "so true a flame of liking"?

SARAH: A love that burns steadily.

MR. KAY: What do you mean by "that her search implies"?

SARAH: What she's searching for.

MR. KAY: And what do you mean by "riddle-like"?

SARAH: Paradoxically.

MR. KAY: Good, good, Sarah. Okay, now let's talk a bit about this scene.

Helena's one of Shakespeare's complex female characters, who makes a big psychological journey during the course of the play.

She's a very intelligent character—intense and passionate, obsessive and tenacious, and of course, by the end of the story she becomes quite confident and even courageous.

But here, at the *beginning* of the play, she's still a tentative and apprehensive young woman, self-conscious and apologetic, and afraid to speak her mind.

So, let's go through this again, Sarah, and this time, let's try a spoken subtext exercise that I call *secret fears.*

(The class writes "secret fears" in their notebooks.)

Here's how this works: I'd like you to complete the phrase "I'M AFRAID THAT . . ." before you speak each speech measure.

(The students write "I'm afraid that . . ." in their notebooks.)

SARAH: I'm afraid that . . . ?

MR. KAY: Yes. You say your secret fear *aloud,* then allow the statement of that fear to springboard you into the next bit of text. Got it?

SARAH: I'm afraid that I don't . . . *(the class laughs)* . . . but I'm willing to give it a try.

MR. KAY: Good. Now, as we work, please keep in mind that your subtext must be inspired by the text—by clues inside the speech measure. It shouldn't be pulled out of thin air and arbitrarily imposed upon the text.

In other words, your subtext is your springboard to text.

Make sense?

SARAH: Yes.

MR. KAY: All right then. If you restore the beginning of your scene, please.

(Sarah does so.)

And remind us, what's the objective again?

SARAH: I want the Countess to take pity on me.

MR. KAY: Okay, then, you want her to take pity on you, but you're afraid. So what's the first thing you're afraid of?

SARAH: Um . . . I'm not sure.

MR. KAY: Well, what's the first speech measure?

SARAH: Then I confess . . .

MR. KAY: Why must you *confess*? What are you afraid of?

SARAH: I'm afraid that it's a sin.

MR. KAY: What's a sin?

SARAH: My feelings for Bertram.

MR. KAY: Good, then say it aloud. I'm afraid that . . . ? What?

SARAH: I'M AFRAID THAT MY FEELINGS FOR BERTRAM ARE SINFUL.

MR. KAY: Yes, but don't just *say* it—fill yourself with that fear! And again, please—secret fear?

(Sarah's eyes soften, and her breathing deepens.)

SARAH: I'M AFRAID THAT MY FEELINGS FOR BERTRAM ARE SINFUL.

MR. KAY: Good! Now let that statement propel you into your text.

SARAH: Then I confess
Here on my knee, before high heaven and you,
That before you, and next unto high heaven,
I love your son.

MR. KAY: Excellent! Next secret fear? I'm afraid that . . . what?

SARAH: *(Unsure)* Um . . .

MR. KAY: What does the text in the next measure say?

SARAH: My friends were poor, but honest . . .

MR. KAY: Yes. Why would you say that? What are you afraid of?

SARAH: I'M AFRAID THAT I'M NOT WORTHY.

MR. KAY: Yes! And text, Helena?

SARAH: My friends were poor, but honest, so's my love.

MR. KAY: *(To the class)* And do you see, folks, how the statement of that fear launches her directly into her text?

(To Sarah) Next secret fear? I'm afraid that . . . ?

SARAH: I'M AFRAID THAT I'VE OFFENDED HER.

MR. KAY: And text?

SARAH: Be not offended, for it hurts not him
That he is lov'd of me;

MR. KAY: Good! And continue now, Helena, on your own . . .

SARAH: I'M AFRAID THAT SHE'S DISGUSTED.

> I follow him not
> By any token of presumptuous suit,

I'M AFRAID THAT I DON'T DESERVE HIM.

> Nor would I have him till I do deserve him,
> Yet never know how that desert should be.

I'M AFRAID THAT SHE'LL THINK I'M A FOOL.

> I know I love in vain, strive against hope,

I'M AFRAID THAT IT WILL NEVER STOP HURTING.

> Yet in this captious and intenible sieve,
> I still pour the waters of my love
> And lack not to lose still.

I'M AFRAID THAT BERTRAM WILL NEVER LOVE ME.

> Thus Indian-like,
> Religious in mine error, I adore
> The sun, that looks upon his worshipper,
> But knows of him no more.

I'M AFRAID THAT NOW SHE HATES ME.

> My dearest madam,
> Let not your hate encounter with my love
> For loving where you do;

I'M AFRAID THAT SHE DOESN'T UNDERSTAND.

> but if yourself,
> Whose agèd honor cites a virtuous youth,
> Did ever in so true a flame of liking
> Wish chastely and love dearly,

I'M AFRAID THAT SHE'LL DISOWN ME.

> O then give pity
> To her whose state is such that cannot choose
> But lend and give where she is sure to lose;

I'M AFRAID THAT SHE'LL THROW ME OUT OF THE HOUSE.

> That seeks not to find that her search implies,
> But riddle-like, lives sweetly where she dies.

MR. KAY: Good, Sarah. Thank you.

(Sarah comes down off the stage.)

(To the class) Please keep in mind, folks, that the statement of all these fears makes Helena a *courageous* individual, not a coward. Because, *despite* all these fears, she keeps pursuing her objective, undaunted.

And I think you can see, folks, that these spoken subtext exercises can be very powerful tools, which require a great deal of courage as an *actor.*

Because they allow you to *personalize* the character's experience in a very immediate way, in a way that can make you feel intensely vulnerable emotionally.

But again, I would remind you that that is *precisely* why we come to the theater—to see a great actor breathe life into exquisite words spoken by complex characters in extraordinary circumstances.

So you must commit fully to these tools *despite* that fact that they make you feel intensely vulnerable.

Otherwise, the audience might just as well stay home and read the play by a warm fire.

Let's work some more. Who wants to go next?

⮽ SECRET HOPES AND DREAMS ⮽

TAYO: Me!

(Tayo goes up onto the stage.)

MR. KAY: All right, Tayo. And what are you going to show us?

TAYO: Portia, from *The Merchant of Venice.*

MR. KAY: Fine. If you would place yourself in your scene, please, so I can ask you a few questions.

(Tayo stands center stage, gazing outward.)

Where are you, Portia?

TAYO: In my house, in Belmont.

MR. KAY: And who are you talking to?

TAYO: To Bassanio.

MR. KAY: Who is he?

TAYO: He's a suitor for my hand in marriage.

MR. KAY: And what's he doing in your house?

TAYO: He's come to choose between three caskets, because the suitor who chooses the right casket gets to marry me.

MR. KAY: I see. And who set up this crazy test?

TAYO: My dead father.

MR. KAY: I see. So what do *you* want? What do you hope to accomplish by talking to Bassanio?

TAYO: I want to convince him to postpone his choosing a casket.

MR. KAY: Why do you want to postpone his choosing a casket?

TAYO: Well, I'm in love with him, and I want him to choose the *right* casket, so I can marry him. But I can't bear to let him choose, because if he chooses the *wrong* one, I'll never see him again. So I want to postpone the whole thing for a month or two.

MR. KAY: I see. And what's the obstacle to that? Why is it difficult to convince him to postpone his choice?

TAYO: He's eager to choose *right now.*

MR. KAY: I see. Any other obstacles?

TAYO: Um . . . well, I can't really say what's on my mind. I can't speak my true feelings out loud because everyone's listening.

MR. KAY: I see. So, it's a *private* scene that takes place in *public*?

TAYO: Yes.

MR. KAY: Good. Let's see if you can get him to postpone his choice. Begin, please.

PORTIA: I pray you tarry; pause a day or two
    Before you hazard, for in choosing wrong
    I lose your company. Therefore forbear a while.
    There's something tells me (but it is not love)
    I would not lose you; and you know yourself
    Hate counsels not in such a quality.
    But lest you should not understand me well—
    And yet a maiden hath no tongue but thought—
    I would detain you here some month or two
    Before you venture for me. I could teach you
    How to choose right, but then I am forsworn.
    So will I never be. So may you miss me.
    But if you do, you'll make me wish a sin,
    That I had been forsworn. Beshrew your eyes!
    They have o'erlook'd me and divided me:
    One half of me is yours, the other half yours—
    Mine own I would say; but if mine, then yours,
    And so all yours. O these naughty times
    Puts bars between the owners and their rights.
    And so, though yours, not yours. Prove it so,
    Let fortune go to hell for it, not I.

I speak too long, but 'tis to peize the time,
To eke it, and draw it out in length,
To stay you from election.

MR. KAY: Good, Tayo. And before we go back and look at this again, let's make sure we understand the text completely.

What do you mean by "you know yourself hate counsels not in such a quality"?

TAYO: You know that hate doesn't tell me to delay your choice.

MR. KAY: What do you mean by "So may you miss me"?

TAYO: You might not win me, because I won't disobey my father's will.

MR. KAY: What do you mean by "They have o'erlook'd me"?

TAYO: Your eyes have bewitched me.

MR. KAY: What do you mean by "Prove it so, let fortune go to hell for it, not I"?

TAYO: If this ends up badly, it's fortune's fault, not mine.

MR. KAY: What do you mean by "to peize the time"?

TAYO: It means "to stall, or delay, or procrastinate."

MR. KAY: And what do you mean by "To eke it"?

TAYO: To stretch time out.

MR. KAY: Good. So, let's talk about this speech for a moment.

Portia is a woman with a lot of hopes and dreams and desires, which she's not allowed to reveal because of the test her dead father has set up for her suitors.

The challenge of the speech is: how do you reveal these things to the *audience,* when you're not allowed to reveal them to *Bassanio*?

One way to answer that question is to say some of her subtext *aloud,* and use it to orchestrate the speech.

So, let's try an exercise that I call *secret hopes and dreams.*

(The students write "secret hopes and dreams" in their notebooks.)

Would you please say aloud, Tayo, before each speech measure, one of the following phrases? Please repeat after me: I wish—

TAYO: I wish—

MR. KAY: I want—

TAYO: I want—

MR. KAY: I hope—

TAYO: I hope—

MR. KAY: I need—

TAYO: I need—

MR. KAY: I must—

TAYO: I must.

(The students write "I wish, I want, I hope, I need, I must" in their notebooks.)

MR. KAY: Yes! So let's do the speech again, Tayo, and this time I'd like you to *complete* any of those phrases—"I WISH," "I WANT," "I HOPE," "I NEED," or "I MUST"—before you speak each measure of the text. Got it?

TAYO: I hope so.

(The class laughs.)

MR. KAY: Good. Now, as we work, please remember that your secret hopes and dreams must be inspired by what the character actually says in each speech measure. Your choices must be based in the text, not in your opinions or feelings about the character. Make sense?

TAYO: Yes.

MR. KAY: Good! So, let's go back to the top, please.

(Tayo restores the scene in her imagination.)

And remind us, please, what's your objective, Portia?

TAYO: To postpone his choice.

MR. KAY: Yes, and what's your first speech measure?

TAYO: I pray you tarry;

MR. KAY: Yes, and secret hopes and dreams before you speak? I wish, I want, I hope, I need, I must?

TAYO: Um . . . I MUST STOP HIM FROM CHOOSING.

MR. KAY: Good, then stop him!

TAYO: I pray you tarry;

MR. KAY: Good! *(To the class)* And did you see how she used the subtext as a springboard to her text?

(To Tayo) And continue, please, Portia—I wish, I want, I hope, I need, I must?

TAYO: I HOPE I CAN CONVINCE HIM TO WAIT.

pause a day or two
Before you hazard,

MR. KAY: Yes, but don't just *say* it—fill yourself up with that secret hope! And again, please?

TAYO: I HOPE I CAN CONVINCE HIM TO WAIT.

(Tayo's eyes open wide, and her voice softens.)

pause a day or two
Before you hazard,

MR. KAY: Good! *(To the class)* Do you see how this works, folks? You fill yourself up with those secret unspoken desires; you say them out loud and permit them to affect you; you inhale; you let them permeate the speech measure which follows.

(To Tayo) And continue, please, Portia—I wish, I want, I hope, I need, I must?

TAYO: I MUST GIVE HIM A REASON.

for in choosing wrong
I lose your company.

I NEED TO BE FIRM.

Therefore forbear a while.

I WISH I COULD TELL HIM HOW I REALLY FEEL.

There's something tells me

I MUST HIDE MY TRUE FEELINGS.

(but it is not love)

I WANT TO LIVE WITH THIS MAN FOREVER.

I would not lose you;

I HOPE HE KNOWS HOW I FEEL ABOUT HIM.

and you know yourself
Hate counsels not in such a quality.

I MUST BE DIRECT WITH HIM.

But lest you should not understand me well—

I WANT TO TELL HIM EVERYTHING.

And yet a maiden hath no tongue but thought—

I WISH THERE WERE MORE TIME.

I would detain you here some month or two
Before you venture for me.

I WISH I COULD TELL HIM TO CHOOSE THE LEAD CASKET.

I could teach you
How to choose right,

I MUST NOT BREAK MY PROMISE.

but then I am forsworn.

MR. KAY: *(Stopping her)* And I pray you tarry, Portia, because I'd like you to rephrase that intention *positively,* rather than negatively! In other words, don't tell us what you must *not* do, tell us what you must *do!*

TAYO: Um . . . I MUST DO WHAT MY FATHER'S WILL DEMANDS.

but then I am forsworn.

MR. KAY: Good! *(To the class)* And do you all see how much easier it is to play a *positive* intention, rather than a *negative* one? You must always remember to phrase all your spoken subtext in this manner!

(To Tayo) And continue, please, Portia.

TAYO: I WANT TO DO WHAT IS RIGHT.

So will I never be.

I NEED TO BE STRONG.

So may you miss me.

I WANT TO CRY.

But if you do, you'll make me wish a sin,
That I had been forsworn.

I NEED TO LOOK AWAY.

(Looking away)

Beshrew your eyes!

I HOPE HE LIKES WHAT HE SEES.

They have o'erlook'd me and divided me:
One half of me is yours,

I WANT TO LOOK AT HIM AGAIN.

(Looking back at him)

the other half yours—

I MUST CONTROL MYSELF.

Mine own I would say;

I WANT HIM TO KISS ME.

but if mine, then yours,

I WANT HIM IN MY BED.

And so all yours.

I WANT TO SHOUT OUT MY FRUSTRATION!

(Looking up)

O these naughty times
Puts bars between the owners and their rights.

MR. KAY: You shifted you focal point *up,* Portia. Why? What's up there?

TAYO: I'm shouting up to my dead father!

MR. KAY: I see! And continue, please.

TAYO: I MUST PREPARE MYSELF TO LOSE HIM.

> And so, though yours, not yours.

> I WANT TO CURSE THIS STUPID TEST.

> Prove it so,
> Let fortune go to hell for it, not I.

> I NEED TO SHUT UP NOW.

> I speak too long,

> I MUST LET HIM CHOOSE.

> but 'tis to peize the time,
> To eke it, and draw it out in length,
> To stay you from election.

MR. KAY: Excellent! Thank you, Tayo.

(Tayo comes down off the stage.)

(To the class) Do you all see how filling yourself up with the secret hopes and dreams of the character, and saying them *aloud,* can help you to orchestrate a speech?

(To Tayo) Of course, the next step in the process, Tayo, now that we've carefully orchestrated this speech, is to fill yourself up with those secret hopes and dreams from moment to moment, permit them to affect you deeply, and then *keep them to yourself!*

So even though Portia cannot tell Bassanio, in this public ritual, how she truly feels, her private thoughts will nevertheless be revealed to the audience through her behavior, through voice and body, rather than the words.

Let's look at another speech. Who's next?

⊸ SECRET INTENTIONS ⊸

TRINITY: I am!

(Trinity goes up onto the stage.)

MR. KAY: What are you going to show us, today, Trinity?

TRINITY: Cleopatra, from *Antony and Cleopatra.*

MR. KAY: All right, and if you'd place yourself in your scene, please, so I can ask you a few questions.

(Trinity stands stage right, gazing outward.)
Where are you, Cleopatra?

TRINITY: I'm in my palace on the Nile.

MR. KAY: Yes, and what room are you in?

TRINITY: In my bedchamber.

MR. KAY: I see. And who are you talking to?

TRINITY: Well, first to my servant, Charmian, but mostly to my lover, Antony.

MR. KAY: And what do you want from Antony? What do you hope to accomplish?

TRINITY: I want to make him stay with me in Egypt.

MR. KAY: And what's the obstacle to that? Why must he leave?

TRINITY: Well, there's a war going on back in Rome . . .

MR. KAY: A war?

TRINITY: Yes, a civil war. And, he's married, and his wife is back in Rome waiting for him.

MR. KAY: His wife?

TRINITY: Yes. Fulvia.

TRINITY: I see. Let's see if you can get Antony to stay in Egypt. Begin, please.

CLEOPATRA: But here comes Antony. I'm sick and sullen.
Help me away, dear Charmian, I shall fall!
It cannot be thus long; the sides of nature
Will not sustain it. Pray you stand farther from me.
I know by that same eye there's some good news.
What, says the married woman you may go?
Would she had never giv'n you leave to come!
Let her not say 'tis I that keep you here.
I have no pow'r upon you; hers you are.
O, never was there a queen
So mightily betray'd! Yet at the first
I saw the treasons planted.
Why should I think you can be mine and true
(Though you in swearing shake the thronèd gods)
Who have been false to Fulvia? Riotous madness,
To be entangl'd with those mouth-made vows
Which break themselves in swearing!
Nay, pray you seek no color for your going,
But bid farewell and go. When you sued staying,

Then was the time for words; no going then.
Eternity was in our lips and eyes,
Bliss in our brows' bent; none our parts so poor
But was a race of heav'n. They are so still.
Or thou, the greatest soldier of the world,
Art turn'd the greatest liar.
I would I had thy inches; thou shouldst know
There were a heart in Egypt.

MR. KAY: Good, Trinity. I like the way you've cut and pasted that speech together from a scene with Antony. Very clever.

TRINITY: Thank you.

MR. KAY: Now, before we look at this again, Trinity, let's make sure we all understand the text completely.

What do you mean by "the sides of nature"?

TRINITY: Um . . . the human body.

MR. KAY: What do you mean by "mouth-made vows"?

TRINITY: Empty promises.

MR. KAY: What do you mean by "Would she had never giv'n you leave to come"?

TRINITY: I wish she'd never given you permission to come here.

MR. KAY: What do you mean by "our brows' bent"?

TRINITY: Well, the "our" is the "royal we," so I mean "the arch of my eyebrow."

MR. KAY: What do you mean by "none our parts so poor"?

TRINITY: It means "none of my features, no matter how small."

MR. KAY: What do you mean by "But was a race of heav'n"?

TRINITY: It means "was of divine origins."

MR. KAY: What do you mean by "I would I had thy inches"?

TRINITY: I wish I had your height and strength . . .

MR. KAY: But also . . . ?

TRINITY: I wish I were a man.

MR. KAY: And also . . . ?

(A pregnant pause.)

TRINITY: I wish I had you inside me.

MR. KAY: Yes, good, kind of a sexy triple-meaning there, yes?

TRINITY: Uh-huh!

(The class laughs.)

MR. KAY: All right then, let's talk a bit about this scene. What's Cleopatra's objective again? What do you want to accomplish?

TRINITY: I want to make Antony stay in Egypt.

MR. KAY: Yes. And how many different *ways* do you try to make him stay?

TRINITY: How many different ways? Well, I'm not sure . . . I mean . . . I didn't really think about that.

MR. KAY: And you see, that's the main problem with the scene right now, Trinity.

Because you haven't orchestrated the speech from moment to moment, we see Cleopatra trying only two or three very generalized ways to keep Antony in Egypt.

But Cleopatra, the master manipulator, a woman of "infinite variety," might try eighteen or twenty different ways to make Antony stay in this short speech.

So, let's work on that right now. Let's look at some of the ways you might try to make Antony stay in Egypt with you.

. For example, what's the first thing you try? What do you tell Charmian when you realize Antony is on his way in?

TRINITY: "But here comes Antony. I'm sick and sullen."

MR. KAY: So, you see Antony coming, and you decide—in that instant—what you're going to do. You tell Charmian that you want him to think you're *sick.* Why?

TRINITY: Well, I want to alarm him, I want him to feel concerned about me.

MR. KAY: So you deliberately, willfully, and consciously intend to manipulate his feelings to get what you want?

TRINITY: Well . . . yes, of course!

(The class laughs.)

MR. KAY: All right then, let's continue with that idea. Let's continue with the idea that you're going to tell us your secret intention *aloud,* as you do with Charmian in that moment, just before you play it.

I'd like you to *keep* telling us your *secret intentions,* aloud, from moment to moment, throughout the entire speech.

(The students write "secret intentions" in their notebooks.)

And I'd like you to do that in a very specific way. I'd like you to complete the phrase "I WANT TO MAKE HIM FEEL . . ."

(The students write "I want to make him feel . . . " in their notebooks.)

For example, you might say "I want to make him feel *angry*." Then you'll use that statement to springboard you directly into your text.

Got that?

TRINITY: I think so.

MR. KAY: Good. Remember that your secret intentions must be inspired by textual clues inside the speech measure, rather than plucked from the ether.

TRINITY: Yes.

MR. KAY: Very good. So, if you would, immerse yourself in your scene again, please.

(Trinity does so.)

Ready? You see Antony coming! And, first line?

TRINITY: But here comes Antony. I'm sick and sullen.

MR. KAY: First secret intention? I want to make him feel . . . ?

TRINITY: Um . . . I WANT TO MAKE HIM FEEL . . . ALARMED.

MR. KAY: Yes, and text?

TRINITY: Help me away, dear Charmian, I shall fall!

MR. KAY: Is he alarmed?

TRINITY: Yes. I think so. He looks shocked to see me sick!

MR. KAY: Good! Next intention? I want to make him feel . . . what?

TRINITY: I WANT TO MAKE HIM FEEL ANXIOUS.

MR. KAY: And text . . .

TRINITY: It cannot be thus long; the sides of nature
Will not sustain it.

MR. KAY: Have you made him feel anxious, Cleo?

TRINITY: Yes. He's upset that I might be dying.

MR. KAY: How do you know?

TRINITY: I can see it in his eyes.

MR. KAY: Good. And continue, please, Cleo . . . I want to make him feel . . . what?

TRINITY: I WANT TO MAKE HIM FEEL SPURNED.

MR. KAY: And text?

TRINITY: Pray you stand farther from me.

MR. KAY: Again, please, but *stronger!* Make him feel *spurned!*

TRINITY: Pray you stand farther from me.

MR. KAY: Does he feel spurned?

TRINITY: Yes. He's stopped dead in his tracks, and he has a hurt expression on his face.

MR. KAY: Good. And going on . . . next intention, Cleo?

TRINITY: I WANT TO MAKE HIM FEEL TRANSPARENT.

MR. KAY: Good! But say that again with your *intention* behind it!

TRINITY: I WANT TO MAKE HIM FEEL TRANSPARENT.

MR. KAY: Good! Now let that intention bleed vocally and physically into your text!

TRINITY: I know by that same eye there's some good news.

MR. KAY: Excellent! Next . . . ?

TRINITY: I WANT TO MAKE HIM FEEL CHILDISH.

What, says the married woman you may go?

MR. KAY: Again, please—speak to him like a little boy—make him feel *childish!*

TRINITY: What, says the married woman you may go?

MR. KAY: Good! Next intention?

TRINITY: I WANT TO MAKE HIM FEEL MY MISERY.

Would she had never giv'n you leave to come!

MR. KAY: Yes, but *stronger*—make him feel your misery, Cleo!

TRINITY: Would she had never giv'n you leave to come!

MR. KAY: Good! *Now* he's miserable! Next intention?

TRINITY: I WANT TO MAKE HIM FEEL RESPONSIBLE.

Let her not say 'tis I that keep you here.
I have no pow'r upon you; hers you are.

I WANT TO MAKE HIM FEEL GUILTY.

O, never was there a queen
So mightily betray'd!

I WANT TO MAKE HIM FEEL TREASONOUS.

Yet at the first
I saw the *treasons* planted.

MR. KAY: Excellent. *(To the class)* And did you all hear how she used the word "treasons" to make him feel *treasonous*?

Whenever possible, choose a secret intention that will allow you to stress the operative word.

(To Trinity) Continue, Cleo.

TRINITY: I WANT TO MAKE HIM FEEL DECEITFUL.

Why should I think you can be mine and *true*
(Though you in swearing shake the thronèd gods)
Who have been *false* to Fulvia?

MR. KAY: Yes! *(To the class)* And did you notice how she used "true" and "false" as her operative words to make him feel *deceitful*?

Whenever possible, choose a secret intention that will allow you to use a figure of rhetoric—in this case an *antithesis*—as part of the tactic.

(To Trinity) Next . . . ?

TRINITY: I WANT TO MAKE HIM FEEL RIDICULOUS.

Riotous madness,
To be entangl'd with those mouth-made vows
Which break themselves in swearing!

MR. KAY: Yes—she wants to make him feel ridiculous, so she *ridicules* him, yes?

TRINITY: I WANT TO MAKE HIM FEEL INSIGNIFICANT.

Nay, pray you seek no color for your going,
But bid farewell and go.

MR. KAY: She wants to make him feel insignificant, so she *dismisses* him . . .

TRINITY: I WANT TO MAKE HIM FEEL REGRETFUL.

When you sued *staying,*
Then was the time for words; no *going* then.

MR. KAY: Yes. *(To the class)* And did you all hear how she balanced the words "staying" and "going"—another antithesis—in order to make him feel *regretful*?

(To Trinity) Very good, Cleo, continue . . .

TRINITY: I WANT TO MAKE HIM FEEL LUSTFUL.

Eternity was in our lips and eyes,
Bliss in our brows' bent;

MR. KAY: She wants to make him feel lustful, so she plays *to entice* . . .

TRINITY: I WANT TO MAKE HIM FEEL IN AWE.

> none our parts so poor
> But was a race of heav'n. They are so still.

> I WANT TO MAKE HIM FEEL ASHAMED.

> Or thou, the greatest soldier of the world,
> Art turn'd the greatest liar.

MR. KAY: And what action does she use there to make him feel ashamed? To *shame,* of course!

TRINITY: I WANT TO MAKE HIM FEEL LOVED.

> I would I had thy inches; thou shouldst know
> There were a heart in Egypt.

MR. KAY: Good! Very good work, Trinity. Thank you.

(Trinity comes down off the stage.)

(To the class) Now, do you all see how committing yourself to these statements of intention leads you to playing a very specific sequence of actions or tactics?

Cleopatra wants Antony to stay in Egypt, and she'll manipulate his feelings relentlessly until she gets her way.

She plays one intention, then another, then another, then another, without letting up, until she succeeds.

This is what Enobarbus calls "her infinite variety."

But this "infinite variety" must be orchestrated, moment by moment, based on what the text tells you. You must try a hundred different possibilities in rehearsal until you hit upon a sequence that works.

Let's look at another speech. Who hasn't worked yet?

ᗯ᠑ REALIZATIONS ᗰ᠑

CLAIRE: I haven't.

(Claire goes up onto the stage.)

MR. KAY: All right, Claire. What are you going to show us today?

CLAIRE: Viola, from *Twelfth Night.*

MR. KAY: Very good. And place yourself in your scene, please, and I'll ask you a few questions.

(Claire stands center stage, looking at a ring she holds in her hand.)

Where are you, Viola?

CLAIRE: I'm on a road in Illyria.

MR. KAY: Where are you going?

CLAIRE: I'm walking back to Count Orsino's house.

MR. KAY: And who's Count Orsino?

CLAIRE: He's my master.

MR. KAY: I see. And where are you coming from?

CLAIRE: From Countess Olivia's house.

MR. KAY: What were you doing there?

CLAIRE: I went to woo Olivia for Count Orsino.

MR. KAY: He sent a *woman* to woo for him?

CLAIRE: Well, no—I'm in disguise. I'm dressed as *boy.*

MR. KAY: Why are you dressed as a boy?

CLAIRE: Well, I was shipwrecked here in Illyria, and lost everything. So, for safety, I dressed up as a boy and offered myself as a servant to Orsino.

MR. KAY: I see. And does *Orsino* know that you're a woman?

CLAIRE: No, he thinks I'm a boy. He calls me Cesario.

MR. KAY: That must be awkward!

CLAIRE: Yes, it is—because I've fallen in love with him!

MR. KAY: I see. So who are you talking to now?

CLAIRE: Myself.

MR. KAY: Why? What just happened?

CLAIRE: Olivia's servant, Malvolio, just gave me this ring, telling me that Olivia refuses to keep it. But I never gave her any ring!

MR. KAY: I see. So why are you talking to yourself? What do you hope to accomplish?

CLAIRE: I want to sort out this mess I've gotten myself into.

MR. KAY: And what's the obstacle to that?

CLAIRE: I haven't a clue how to do it!

MR. KAY: Good, then let's see if you can sort things out. Begin, please.

VIOLA: I left no ring with her. What means this lady?
Fortune forbid my outside have not charm'd her.
She made good view of me, indeed so much

That methought her eyes had lost her tongue,
For she did speak in starts distractedly.
She loves me sure! The cunning of her passion
Invites me in this churlish messenger.
None of my lord's ring? Why, he sent her none.
I am the man. If it be so, as 'tis,
Poor lady, she were better love a dream.
Disguise, I see thou art a wickedness
Wherein the pregnant enemy does much.
How easy is it for the proper false
In women's waxen hearts to set their forms!
Alas, our frailty is the cause, not we,
For such as we are made of, such we be.
How will this fadge? My master loves her dearly;
And I, poor monster, fond as much on him;
And she, mistaken, seems to dote on me.
What will become of this? As I am a man,
My state is desp'rate for my master's love.
As I am a woman (now, alas the day!)
What thriftless sighs shall poor Olivia breathe?
O Time, thou must untangle this, not I;
It is too hard a knot for me t' untie.

MR. KAY: Good, Claire. Now, before we look at this again, let me ask you about a phrase or two that we may not understand.

What do you mean by "she made good view of me"?

CLAIRE: She took a good look at me.

MR. KAY: What do you mean by "methought her eyes had lost her tongue"?

CLAIRE: What she saw seemed to make her tongue-tied.

MR. KAY: What do you mean by "The cunning of her passion invites me in this churlish messenger"?

CLAIRE: Olivia is cleverly using Malvolio to get me to return to her house.

MR. KAY: What do you mean by "I am the man"?

CLAIRE: I'm the man of her dreams!

MR. KAY: What do you mean by "the pregnant enemy"?

CLAIRE: That clever old devil, Satan.

MR. KAY: What do you mean by "the proper false"?

CLAIRE: Handsome, untrustworthy men.

MR. KAY: What do you mean by "In women's waxen hearts to set their forms"?

CLAIRE: To make a strong impression on our soft hearts.

MR. KAY: What do you mean by "Such as we are made of, such we be"?

CLAIRE: Women are frail, because we're made of frail stuff.

MR. KAY: What do you mean by "How will this fadge?"

CLAIRE: How will this all turn out?

MR. KAY: What do you mean by "And I, poor monster"?

CLAIRE: I'm a monster, because I'm a woman dressed as a man.

MR. KAY: What do you mean by "fond as much on him"?

CLAIRE: I dote on Orsino as much as Orsino dotes on Olivia.

MR. KAY: What do you mean by "thriftless sighs"?

CLAIRE: Pointless yearning.

MR. KAY: Yes, good, Claire. Now, let's talk about this scene for a bit.

Viola is just beginning to get a glimpse of reality here on the road between Orsino and Olivia's estates. For the first time since washing up onto the shores of Illyria, she's drawing back the curtains of illusion and delirium, and can clearly see the hard knot she's tied for herself by dressing up as a boy.

So I think you're absolutely right, Claire, about the *objective* of the speech—that Viola wants to sort out the mess she's gotten herself into. And I think you're *playing* that objective very strongly.

The problem is that you're so focused on your *objective,* that you're not playing the specific series of *discoveries* that Viola makes as she pursues that objective.

You're pushing so hard to solve the puzzle that you're forgetting to illuminate the moments when a piece of that puzzle actually falls into place.

So I think we need to go back, Claire, and figure out—what exactly does Viola *realize,* and when does she *realize* it?

CLAIRE: Okay.

MR. KAY: So let's go through the speech again, and this time, let's try a spoken subtext exercise that I call *realizations.*

(The students write "realizations" in their notebooks.)

CLAIRE: Okay, I'm game.

MR. KAY: Good. Then, here's how this works. Would you put the back of your fist up on your forehead, please? Like this.

(Mr. Kay demonstrates; Claire does the same.)

Then, *slowly,* open your fingers, like a flower blossoming—like this.

(Mr. Kay demonstrates; Claire does the same.)

Now, let's do that again, and this time, when your fingers open, please complete the phrase "I REALIZE THAT . . ."

(The students write "I realize that . . . " in their notebooks.)

(Claire puts her fist to her forehead again, and unfurls her fingers.)

CLAIRE: I REALIZE THAT . . . this feels very silly.

(The class laughs.)

MR. KAY: Yes, it feels silly at first, but that's okay—it's a comedy.

So, the idea here, you understand, is to *physicalize* your realization with your hand. Then you say your realization *aloud,* then use that realization as a *springboard* into text. Follow that?

CLAIRE: Yes, I follow.

MR. KAY: Good, let's give it a try. From Malvolio's exit. The ring is your first focal point.

(Claire stands center stage, staring at the ring in her hand.)

And remind us, please, what's your objective, Viola?

CLAIRE: To sort out this mess.

MR. KAY: Good, and first realization, Viola, before you speak?

(She puts her fist to her forehead, and unfurls her fingers, slowly.)

CLAIRE: I REALIZE THAT I'VE NEVER SEEN THIS RING BEFORE.

MR. KAY: Good, but don't *just* say it! This is first time you've ever seen this ring—the first time you've ever had this thought! *Here,* in this place, *now,* in this moment! And again, please, Viola—first realization?

(She stares at the ring in absolute bewilderment.)

CLAIRE: I REALIZE THAT I'VE NEVER SEEN THIS RING BEFORE.

MR. KAY: Good! And text?

CLAIRE: I left no ring with her. What means this lady?

MR. KAY: Good, Claire. *(To the class)* And did you all notice how the realization carried over into the speech measure that followed?

(To Claire) Next realization, Viola?

CLAIRE: I REALIZE THAT OLIVIA MAY BE SMITTEN WITH ME.

Fortune forbid my outside have not charm'd her.

MR. KAY: Good. Let the realization *bleed*—vocally and physically—into the action. Next realization?

CLAIRE: I REALIZE THAT SHE STARED AT ME.

She made good view of me,

MR. KAY: Yes, continue. Next realization?

CLAIRE: I REALIZE THAT SHE STAMMERED WHEN SHE SPOKE TO ME.

indeed so much
That methought her eyes had lost her tongue,
For she did speak in starts distractedly.

MR. KAY: Good. Next realization?

CLAIRE: I REALIZE THAT OLIVIA'S IN LOVE WITH ME.

(A big inhalation.)

She loves me sure!

MR. KAY: Excellent! That's a *big* realization! *(To the class)* And do you see, folks, how the realization instantly transports her into the here and now?

(To Claire) Continue, please, Viola.

CLAIRE: I REALIZE THAT OLIVIA SENT MALVOLIO TO GET ME TO RETURN.

The cunning of her passion
Invites me in this churlish messenger.

I REALIZE THAT ORSINO NEVER SENT A RING.

None of my lord's ring? Why, he sent her none.

I REALIZE THAT I AM THE MAN.

I am the man.

I REALIZE THAT OLIVIA IS IN LOVE WITH A SHADOW.

If it be so, as 'tis,
Poor lady, she were better love a dream.

I REALIZE THAT DISGUISE IS DANGEROUS.

Disguise, I see thou art a wickedness
Wherein the pregnant enemy does much.

I REALIZE THAT WOMEN ARE TOO IMPRESSIONABLE.

How easy is it for the proper false
In women's waxen hearts to set their forms!

I REALIZE THAT WOMEN ARE MADE OF FRAIL STUFF.

Alas, our frailty is the cause, not we,
For such as we are made of, such we be.

I REALIZE THAT I CAN'T FORSEE THE OUTCOME OF THIS.

How will this fadge?

I REALIZE THAT I MUST SKETCH THIS OUT.

(Using her finger in the air to make a sketch)

My master loves her dearly;
And I, poor monster, fond as much on him;
And she, mistaken, seems to dote on me.

MR. KAY: Excellent! *(To the class)* Did you all see how that one realization propelled her through the next three speech measures?

A single realization can encompass *many* speech measures.

(To Claire) Continue, please, Viola.

CLAIRE: I REALIZE THAT THIS IS A TRIANGLE.

(Seeing the triangle for the first time)

What will become of this?

MR. KAY: *(To the class)* And in that moment, she's suddenly able to see all three sides of the love triangle! Wonderful.

(To Claire) Continue, please.

CLAIRE: I REALIZE THAT I AN DESPERATE FOR ORSINO'S LOVE.

As I am a man,
My state is desp'rate for my master's love.

I REALIZE THAT OLIVIA WILL HAVE HER HEART BROKEN.

As I am a woman (now, alas the day!)
What thriftless sighs shall poor Olivia breathe?

I REALIZE THAT ONLY TIME CAN SORT OUT THIS MESS.

O Time, thou must untangle this, not I;
It is too hard a knot for me t' untie.

MR. KAY: Good. Very good, Claire. Thank you.

(Claire comes down off the stage.)

(To the class) Of course, the "ring speech" is the quintessential realization speech in Shakespeare. My guess is that this is probably the largest number of realizations a character has in any one speech in the entire canon. Most of the speeches you'll encounter will contain just *one* realization that moves the character forward in the story.

Can you think of other examples of realizations in Shakespeare? Anybody?

JAKE: Othello realizes that Iago has tricked him.

MADISON: Juliet realizes that Romeo is dead.

RACHEL: Proteus realizes that he loves Sylvia.

TIM: Isabella realizes that Angelo wants to sleep with her.

TAYO: Shylock realizes that he has lost his pound of flesh.

JESSE: Macbeth realizes that the witches have tricked him.

ELENA: Troilus realizes that Cressida is false.

NOAH: Falstaff realizes that Hal no longer loves him.

SAM: Titania realizes that she's slept with an ass.

GABRIELLA: That's happened to me!

(The entire class laughs.)

MR. KAY: Excellent!

Let's look at another speech. Who wants to work?

⟡ DECISIONS ⟡

LUKE: I do!

(Luke goes up onto the stage.)

MR. KAY: Good, Luke. So, what are you going to show us?

LUKE: Edgar, from *King Lear.*

MR. KAY: All right. And if you would place yourself in your scene, please, and I'll ask you a few questions.

(Luke stands upstage center, gazing outward.)

Where are you, Edgar?

LUKE: I'm in a field in Gloucestershire.

MR. KAY: What are you doing there?

LUKE: I've been hiding in a hollow tree to avoid being caught.

MR. KAY: Why? What did you do?

LUKE: Nothing! But I've been falsely accused of trying to murder my father.

MR. KAY: I see. And who are you talking to now?

LUKE: Myself.

MR. KAY: Why? What do you hope to accomplish?

LUKE: I need to figure out how I'm going to elude capture.

MR. KAY: I see. And what are the obstacles you face?

LUKE: Well, there are guards stationed everywhere . . . and everyone knows what I look like . . . and I have no one to help me . . .

MR. KAY: Good, then let's see if you can come up with a plan. Begin, please.

EDGAR: I heard myself proclaim'd,
  And by the happy hollow of a tree
  Escap'd the hunt. No port is free, no place
  That guard, and most unusual vigilance
  Does not attend my taking. Whiles I may 'scape
  I will preserve myself: and am bethought
  To take the basest and most poorest shape
  That ever penury in contempt of man
  Brought near to beast. My face I'll grime with filth,
  Blanket my loins, elf all my hairs in knots,
  And with presented nakedness outface
  The winds and persecutions of the sky.
  The country gives me proof and precedent
  Of Bedlam beggars, who with roaring voices
  Strike in their numb'd and mortifièd arms,
  Pins, wooden pricks, nails, sprigs of rosemary;
  And with this horr'ble object, from low farms,
  Poor pelting villages, sheep-cotes, and mills,
  Sometimes with lunatic bans, sometime with prayers,
  Enforce their charity. "Poor Turlygod! Poor Tom."
  That's something yet: Edgar I nothing am.

MR. KAY: Good, Luke. First of all, let me ask you about a few words we may not understand.
  What do you mean by "proclaim'd"?

LUKE: Publicly declared an outlaw.

MR. KAY: What do you mean by "by the happy hollow of a tree"?

LUKE: I was lucky enough to find a hiding place inside a hollow tree.

MR. KAY: What do you mean by "Does not attend my taking"?

LUKE: There's no place to go where they aren't hoping to capture me.

MR. KAY: What do you mean by "am bethought"?

LUKE: Am resolved.

MR. KAY: What do you mean by "penury in contempt of man?"

LUKE: Um . . . that means . . . "poverty too harsh for a man to bear."

MR. KAY: What do you mean by "elf all my hairs in knots"?

LUKE: Twist and tangle my hair into matted locks.

MR. KAY: What do you mean by "with presented nakedness"?

LUKE: With my naked body completely exposed.

MR. KAY: What do you mean by "outface"?

LUKE: Confront.

MR. KAY: What do you mean by "gives me proof and precedent"?

LUKE: Provides me with previous examples.

MR. KAY: What's a Bedlam beggar?

LUKE: A beggar who claims to have a license to beg.

MR. KAY: What do you mean by "Strike in their numb'd and mortifièd arms"?

LUKE: Stick things into their cold, unfeeling arms.

MR. KAY: What do you mean by "wooden pricks"?

LUKE: A skewer.

MR. KAY: What do you mean by "this horrible object"?

LUKE: This grisly sight.

MR. KAY: What's a "low farm"?

LUKE: A humble farm.

MR. KAY: What's a "Poor pelting village"?

LUKE: An impoverished and insignificant little town.

MR. KAY: What do you mean by "lunatic bans"?

LUKE: Insane cursing.

MR. KAY: What do you mean by "enforce their charity"?

LUKE: Beg for food.

MR. KAY: What's a "Turleygod"?

LUKE: That's a made-up name, like "Tom o' Bedlam."

MR. KAY: What do you mean by "Edgar I nothing am"?

LUKE: I'm no longer Edgar.

MR. KAY: Excellent. Now, let's talk about this speech for a few minutes.
(To the class) Keep in mind, folks, that Edgar is the son of a Duke—the Duke of Gloucester—and up to this moment, he's lived the life of a genteel and well-educated nobleman. That is, until Edmund, his bastard brother, framed him to get his lands.

So now, for the first time in his life, he's having to use his wits in order to *survive*. He needs to decide how he's going to elude capture, and take action immediately in order to preserve himself. So he makes a series of quick decisions and transforms himself into Poor Tom, a beggar who wanders about half-naked on the heath.

(To Luke) The problem is, Luke, we're having a hard time following the speech for two reasons.

First, you haven't orchestrated Edgar's decision-making process from moment to moment, so we can't come along with you, can't follow your thinking.

Second, when we *do* see and hear you make a decision as Edgar, we don't see you *act* upon it. Your decisions don't move the character forward, don't spur you into *action*.

So, I think you need to do two things.

First, you need to be more specific about *what* Edgar decides to do, and *when* he decides to do it.

Second, having made a decision, you need to *act* upon it *immediately*.

So, with those two things in mind, let's look at this speech again, Luke, and I'd like to suggest that we orchestrate it by using another spoken subtext exercise that I call *decisions*.

(The students write "decisions" in their notebooks.)

What I'd like you to do, Luke, as we go through the speech again, is tell us exactly what decision you make, and when you make it. All right?

LUKE: Yes.

MR. KAY: And I'd like you to do that in a very specific way. I'd like you to *snap* your fingers, and then tell us your decision *aloud* by completing the phrase "I'M GOING TO . . ."

(The students write "I'm going to . . . " in their notebooks.)

LUKE: *(Snapping his fingers)* I'm going to . . .

MR. KAY: Yes. The idea is to *physicalize* your decision with your hand, just as we did with realizations. But unlike realizations, which blossom slowly, decisions are *quick* and *impulsive*.

So, you snap your fingers, and state your decision aloud. Then, you immediately *act* upon that decision. You *do* what you decided to do, right then and there, while speaking the text. Got it?

LUKE: Yes, I think so.

MR. KAY: Good, then let's give it a try. From the top, please.

(Luke runs in place at upstage center.)

And remind us, please, what's your objective, Edgar?

LUKE: To decide how I'm going to elude capture.

MR. KAY: Good, and first decision, Edgar, before you speak?

LUKE: *(Snaps fingers)* I'M GOING TO STOP RUNNING.

MR. KAY: And text?

(Luke stops running in place, and catches his breath.)

EDGAR: I heard myself proclaim'd,
And by the happy hollow of a tree
Escap'd the hunt.

MR. KAY: Good. *(To the class)* He decides to stop running, so he immediately tries to catch his breath and calm himself down.

Did you all notice, by the way, how all the "h" sounds in the verse help him to do that?

(To Luke) Next decision, Edgar?

LUKE: *(Snaps fingers)* I'M GOING TO REVIEW MY OPTIONS.

(Luke looks in several directions.)

No port is free, no place
That guard, and most unusual vigilance
Does not attend my taking.

MR. KAY: Yes. *(To the class)* He decides to review his options, so he immediately checks possible escape routes.

(To Luke) Next decision?

LUKE: *(Snaps fingers)* I'M GOING TO HOLD OUT AS LONG AS I CAN.

(Luke makes a vow to himself.)

Whiles I may 'scape
I will preserve myself:

MR. KAY: *(to the class)* He decides to hold out for as long as he can, so he immediately makes a vow to himself to survive.

(To Luke) Next decision?

LUKE: *(Snaps fingers)* I'M GOING TO DISGUISE MYSELF AS A BEGGAR.

and am bethought
To take the basest and most poorest shape
That ever penury in contempt of man
Brought near to beast.

MR. KAY: *(To the class)* He decides to disguise himself as a beggar—and this is where it gets interesting. Because now, instead of waiting until after intermission to see Poor Tom, Edgar is going to transform into Poor Tom right here in front of us!

Next decision, Edgar?

LUKE: *(Snaps fingers)* I'M GOING TO MAKE MYSELF FILTHY.

MR. KAY: Good, now *act* upon that decision, Edgar! Make yourself filthy!
(Luke puts mud on his face, and pulls at his hair.)

LUKE: My face I'll grime with filth,
Blanket my loins, elf all my hairs in knots,

MR. KAY: Yes! Next decision?

LUKE: *(Snaps fingers)* I'M GOING TO STRIP MYSELF NAKED.

MR. KAY: Good, now *act* upon that decision! Strip yourself naked!
(Luke strips off his shirt.)

LUKE: And with presented nakedness outface
The winds and persecutions of the sky.

MR. KAY: Good! Next decision?

LUKE: *(Snaps fingers)* I'M GOING TO CREATE A BEDLAM BEGGAR.

MR. KAY: Good, now *act* upon that decision! Begin to create a Bedlam beggar!
(Luke squats down, and rubs his arms with his hands.)

LUKE: The country gives me proof and precedent
Of Bedlam beggars, who with roaring voices
Strike in their numb'd and mortifièd arms,
Pins, wooden pricks, nails, sprigs of rosemary;

MR. KAY: Good. Next decision?

LUKE: *(Snaps fingers)* I'M GOING TO ROAM GLOUCESTERSHIRE COLLECTING CHARITY.

MR. KAY: Good, now *act* upon that decision! Show us how you'll roam
Gloucestershire!
(Luke walks about like a madman.)

LUKE: And with this horr'ble object, from low farms,
Poor pelting villages, sheep-cotes, and mills,
Sometimes with lunatic bans, sometime with prayers,
Enforce their charity.

MR. KAY: Next decision, Edgar?

LUKE: *(Snaps fingers)* I'M GOING TO TRY ON A MADMAN'S VOICE.

MR. KAY: Good, now *act* upon that decision! Let's hear your madman's voice!
(Luke changes his voice.)

LUKE: "Poor Turlygod! Poor Tom."

MR. KAY: Excellent. *(To the class)* And can you all see how Edgar is building a madman right before our eyes?

(To Luke) And continue, please.

LUKE: *(Snaps fingers)* I'M GOING TO KEEP WORKING ON MY DISGUISE.

That's something yet:

(Snaps fingers) I'M GOING TO OBLITERATE EDGAR.

Edgar I nothing am.

(Snaps fingers) I'M GOING TO FIND SHELTER.

(Luke runs off stage left.)

MR. KAY: Excellent, Luke!

(To the class) This speech is so much more interesting when we get to see the transformation of Edgar into Poor Tom right before our eyes, rather than having it take place backstage in the dressing room! It's worth the price of admission!

(To Luke) You can put your clothes back on now, Luke.

(The class laughs.)

LUKE: *(Putting his shirt back on.)* Was it good for you?

(The class laughs.)

MR. KAY: Yes, it was actually. Thank you, Luke.

(Luke comes down off the stage.)

(To the class) The point I'm trying to make here, folks, which I think Luke demonstrated quite well, is that *decisions* must lead to *action*.

Decisions are brisk and impulsive. They are not made in the mind, but in the guts. They convert needs and wants into *action*. They propel the character into the *future*.

(The students write all this down in their notebooks.)

Now Edgar's speech is unique, folks, because it contains so *many* decisions. Most of the speeches you'll encounter will not contain nearly as many decisions as this.

But I think you'll find that most of the solo scenes in Shakespeare contain at least *one* decision, very often in the last line or two of the speech, because Shakespeare regularly uses decisions to move his plots forward.

Can you think of any examples of this?

GABRIELLA: Hamlet decides to put on a play.

CLAIRE: Malvolio decides to dress in yellow stockings.

NOAH: Prospero decides to break his staff.

MADISON: Juliet decides to drink the Friar's potion.

TIM: Isabella decides to remain chaste and let her brother die.

SAM: Prince Hal decides to change his ways.

MR. KAY: Good! And do you see how each decision in that list drives the character to take action, and surges the story of the play forward in time?

(Looking up at the clock) And speaking of time . . .

(Putting his hand to his forehead) I REALIZE THAT we're just about out of time, so . . .

(Snapping his fingers) I'M GOING TO dismiss you.

(The class laughs.)

Please keep working on these speeches, everyone. I'd like you to keep incorporating the work we've been doing the past few days on speech measures, focal points, images, and spoken subtext into your orchestrations.

See you tomorrow.

BLACKOUT.

SCENE 5

Actions

The Acting Studio. Friday.

MR. KAY: Good morning, folks. Yesterday we looked at spoken subtext. Today we're going to look at *actions*.

(The students write "actions" in their notebooks.)

By *actions,* I mean *verbs* or *tactics* played in pursuit of *objectives* against *obstacles.*

Today, we're going to look at orchestrating a speech by selecting, arranging, and heightening a character's actions.

(Scanning the class) So, who wants to go first today?

༒ PURELY PHYSICAL ACTIONS ༒

ELENA: I will!

MR. KAY: All right, Elena. What are you going to show us?

ELENA: Cressida, from *Troilus and Cressida.*

MR. KAY: Good. And if you would place yourself in your scene, please, so I can ask you a few questions.

(Elena stands center stage, gazing outward.)

Where are you, Cressida?

ELENA: In Troy, in an orchard, just outside my father's house.

MR. KAY: Yes, and why are you there?

ELENA: Pandarus, my uncle, brought me here to meet with Troilus.

MR. KAY: And who are you talking to now?

ELENA: Troilus.

MR. KAY: And who is Troilus?

ELENA: He's a Trojan prince—one of the sons of Priam and Hecuba.

MR. KAY: And why are you talking to him? What do you hope to accomplish?

ELENA: I want him to kiss me, to take me to bed, to fall in love with me.
(The class laughs.)

MR. KAY: Yes. Of course you want all those things! But which of those is your *speech* objective?

ELENA: Um . . . to get him to kiss me.

MR. KAY: Yes, I agree. And what's making it difficult for you to get that kiss? What are the obstacles?

ELENA: My inexperience with men, my shyness, my embarrassment in front of Pandarus, my overblown sense of propriety, my fear of being hurt by him . . .

MR. KAY: *(Interrupting)* Yes, I agree with all of those, Cressida. But let me ask you this—why haven't you said anything to Troilus about your feelings before this?

ELENA: Well, I've been playing hard-to-get because I wanted him to want me even more. So I've deliberately held him off.

MR. KAY: Good, then let's see if you can get that kiss. Begin, please.

CRESSIDA: Boldness comes to me now, and brings me heart.
Prince Troilus, I have lov'd you night and day
For many weary months—O pardon me;
If I confess too much, you will play the tyrant.
I love you now, but till now, not so much
But I might master it. In faith, I lie;
My thoughts were like unbridl'd children, grown
Too headstrong for their mother. See, we fools!
Why have I blabb'd? Who shall be true to us
When we are so unsecret to ourselves?
But though I lov'd you well, I woo'd you not;
And yet, good faith, I wish'd myself a man,
Or that we women had men's privilege
Of speaking first. Sweet, bid me hold my tongue,
For in this rapture I shall surely speak
The thing I shall repent. See, see, your silence,
Cunning in dumbness, in my weakness draws

My soul of counsel from me. Stop my mouth.

MR. KAY: Good, Elena. And I think boldness came to you when you cut that speech!

(Elena hides a guilty smile with a hand over her mouth.)

But let's talk about that a bit later. First, let's just be sure we understand every word of the text.

What do you mean by "My thoughts were like unbridl'd children"?

ELENA: My thoughts were like spoiled little brats that won't obey their mother.

MR. KAY: Yes. And what do you mean by "in this rapture"?

ELENA: In this aroused state.

MR. KAY: And what do you mean by "My soul of counsel"?

ELENA: My most secret, unspoken thoughts.

MR. KAY: What do you mean by "Stop my mouth"?

ELENA: Kiss me, you fool!

(The class laughs.)

MR. KAY: Good, good. Now let's talk about this scene for a minute.

Cressida is clearly at odds with herself here. She aches to lean forward and kiss this man, but her shyness, her inexperience, her sense of propriety, her embarrassment, and her fear keep pulling her back.

In other words, sometimes boldness comes to her, and she *advances* towards her objective, and sometimes the obstacles overwhelm her, and she *retreats.*

So let's use this observation as an entry point into the speech, Elena.

Let's look at this speech again, and orchestrate it from speech measure to speech measure by using two simple *opposing physical movements.*

(The students write "opposing physical movements" in their notebooks.)

I'd like you to say "ADVANCE" and step *towards* Troilus when you're pursuing your objective, or say "RETREAT" and step *away* from Troilus when the obstacles overcome you. Make sense?

ELENA: Yes.

(The students write "advance and retreat" in their notebooks.)

MR. KAY: Good, then if you'll place yourself in your scene, please, we'll look at this again.

(Elena does so.)

And remind us, please, what's your objective, Cressida?

ELENA: To get Troilus to kiss me.

MR. KAY: Good, and first speech measure, please—advance or retreat?

ELENA: ADVANCE.

(Stepping forward)

Boldness comes to me now, and brings me heart.

MR. KAY: Good. Second speech measure—advance or retreat?

ELENA: ADVANCE.

(Stepping forward)

Prince Troilus,

MR. KAY: Good, and continue, please.

ELENA: ADVANCE.

(Stepping forward)

I have lov'd you night and day
For many weary months—

RETREAT.

(Stepping back)

O pardon me;

MR. KAY: Good! *(To the class)* And there the obstacle overwhelms her and forces her to retreat.

(To Elena) And continue, please, Cressida.

ELENA: RETREAT.

(Stepping back)

If I confess too much, you will play the tyrant.

ADVANCE.

(Stepping forward)

I love you now,

ADVANCE.

(Stepping forward)

but till now, not so much
But I might master it.

RETREAT.

(Stepping back)

In faith, I lie;

ADVANCE.

(Stepping forward)

My thoughts were like unbridl'd children, grown
Too headstrong for their mother.

RETREAT.

(Stepping back)

See, we fools!

RETREAT.

(Stepping back)

Why have I blabb'd?

RETREAT.

(Stepping back)

Who shall be true to us
When we are so unsecret to ourselves?

ADVANCE.

(Stepping forward)

But though I lov'd you well, I woo'd you not;

RETREAT.

(Stepping back)

And yet, good faith, I wish'd myself a man,

RETREAT.

(Stepping back)

Or that we women had men's privilege
Of speaking first.

ADVANCE.

(Stepping forward)

Sweet,

ADVANCE.

(Stepping forward)

bid me hold my tongue,

ADVANCE.

(Stepping forward)

For in this rapture I shall surely speak
The thing I shall repent.

RETREAT.

(Stepping back)

See,

RETREAT.

(Stepping back)

see,

RETREAT.

(Stepping back)
your silence,

RETREAT.

(Stepping back)
Cunning in dumbness,

RETREAT.

(Stepping back)
in my weakness draws
My soul of counsel from me.

ADVANCE.

(Stepping forward)
Stop my mouth.

MR. KAY: Very good. Thank you, Elena.

(Elena comes down off the stage.)

(To the class) Remember folks, this is *process*, not *product*. And this exercise is just a *first* step in the process of orchestrating the verbs or tactics or *actions* in this speech.

By using two opposing physical movements, Elena has sketched out where the major changes in tactics in the speech might be, and begun to *physicalize* the pursuit of her objective through text.

But there are many other steps to follow, as you'll see.

By the way, you can do this same exercise with a chair, by sitting and rising. Or by facing one wall of a room, and then turning to a different wall. Any two opposing physical movements will work.

Now, before we move on, let's talk about Elena's cutting for a minute. Did anybody notice the line that Elena cut in order to make this work as a monologue?

RACHEL: Hard to seem won, but I was won, my lord,
With the first glance that ever—

MR. KAY: Yes, exactly, Rachel. Elena has rather brazenly cut the most famous line in the speech, which I must say is either incredibly gutsy, or incredibly foolish, or both.

(To Elena) Tell us why you made that cut, would you, Elena?

ELENA: Well . . . I didn't really think of it as a famous line. I just wanted to start the speech by saying his *name*. And the only way I could do that was by gluing an earlier line in the dialogue to the beginning of the speech, and cutting "Hard to seem won."

MR. KAY: I see. *(To the class)* Well, I have to say, I missed those lines because I know them so well as part of this speech.

RACHEL: So did I!

MR. KAY: But, on the other hand, the cut does seem to make the speech work better as an audition monologue.

TRINITY: I think so.

MR. KAY: So there you have it in a nutshell: the scholars and purists on one hand, like Rachel and me, who want every word of Shakespeare to be honored and revered, and theater artists like Elena and Trinity on the other hand, who want to use the text as raw material to be cut, pasted, rescripted, conflated, contemporized, and adapted to serve their own artistic ends.

And this same conflict has been going on now for over four hundred years!

Let's work on another speech. Who's next?

᥯ OPPOSING ACTIONS ᥯

GABRIELLA: I'll go!

(Gabriella goes up onto the stage.)

MR. KAY: What are you going to show us today, Gabriella?

GABRIELLA: Phoebe, from *As you Like It*.

MR. KAY: All right. Would you place yourself in your scene, please, Gabriella, so I can ask you a few questions.

(Gabriella sits center stage, gazing outward.)

Where are you, Phoebe?

GABRIELLA: In the forest of Arden.

MR. KAY: And who are you talking to?

GABRIELLA: Silvius.

MR. KAY: Is he your boyfriend?

GABRIELLA: No, no, he's just a boy who says he loves me, but I'm not interested in him.

MR. KAY: I see. So why are you talking to him?

GABRIELLA: Well, I'm trying to sort out my feelings about this other boy I just met.

MR. KAY: Yes? Who was that?

GABRIELLA: His name is Ganymede.

MR. KAY: And why are trying to sort out your feelings for him? What just happened?

GABRIELLA: He appeared out of nowhere, and chided me for mistreating Silvius. Then he left just as suddenly.

MR. KAY: I see. So what do you hope to accomplish by talking to Silvius? What's the objective?

GABRIELLA: I want to prove that I'm not in love with Ganymede.

MR. KAY: And what's the obstacle to that?

GABRIELLA: I'm head over heels in love with him.

MR. KAY: Good, then let's hear how you prove you're not in love. Begin, please.

PHOEBE: Think not I love him, though I ask for him.
    'Tis but a peevish boy. Yet he talks well.
    But what care I for words? Yet words do well
    When he that speaks them pleases those that hear.
    It is a pretty youth—not very pretty—
    But sure he's proud; and yet his pride becomes him.
    He'll make a proper man. The best thing in him
    Is his complexion; and faster than his tongue
    Did make offense, his eye did heal it up.
    He is not very tall; yet for his years he's tall.
    His leg is but so so; and yet 'tis well.
    There was a pretty redness in his lip,
    A little riper and more lusty red
    Than that mix'd in his cheek. 'Twas just the difference
    Betwixt the constant red and mingled damask.
    There be some women, Silvius, had they mark'd him
    In parcels as I did, would have gone near
    To fall in love with him; but for my part,
    I love him not, nor hate him not. And yet
    Have more cause to hate him than to love him,
    For what had he to do to chide at me?
    He said mine eyes were black, and my hair black,
    And now I am remember'd, scorn'd at me.
    I marvel why I answer'd not again.
    But that's all one. Omittance is no quittance.
    I'll write to him a very taunting letter,
    And thou shalt bear it. Wilt thou, Silvius?

MR. KAY: Good, Gabriella, good. Before we look at this again, let's make sure we understand everything you say.

What do you mean by "He'll make a proper man"?

GABRIELLA: He'll be handsome when he gets a little older.

MR. KAY: What do you mean by "the constant red"?

GABRIELLA: Totally red.

MR. KAY: What do you mean by "mingled damask"?

GABRIELLA: Red and white mixed together, like a damask rose.

MR. KAY: What do you mean by "mark'd him in parcels"?

GABRIELLA: Checked him out, one piece at a time.

MR. KAY: What do you mean by "gone near"?

GABRIELLA: Come close.

MR. KAY: What do you mean by "what had he to do"?

GABRIELLA: What business did he have.

MR. KAY: What do you mean by "Omittance is no quittance"?

GABRIELLA: Just because I didn't answer him *then,* doesn't mean I can't do it *now.*

MR. KAY: Good, good, Gabriella. Now, let's talk about this speech for a minute.

I think one of the things that makes this speech so much fun is watching how Phoebe struggles to sort out her feelings for this boy Ganymede. As you said, she wants to prove that she doesn't love him, but we can see with our own eyes that she's head over heels for him.

The challenge of the speech, of course, is to avoid trying to play both love and hate *simultaneously,* because that leads to generalized, unspecific, undetailed mush.

You've got to orchestrate the speech so that the pendulum swings back and forth between these *two opposing actions.*

(The students write "two opposing actions" in their notebooks.)

One moment you *love* Ganymede, and the very next moment you're trying to prove you *hate* him.

So with that in mind, let's work through the speech again, and would you tell us aloud, speech measure by speech measure, whether you're going to play "TO LOVE" or "TO HATE." Got it?

GABRIELLA: Love it!

(The class laughs.)

MR. KAY: Good! So, please restore your scene in your imagination.

(Gabriella sits down again, and gazes outward.)

And remind us, please, Phoebe—what's your objective?

GABRIELLA: To prove that I'm not in love with Ganymede.

MR. KAY: And first action, please—*to love* or *to hate*?

GABRIELLA: TO HATE.

MR. KAY: And text?

GABRIELLA: Think not I love him,

MR. KAY: Yes, but make that action *stronger.* Fill yourself up with "to hate" before you inhale to speak. First action again, please.

GABRIELLA: *(Strongly)* TO HATE.

MR. KAY: Yes! And text?

GABRIELLA: *(Strongly)* Think not I love him,

MR. KAY: Good! Second action?

GABRIELLA: TO LOVE.

though I ask for him.

MR. KAY: Yes, but really *commit* yourself to that action. Love with all of your body and all of your voice. And again, please.

GABRIELLA: *(With a sigh)* TO LOVE.

though I ask for him.

MR. KAY: Good! And continue, please, Phoebe, on your own.

GABRIELLA: TO HATE.

MR. KAY: And text?

GABRIELLA: 'Tis but a peevish boy.

MR. KAY: And continue, please, on your own.

GABRIELLA: TO LOVE.

Yet he talks well.

TO HATE.

But what care I for words?

TO LOVE.

Yet words do well
When he that speaks them pleases those that hear.

TO LOVE.

It is a pretty youth—

TO HATE.

not very pretty—

TO HATE.

But sure he's proud;

TO LOVE.

and yet his pride becomes him.

TO LOVE.

He'll make a proper man.

TO LOVE.

The best thing in him
Is his complexion;

TO LOVE.

and faster than his tongue
Did make offense,

TO LOVE.

his eye did heal it up.

TO HATE.

He is not very tall;

TO LOVE.

yet for his years he's tall.

TO HATE.

His leg is but so so;

TO LOVE.

and yet 'tis well.

TO LOVE.

There was a pretty redness in his lip,

TO LOVE.

A little riper and more lusty red
Than that mix'd in his cheek.

TO LOVE.

'Twas just the difference
Betwixt the constant red and mingled damask.

TO HATE.

There be some women, Silvius,

TO LOVE.

had they mark'd him
In parcels as I did,

TO LOVE.

would have gone near
To fall in love with him;

TO LOVE.

but for my part,
I love him not,

TO HATE.

nor hate him not.

TO HATE.

And yet
Have more cause to hate him than to love him,

TO LOVE.

For what had he to do to chide at me?

TO LOVE.

He said mine eyes were black,

TO LOVE.

and my hair black,

TO HATE.

And now I am remember'd, scorn'd at me.

TO LOVE.

I marvel why I answer'd not again.

TO HATE.

But that's all one.

TO LOVE.

Omittance is no quittance.

TO HATE.

I'll write to him a very taunting letter,

TO LOVE.

And thou shalt bear it.

TO LOVE.

Wilt thou, Silvius?

MR. KAY: Good, Gabriella, that's excellent work. But, remember, this is just the *first* step in the process.

So, let me ask you this—now that you've orchestrated this speech using just two strong actions, "to love" and "to hate"—what do you think should be the *next* step in the process?

GABRIELLA: Well, to find a *variety* of ways to play "to love" and "to hate"?

MR. KAY: Yes, exactly. To continue the process of orchestration by becoming more *specific* with each of these verbs.

So, for example, what are some possible actions that reveal "to hate"?

GABRIELLA: Um . . . to scorn, to loath, to despise, to criticize . . .

MR. KAY: Yes, good. And what are some possible actions that reveal "to love"?

GABRIELLA: Um . . . to admire, to compliment, to desire, to adore, to lust after . . .

MR. KAY: Good. And when you can't think of any more actions off the top of your head, where might you look for some other good verbs?

GABRIELLA: A thesaurus?

MR. KAY: Yes. You go to your thesaurus and look up "love" and "hate," and you'll find a dozen more ideas.

AVI: *(Jumping in)* But, isn't that, kind of, I don't know, kind of an *intellectual* way to work on a speech?

MR. KAY: That's an excellent question, Avi. Yes, absolutely, there's always a danger of becoming so *analytical* about your work that you fail to *act.*

You have to remember that creating a score is not the end of the process. A performance is not a term paper. We go to the theater and pay our money to see *behavior,* not a research project. And it doesn't matter if you've created the most brilliant score on *paper* if you can't *play* what you've scored.

So, there's no law that says you can't use a few resources to inspire you. Just so long as you always remember that writing down the ideas you get from a thesaurus, or a novel, or a movie, or a painting, or a photograph, or a song, or *whatever* inspires you, cannot be the end of the process. It's just the beginning. You'll be testing those ideas *on your feet,* trying each action, with body and with voice, before you decide which ones work best, and *how* they work best, and *where* they work best.

Remember—orchestration is the art of *selecting, arranging,* and *heightening* each moment of your performance, not researching, recording, and rearranging words on a piece of paper.

(To Gabriella) Thank you, Gabriella. Well done.

(Gabriella comes down off the stage.)

Who's up next?

怀 LABAN EFFORT ACTIONS

AVI: I am!

(Avi goes up onto the stage.)

MR. KAY: Good. And what are you going to show us, today, Avi?

AVI: King Richard, from *Richard the Second.*

MR. KAY: All right. And if you would place yourself in your scene, please, while I ask you a few questions.

(Avi stands center stage, and gazes outward.)

Where are you, Richard?

AVI: I'm on the walls at Flint Castle.

MR. KAY: And where is Flint Castle?

AVI: It's in Wales.

MR. KAY: And who are you talking to?

AVI: The Earl of Northumberland.

MR. KAY: Why are you talking to Northumberland? What do you hope to accomplish?

AVI: I want to stop Henry Bolingbroke from taking my crown.

MR. KAY: And where is he? Where is Bolingbroke?

AVI: He's out in the nearby fields with his army.

MR. KAY: Can you see him from where you are?

AVI: Yes. I can see him in the distance.

MR. KAY: Good, and what are the obstacles? What's making it difficult to stop Bolingbroke from taking your crown?

AVI: Well, all of my allies have deserted me, and I've dismissed my army, so I have no way to back up any of my threats. All I can do at this point is look and sound kingly, and bluff.

MR. KAY: Yes. Anything else? Other obstacles?

AVI: Well, my own insecurities and fears. I don't truly believe that I can stop Bolingbroke if he wants to usurp my throne.

MR. KAY: Good, then let's see how you try to stop him. Begin, please.

KING RICHARD: We are amaz'd; and thus long have we stood
To watch the fearful bending of thy knee,

Because we thought ourself thy lawful king.
And if we be, how dare thy joints forget
To pay their awful duty to our presence?
If we be not, show us the hand of God
That hath dismiss'd us from our stewardship;
For well we know no hand of blood and bone
Can grip the sacred handle of our scepter,
Unless he do profane, steal, or usurp.
And though you think that all, as you have done,
Have torn their souls by turning them from us
And we are barren and bereft of friends,
Yet know, my master, God omnipotent,
Is must'ring in his clouds on our behalf
Armies of pestilence, and they shall strike
Your children yet unborn and unbegot
That lift your vassal hands against my head
And threat the glory of my precious crown.
Tell Bolingbroke, for yond methinks he stands,
That every stride he makes upon my land
Is dang'rous treason. He is come to open
The purple testament of bleeding war.
But ere the crown he looks for live in peace,
Ten thousand bloody crowns of mothers' sons
Shall ill become the flow'r of England's face,
Change the complexion of her maid-pale peace
To scarlet indignation, and bedew
Her pastures' grass with faithful English blood.

MR. KAY: Good, Avi. Now, before we look at this again, let's make sure we all understand every word of Richard's speech.

What do you mean by "To pay their awful duty"?

AVI: To show reverence for the king.

MR. KAY: I don't understand—why is that so "awful"?

AVI: "Awful" doesn't mean "lousy." It means "full of awe."

MR. KAY: Ah, I see. What do you mean by "profane"?

AVI: To desecrate.

MR. KAY: What do you mean by "Have torn their souls by turning them from us"?

AVI: Will burn in hell for becoming traitors to the King.

MR. KAY: What do you mean by "your vassal hands"?

AVI: The hands of a subject.

MR. KAY: What do you mean by "the purple testament"?

AVI: A bloody inheritance for the people of England.

MR. KAY: What do you mean by "ten thousand bloody crowns"?

AVI: Ten thousand bloodied heads.

MR. KAY: What is "the flow'r of England's face"?

AVI: The English countryside.

MR. KAY: What do you mean by "maid-pale peace"?

AVI: As pale as the face of a maiden.

MR. KAY: Good, Avi. Now, let's talk about this speech for a moment.

One of the biggest challenges of performing in *Richard the Second,* or *any* of Shakespeare's history plays, is that you often find yourself standing in one place, spouting dozens of lines of verse, and praying you'll figure out some way to make it interesting and exciting.

Unfortunately, praying for inspiration is not an effective rehearsal technique.

(The class laughs.)

You've got to find something to *do* while you're standing stock still on that upstage platform.

You've got to find *strong* actions to play. You've got to find a *variety* of actions to play. You've got to find a *progression* of actions to play.

You've got to find ways to pursue your objective using mostly your voice, and the text.

In other words, you've got to find *action* in *stillness.*

And because you haven't made strong choices, Avi, through trial and error, about each moment in the speech, you're repeating the same generalized action over and over again, showing us the same kingly quality from start to finish.

So, let's go back, Avi, and orchestrate the speech, one speech measure at a time, and look for ways to play a variety of strong actions in a repeatable linear progression.

To help us accomplish this, we're going to borrow some terms from Rudolf Laban. Does anyone know who he was?

SARAH: Wasn't he a choreographer?

MR. KAY: Yes. Laban was a dance choreographer who came up with a way to describe movement using terms he called "effort actions."

(The students write "effort actions" in their notebooks.)

And we're going to adapt some of his ideas to help us with this speech.

So, Avi, let me show you four of these "effort actions."

First, "STROKE"—imagine you're stroking a cat with your hand.

(Avi strokes an imaginary cat with his hand.)

Now, "WRING"—imagine you're wringing out a wet washcloth with two hands.

(Avi wrings out an imaginary washcloth.)

Now, "FLICK"—imagine you're flicking a bug off of someone's shoulder.

(Avi flicks his fingers at an imaginary bug.)

Now, "SLASH"—imagine you're slashing through a canvas with a knife.

(Avi slashes at the air with an imaginary knife.)

Good. Now, when we look at the speech again, I'd like you to use one of these four effort actions in each measure to help you get your objective.

AVI: *(Trying each effort action again)* Stroke . . . wring . . . flick . . . or slash.

MR. KAY: Yes, you've got it.

(The students write "stroke, wring, flick, slash" in their notebooks.)

AVI: Do I need to say the the effort action *aloud* before I do it?

MR. KAY: Yes, be sure to tell us your choice aloud before each speech measure.

AVI: Okay.

MR. KAY: Also, keep in mind, Avi, that because stroke and wring are *sustained* effort actions, they'll happen on *phrases*. And because flick and slash are *sudden* effort actions, they'll happen on *operative words*. Make sense?

AVI: Yes, I think so.

(The students write "sustained" and "sudden" in their notebooks.)

MR. KAY: Should we give it a try?

AVI: Absolutely.

MR. KAY: Good. Then would you please restore your scene in your imagination?

(Avi does so.)

And, remind us, please, King Richard, what's your objective?

AVI: To stop Bolingbroke from taking my crown.

MR. KAY: And first effort action? Stroke, wring, flick, or slash?

AVI: Uh . . . STROKE.

MR. KAY: And text?

AVI: *(One brisk stroke)* We are amaz'd;

MR. KAY: And let's try that again, Avi, because I'd like you to *sustain* that action, slowly and gently—like stroking a cat—through the entire phrase. And again, please.

AVI: *(Stroking, slowly and gently, on the phrase)* We are amaz'd;

MR. KAY: Yes, that's it! And continue with next measure, please. Stroke, wring, flick, or slash?

AVI: FLICK.

(Flicking repeatedly) and thus long have we stood

MR. KAY: And let me stop you again, Avi, because I'd like you to flick just once—*suddenly*—on the operative word. What's the operative word in that measure?

AVI: Um . . . stood.

MR. KAY: Then flick that word *(flicking)* "stood"—and *only* that word—at Northumberland. Again, please.

AVI: *(Flicking on the operative word)* and thus long have we *stood*

MR. KAY: Good! You flicked that word at him like a dead little bug! Next measure, please—stroke, wring, flick, or slash?

AVI: WRING.

(Wringing on the phrase) To watch the fearful bending of thy knee,

MR. KAY: Yes! You connected the *words* to the *wringing*, and the *wringing* to the *words*. And continue, please—stroke, wring, flick, or slash?

AVI: SLASH.

(Slashing on the operative word) Because we thought ourself thy lawful *king*.

MR. KAY: An excellent slash! *(To the class)* And do you all sense the *strength* of the actions he's now playing? Do you sense the *variety* of actions? Do you sense the *progression*? *(To Avi)* Keep working this way, King Richard. Keep using these effort actions to win your objective! Next measure, please—stroke, wring, flick, or slash?

AVI: FLICK.

(Flicking) And if we *be,*

SLASH.

(Slashing) how *dare* thy joints forget

WRING.

(Wringing) To pay their awful duty to our presence?

MR. KAY: Good! Now, even though you're standing in one place, Richard, be sure to let these effort actions energize your whole body from the toes up. Continue, please—stroke, wring, flick, or slash?

AVI: STROKE.

(Stroking) If we be not,

WRING.

(Wringing) show us the hand of God

SLASH.

(Slashing) That hath *dismiss'd* us from our stewardship;

MR. KAY: Yes! Now, make sure that each effort action *sounds* different as well. Allow the four physical actions to affect your *voice* in a variety of ways. Continue, please—stroke, wring, flick, or slash?

AVI: STROKE.

(Stroking) For well we know

WRING.

(Wringing) no hand of blood and bone

FLICK.

(Flicking) Can *grip*

STROKE.

(Stroking) the sacred handle of our scepter,

FLICK.

(Flicking) Unless he do *profane*,

WRING.

(Wringing) steal,

SLASH.

(Slashing) or *usurp*.

MR. KAY: And let me stop you there, please, Avi. *(Avi stops.)*
Good, very good. You've got those four, so let's try a few more.
First, "STIR"—imagine stirring a large pot of soup with a spoon.
(Avi stirs an imaginary pot with an imaginary spoon.)
Now, "SQUEEZE"—imagine squeezing out a wet sponge with your hand.
(Avi squeezes an imaginary sponge.)
Now, "PUNCH"—imagine punching a punching bag with your fist.
(Avi punches at an imaginary punching bag.)

Now, "JERK"—imagine jerking on a door handle to open a locked door.
(Avi jerks on an imaginary door handle.)

And please keep in mind, Avi, that stir and squeeze are *sustained*, and happen on *phrases*. Punch and jerk are *sudden*, and happen on *operative words*.
(The students write "stir, squeeze, punch, jerk" in their notebooks.)

So, let's continue, please, using these four effort actions, from where you left off. *(Avi restores the scene in his imagination.)*

First effort action? Stir, squeeze, punch, or jerk?

AVI: STIR.

MR. KAY: And text?

AVI: *(Stirring on the phrase)* And though you think that all,

MR. KAY: Yes, that's good stirring! Next effort action? Stir, squeeze, punch, or jerk?

AVI: JERK.

(Jerking on the operative word) as *you* have done,

MR. KAY: Good—and continue, please.

AVI: SQUEEZE.

(Squeezing on the phrase) Have torn their souls by turning them from us
STIR.

(Stirring) And we are barren and bereft of friends,
PUNCH.

(Punching) Yet *know*,
STIR.

(Stirring) my master,
SQUEEZE.

(Squeezing) God omnipotent,
JERK.

(Jerking) Is *must'ring* in his clouds
STIR.

(Stirring) on our behalf
SQUEEZE.

(Squeezing) Armies of pestilence,
PUNCH.

(Punching) and they shall *strike*
STIR.

(Stirring) Your children yet unborn and unbegot

JERK.

(Jerking) That *lift* your vassal hands against my head

SQUEEZE.

(Squeezing) And threat the glory of my precious crown.

MR. KAY: *(Stopping Avi)* Good! Let's try a few more.

First, "SHAKE"—imagine shaking your fist at someone.

(Avi shakes his fist.)

Then, "PULL"—imagine pulling on a rope with both hands.

(Avi pulls on an imaginary rope with both hands.)

Then, "WHIP"—imagine cracking a whip.

(Avi cracks an imaginary whip.)

Then, "SHOVE"—imagine shoving open a door with both hands.

(Avi shoves a door open with both hands.)

Please keep in mind, Avi, that shake and pull are *sustained*, and happen on *phrases*. Whip and shove are *sudden*, and happen on *operative words*.

(The students write "shake, pull, whip, shove" in their notebooks.)

So, let's continue, please, using these four effort actions, from where you left off.

(Avi restores the scene in his imagination.)

And first effort action? Shake, pull, whip, or shove?

AVI: PULL.

MR. KAY: And text?

AVI: *(Pulling on the phrase)* Tell Bolingbroke,

MR. KAY: Good—and continue, please.

AVI: SHAKE.

(Shaking on the phrase) for yond methinks he stands,

SHOVE.

(Shoving on the operative word) That every *stride* he makes upon my land

WHIP.

(Whipping on the operative word) Is dang'rous *treason*.

PULL.

(Pulling) He is come to open

SHAKE.

(Shaking) The purple testament of bleeding war.

PULL.

(Pulling) But ere the crown he looks for live in peace,

SHOVE.

(Shoving) Ten thousand *bloody* crowns of mother's sons

SHAKE.

(Shaking) Shall ill become the flow'r of England's face,

PULL.

(Pulling) Change the complexion of her maid-pale peace

SHOVE.

(Shoving) To scarlet *indignation*,

SHAKE.

(Shaking) and bedew

Her pastures' grass

WHIP.

(Whipping) with faithful English *blood*.

MR. KAY: Good. Those are just twelve of the possible effort actions you can use, and there are more.

Remember, Avi, that the aim of this rehearsal technique is to find *strong* actions to play, to find a *variety* of actions to play, to find a *progression* of actions to play. To *select*, *arrange*, and *heighten* each moment of the speech in order to find *action* in *stilless*.

Eventually, you'll stop using your arms to play these actions, and they'll be revealed mostly through King Richard's voice and speech, and through subtle, but powerful, changes in King Richard's body.

Thank you, Avi. Well done. *(Avi comes down off the stage.)*

(To the class) By the way, what other medium often requires that you play your actions mostly through voice, limiting you to a very narrow range of physical movement?

(Before anyone can answer) That's right—*television*.

Who's up next?

PSYCHO-PHYSICAL VERBS

DANTE: I'll go!

(Dante goes up onto the stage.)

MR. KAY: Thank you, Dante. And what are you going to show us today?

DANTE: Lewis the Dauphin, from *King John*.

MR. KAY: All right. If you would place yourself in your scene, please, so I can ask you a few questions.

(Dante stands center stage and gazes outward.)

Where are you, Lewis?

DANTE: In a French encampment, in St. Edmundsbury.

MR. KAY: What are you doing in St. Edmundsbury?

DANTE: I have invaded England with an army of Frenchmen, and I'm on my way to London to claim the throne.

MR. KAY: And who are you talking to right now?

DANTE: Cardinal Pandulph.

MR. KAY: And why are you talking to him? What do you hope to accomplish?

DANTE: I want to convince him that England rightfully belongs to me.

MR. KAY: Why must you convince him of that? Isn't he the one who talked you into invading in the first place?

DANTE: Yes, but now he wants me to retreat because he made a deal with King John.

MR. KAY: A deal? What kind of a deal?

DANTE: King John agreed to accept the Pope's authority again, if the Cardinal would convince me to stop my invasion of England.

MR. KAY: I see. So what makes it difficult to convince the Cardinal now that England is yours?

DANTE: Well, I'm young, and the Cardinal has been an advisor to me, so it's not so easy to stand up to him. Also, he represents the Pope, so defying him means defying the Pope as well.

MR. KAY: Good, then let's see if you can convince him that England is yours. Begin, please.

LEWIS: Your grace shall pardon me; I will not back.
I am too high-born to be propertied,
To be a secondary at control,
Or useful servingman and instrument
To any sov'reign state throughout the world.
Your breath first kindled the dead coal of wars
Between this chastis'd kingdom and myself,
And brought in matter that should feed this fire;
And now 'tis far too huge to be blown out

With that same weak wind which enkindled it.
You taught me how to know the face of right,
Acquainted me with interest to this land,
Yea, thrust this enterprise into my heart;
And come ye now to tell me John hath made
His peace with Rome? What is that peace to me?
I, by the honor of my marriage-bed,
After young Arthur, claim this land for mine,
And, now it is half-conquer'd, must I back
Because that John hath made his peace with Rome?
Am I Rome's slave? What penny hath Rome borne,
What men provided, what munition sent
To underprop this action? Is't not I
That undergo this charge? Who else but I,
And such as to my claim are liable,
Sweat in this business and maintain this war?
Have I not heard these islanders shout out
Vive le roi! as I have bank'd their towns?
Have I not here the best cards for the game
To win this easy match play'd for a crown?
And shall I now give o'er the yielded set?
No, no, on my soul, it never shall be said.

MR. KAY: Good, Dante. Now, before we look at this speech again, let's make sure we understand the text completely.

What do you mean by "I will not back"?

DANTE: I refuse to retreat.

MR. KAY: What do you mean by "propertied"?

DANTE: To be used as a tool.

MR. KAY: What do you mean by "a secondary at control"?

DANTE: A subordinate under someone else's command.

MR. KAY: What do you mean by "the face of right"?

DANTE: My true claim to France.

MR. KAY: What do you mean when you say "by the honor of my marriage bed"?

DANTE: In the name of my wife, Blanche of Spain.

MR. KAY: Who is "young Arthur"?

DANTE: King John's nephew.

MR. KAY: What do you mean by "to underprop this action"?

DANTE: To support this war.

MR. KAY: What do you mean by "undergo this charge"?

DANTE: Take on the expense.

MR. KAY: What do you mean by "And such as to my claim are liable"?

DANTE: And those who are subject to my demand for service.

MR. KAY: What do you mean by *"Vive le roi!"*?

DANTE: Long live the king!

MR. KAY: What do you mean by "bank'd their towns"?

DANTE: Sailed past their towns.

MR. KAY: What do you mean by "give o'er the yielded set"?

DANTE: Abandon a game that I've already won.

MR. KAY: Good, Dante. Now, let's talk about this speech for a moment.

(To the class) King John is hardly ever produced because people think it's a boring play. They think it's a boring play because it's full of long speeches like this one, speeches where a character stands in one place and delivers a long diatribe.

Actually, there are lots of great characters and great speeches in *King John,* speeches that don't have to be boring. But they do demand that an actor work painstakingly to orchestrate every moment of a speech using a great variety of *psycho-physical actions.*

(The students write "psycho-physical actions" in their notebooks.)

What do I mean by "psycho-physical actions"?

Psycho-physical actions are usually stated as verbs, in the infinitive form, which contain both a *physical* and a *psychological* element.

For example, "to yearn," "to flatter," and "to tease" are all psycho-physical actions, because they describe *psychological* intentions which can be revealed to the audience *physically*—that is to say, through body and voice.

"To walk," on the other hand, is *not* a psycho-physical action, because it has no *psychological* element. Instead, you should play "to amble," "to march," or "to stride."

"To think" is also not a psycho-physical action, because it has no *physical* element. Instead, you should play "to brood," "to ponder," or "to fantasize."

A psycho-physical action must be able to be directed in pursuit of your objective by using the phrase "in order to." For example, you might play "to stride *in order to* catch the bus," or "to ponder *in order to* decide who to take to the prom."

Psycho-physical actions can also be stated in the form of a *metaphor,* or an *idiomatic expression.* For example, instead of "to walk," you might play "to float on air." Instead of "to think," you might play "to put your thinking cap on."

Finally, psycho-physical actions must be *conscious* and *voluntary.* "To shiver," for example, is not a psycho-physical action, because it is involuntary, and cannot be consciously played in pursuit of an objective. Instead, you must play "to shake in order to warm myself up," or "to calm my nerves in order to defuse the bomb."

So, Dante, let's look at this speech again, and begin to orchestrate it from psycho-physical action to psycho-physical action. All right?

DANTE: Absolutely.

MR. KAY: Good. As we go through the speech again, I'd like you to tell us *aloud* what psycho-physical action you're going to play. Then *inhale* from your focal point. Then speak the text.

Action. Inhale. Text.

Got it?

DANTE: Action. Inhale. Text.

Got it.

MR. KAY: Good. Then, if you would, please restore your scene in your imagination.

(Dante does so.)

And remind us, please, what's the objective?

DANTE: I want to convince the Cardinal that England rightfully belongs to me.

MR. KAY: Yes. And, first psycho-physical action?

DANTE: TO BEG OFF.

MR. KAY: And text, please.

DANTE: Your grace shall pardon me;

MR. KAY: Yes, Lewis, but I think "to beg off" is *stronger* than that. What you're playing is a bit too *polite* vocally and physically—more like "to excuse myself" than "to beg off."

Try it again, please, and this time, play "to beg off" with all of your body and all of your voice.

DANTE: *(Stiffening his spine and lowering his pitch)* Your grace shall pardon me;

MR. KAY: Good, Dante—that's "to beg off"! Second action?

DANTE: TO REJECT.

MR. KAY: And text?

DANTE: I will not back.

MR. KAY: Good, and continue, please.

DANTE: TO BOAST.

I am too high-born to be propertied,

TO BLUSTER.

To be a secondary at control,

TO PROTEST.

Or useful servingman and instrument
To any sov'reign state throughout the world.

TO ACCUSE.

Your breath first kindled the dead coal of wars
Between this chastis'd kingdom and myself,

TO INDICT.

And brought in matter that should feed this fire;

MR. KAY: Yes, Lewis, but your "indict" is almost exactly the same as your "accuse." Either find a way to make those two actions *different,* or choose another action.

DANTE: *(Choosing another action)* TO BLAME.

And brought in matter that should feed this fire;

MR. KAY: Good. "To blame" and "to accuse" are now discernibly different, so we perceive a *progression* of actions, rather than the same action repeated.

And continue, please, Lewis.

DANTE: TO INSULT.

And now 'tis far too huge to be blown out
With that same weak wind which enkindled it.

MR. KAY: Good, Lewis, but speaking of "weak wind," make sure you inhale enough *oxygen* to fuel those two lines of verse on one breath.

Try it again, please, and this time inhale your action—*to insult.*

DANTE: TO INSULT *(He inhales "to insult.")*

And now 'tis far too huge to be blown out
With that same weak wind which enkindled it.

MR. KAY: Excellent. And continue, please.

DANTE: TO ADMONISH.

You taught me how to know the face of right,

TO REPRIMAND.

Acquainted me with interest to this land,

TO SCOLD.

Yea, thrust this enterprise into my heart;

MR. KAY: Good, Lewis, but be sure that those three very similar actions—*to admonish, to reprimand,* and *to scold*—don't bleed into one another and become one thing. You must play the vocal and physical *differences* between these verbs in order to maintain a true progression of actions.

And continue, please.

DANTE: TO CONFRONT.

And come ye now to tell me John hath made
His peace with Rome?

TO DEFY.

What is that peace to me?

TO PROCLAIM.

I, by the honor of my marriage-bed,

TO GLOSS OVER.

After young Arthur,

TO STAKE MY CLAIM.

claim this land for mine,

TO RIDICULE.

And, now it is half-conquer'd, must I back
Because that John hath made his peace with Rome?

TO REBUKE.

Am I Rome's slave?

TO CHALLENGE.

What penny hath Rome borne,

TO BAWL OUT.

What men provided,

TO GIVE HELL.

what munition sent
To underprop this action?

MR. KAY: Excellent! Those last three actions were a superb demonstration of a *vocal build,* Lewis.

(To the class) You understand folks, that there are two ways to create a vocal build.

One way is to play the same action, louder and louder, your pitch rising higher and higher, until you find yourself shouting at the top of your voice.

The other way, as we've just seen, is to play a progression of increasingly strong actions—*to challenge, to bawl out, to give hell*—which naturally create a vocal build.

I recommend the latter, of course.

And how do we know that Shakespeare *wants* a vocal build here? Because he begins those three speech measures in the exact same way. Do you hear it?

"What penny . . . what men . . . what munition . . . "

This is a figure of speech called *anaphora*—the repetition of the same word or words at the beginning of successive phrases. Lincoln used it at Gettysburg:

"We cannot dedicate, we cannot consecrate, we cannot hallow this ground . . ."

Martin Luther King used it in front of the Lincoln Memorial:

"I have a dream today . . . "

And Shakespeare uses it here, to signal a *vocal build.*

(To Dante) And continue, please, Lewis. Next action?

DANTE: TO COMPOSE MYSELF.

Is't not I
That undergo this charge?

TO TAKE CREDIT.

Who else but I,

TO ACKNOWLEDGE.

And such as to my claim are liable,

TO PUT MY FOOT DOWN.

Sweat in this business and maintain this war?

TO BASK IN GLORY.

Have I not heard these islanders shout out
Vive le roi! as I have bank'd their towns?

TO SHOW MY HAND.

Have I not here the best cards for the game
To win this easy match play'd for a crown?

TO SCOFF.

And shall I now give o'er the yielded set?

TO REFUSE.

No,

TO STAND MY GROUND.

no,

TO VOW.

on my soul, it never shall be said.

MR. KAY: Good, that's good work, Dante. You now have a carefully orches-trated, repeatable sequence of psycho-physical actions which you can depend upon to keep the speech vital and theatrical at every performance.

That's a production of *King John* I'd wait in line to see.

Thank you, Dante.

(Dante comes down off the stage.)

(To the class) So these are the things you need to remember, folks, when you work this way with your own speeches.

First, you must be sure that you actually *play* the verbs you choose. Having chosen "to sabotage" for a particular measure, you must make sure that you actually play "to sabotage" with all of your body and all of your voice.

Secondly, you must be sure that you can actually play the *differences* between the actions you choose. Is your "to amuse" really different from your "to entertain"? These verbs must not exist in your head, or on paper, as subtle, literary shades of meaning. If the audience can't perceive the difference *vocally* and *physically* between "to amuse" and "to entertain," you should change your orchestration.

Thirdly, you must never let your actions *bleed* into one another. You must not let "to flatter" overlap with "to praise" in such a way as to make it impossible to perceive when one action ends and the next begins.

Finally, you must be sure that the action begins *before* you inhale to speak. Action. Inhale. Text. This is an inviolable sequence. You must not, as many actors do, inhale, begin to speak, and then hope the action will kick in before too long. The reason for this should be obvious to you by now: nobody inhales to speak without first having an intention they wish to communicate. Except actors.

(The class laughs.)

Who's up next?

Psycho-physical Verbs
with Multiple Focal Points

RACHEL: I'll go!

(Rachel goes up onto the stage.)

MR. KAY: Thanks, Rachel. And what are you going to show us today?

RACHEL: Julia, from *The Two Gentlemen of Verona*.

MR. KAY: All right. And if you would place yourself in your scene, please, so I can ask you a few questions.

(Rachel stands center stage, holding a folded piece of paper.)

Where are you, Julia?

RACHEL: In my house, in Verona.

MR. KAY: Where in the house?

RACHEL: Outside, in the garden.

MR. KAY: And who are you talking to?

RACHEL: To myself.

MR. KAY: I see. And what do you hope to accomplish?

RACHEL: I want to reconstruct the letter that I just tore up.

MR. KAY: Who's the letter from?

RACHEL: From my boyfriend, Proteus.

MR. KAY: And why did you tear it up?

RACHEL: I wanted my servant Lucetta to think I didn't care about it.

MR. KAY: I see. But you *do* care about it?

RACHEL: Oh, yes!

MR. KAY: And did you get a chance to read it before you so rashly tore it up?

RACHEL: *(Heartbroken)* No!

MR. KAY: And what's the obstacle to reconstructing the letter so you can read it?

RACHEL: It's in a million little pieces. And the wind is blowing.

MR. KAY: Good, then let's see how you reconstruct that letter. Begin, please.

JULIA: Go, get you gone, and let the papers lie.
O hateful hands, to tear such loving words!
Injurious wasps, to feed on such sweet honey

And kill the bees that yield it with your stings!
I'll kiss each sev'ral paper for amends.
Look, here is writ "kind Julia." Unkind Julia!
As in revenge of thy ingratitude,
I throw thy name against the bruising stones,
Tramp'ling contemptuously on thy disdain.
And here is writ "love-wounded Proteus."
Poor wounded name! My bosom as a bed
Shall lodge thee till thy wound be throughly heal'd;
And thus I search it with a sov'reign kiss.
But twice or thrice was "Proteus" written down.
Be calm, good wind, blow not a word away
Till I have found each letter in the letter,
Except mine own name; that some whirlwind bear
Unto a ragged, fearful, hanging rock
And throw it thence into the raging sea!
Lo, here in one line is his name twice writ,
"Poor forlorn Proteus, passionate Proteus,
To the sweet Julia." That I'll tear away;
And yet I will not, since so prettily
He couples it with his complaining names.
Thus will I fold them, one upon another.
Now kiss, embrace, contend, do what you will.

MR. KAY: Very good, Rachel. Before we look at this again, let me ask you about a few things in the text that we may not understand.

What's all that about the wasps and the bees? What's the line again?

RACHEL: Injurious wasps, to feed on such sweet honey
And kill the bees that yield it with your stings!

MR. KAY: Yes, what's all that mean?

RACHEL: Well, Proteus' fingers are the *bees* that made the letter, and the letter is the *sweet honey,* and my fingers are the *wasps* that tore the letter up.

MR. KAY: I see. What do you mean by "And thus I search it with a sovereign kiss"?

RACHEL: I'll kiss the wound to help it heal.

MR. KAY: And the wound is?

RACHEL: The piece of paper with Proteus' name on it.

MR. KAY: Good. Now let's chat about this scene a bit.

You told us that Julia talks to *herself* in order to restore the letter. But that's not what we just *saw.* We saw her do a lot more than that.

(To the class) Let me ask you all—who else or *what* else did we see Julia talk to?

TRINITY: She talked to her *hands.*

SAM: She talked to the *papers.*

GABRIELLA: She talked to the *wind.*

SARAH: She talked to her *name.*

MR. KAY: Yes, good. And we'll probably find quite a few more possibilities as we start to orchestrate this speech.

(To Rachel) You understand the distinction I'm making, Rachel? Julia may be *alone* in the scene, but she's not talking to *herself.* She has many different focal points where she directs her actions in order to restore that letter.

So, unlike the last speech we just orchestrated, where all of Lewis' actions were directed towards a *single* focal point—the Cardinal—this speech requires that you play psycho-physical actions towards many *different* focal points.

So, let's go back and orchestrate the speech from psycho-physical action to psycho-physical action.

And as we do that, I'd also like you to tell us aloud the *focal point* for the action, as well as the action itself.

(The students write "action to action using multiple focal points" in their notebooks.)

So, for example, what's your first action?

RACHEL: TO SHOO AWAY.

MR. KAY: Good. And where is that action *directed*? Who or what are you shooing away?

RACHEL: LUCETTA.

MR. KAY: All right. So you'll say: TO SHOO AWAY (LUCETTA).

You'll state the action and the focal point in one statement. Got that?

RACHEL: Yes.

MR. KAY: All right, then, let's go back to the top, please, Rachel.

RACHEL: Okay.

(Rachel throws the pieces of paper back on the floor.)

MR. KAY: And remind us, please, what's your objective, Julia?

RACHEL: To reconstruct the letter.

MR. KAY: And first action and focal point?

RACHEL: TO SHOO AWAY (LUCETTA).

MR. KAY: Good, and text?

RACHEL: Go, get you gone, and let the papers lie.

MR. KAY: Good! Next action and focal point?

RACHEL: TO SPANK (MY HANDS).

(She slaps her hands.)

O hateful hands, to tear such loving words!

MR. KAY: Good. Next action and focal point?

RACHEL: TO SCOLD (MY FINGERS).

(She holds her hands out in front of her.)

Injurious wasps, to feed on such sweet honey
And kill the bees that yield it with your stings!

MR. KAY: I know you're talking to your *fingers* now, Julia, but it looks like you're still talking to your *hands.* Can you make it clear that you're now talking to your *fingers,* rather than your hands?

RACHEL: *(She wiggles her fingers.)*

Injurious wasps, to feed on such sweet honey
And kill the bees that yield it with your stings!

MR. KAY: Excellent! That's very clear now, thank you. Next action and focal point?

RACHEL: TO SMOTHER (THE PAPERS).

I'll kiss each sev'ral paper for amends.

MR. KAY: Good. Continue.

RACHEL: TO CONDEMN (MY NAME).

Look, here is writ "kind Julia."

TO SPITE (MYSELF).

(She pounds her chest with her fist.)

Unkind Julia!

TO CRUMPLE (MY NAME).

(She crumples the paper into a tight wad.)

As in revenge of thy ingratitude,

TO BRUISE (MY NAME).

(She throws down the crumpled paper.)

I throw thy name against the bruising stones,

TO STOMP (MY NAME).

(She stomps on her name.)

Tramp'ling contemptuously on thy disdain.

MR. KAY: Yes, and continue.

RACHEL: TO RESCUE (THE PAPER).

And here is writ "love-wounded Proteus."

TO MOTHER (PROTEUS' NAME).

Poor wounded name!

TO NURSE (THE WOUND).

(She puts the paper into her shirt.)

My bosom as a bed
Shall lodge thee till thy wound be throughly heal'd;

TO KISS (THE BOO BOO).

(She kisses the paper.)

And thus I search it with a sov'reign kiss.

TO SEARCH (THE PILE).

But twice or thrice was "Proteus" written down.

TO CALM (THE WIND).

Be calm, good wind, blow not a word away
Till I have found each letter in the letter,

TO DAMN (MY OWN NAME).

Except mine own name;

TO COMMAND (THE WIND).

that some whirlwind bear

TO CONJURE (A ROCK).

Unto a ragged, fearful, hanging rock

TO HURL (THE FRAGMENT).

And throw it thence into the raging sea!

TO DISCOVER (A TREASURE).

Lo, here in one line is his name twice writ,

TO SAVOR (HIS WORDS).

"Poor forlorn Proteus, passionate Proteus,
To the sweet Julia."

TO DESTROY (THE FRAGMENT).

That I'll tear away;

(She tears and crumples the paper.)

TO RESTORE (THE FRAGMENT).

And yet I will not, since so prettily
He couples it with his complaining names.

(She unfolds and smoothes the paper.)

TO UNITE (THE PAPERS).

Thus will I fold them, one upon another.

TO MATE (THE COUPLE).

(She folds the papers together.)

Now kiss, embrace, contend, do what you will.

MR. KAY: Good, Rachel. And, after this work, do you still think the objective is to reconstruct the letter?

RACHEL: No, it's more like "to resurrect the letter." To bring it back to life.

MR. KAY: To resuscitate the letter? To revive the letter?

RACHEL: To make more letters by breeding this one?

(The class laughs.)

MR. KAY: Yes, very good.

(Noah raises his hand.)

Yes, Noah?

NOAH: Can't this speech be played to the *audience*? I mean, isn't it usually done like that, where she's talking to the audience the whole time?

MR. KAY: That's a great question, Noah.

Right now, Rachel is playing this entire speech behind the *fourth wall,* that is to say, with no connection whatsoever with the audience. And that's fine—I've seen it performed that way, and it works.

But Noah's right, that the speech is often performed with some of the speech measures directed to the *audience,* to keep them included in the action. It is a *comedy*, after all!

So, Rachel, let me ask you this—if you were to reorchestrate this speech so that you sometimes talk to the *audience,* which speech measures might you use?

RACHEL: Um . . .

I'll kiss each sev'ral paper for amends.

MR. KAY: Yes. Another?

RACHEL: Look, here is writ "kind Julia."

MR. KAY: Yes. Another?

RACHEL: Lo, here in one line is his name twice writ.

MR. KAY: Yes . . .

RACHEL: That I'll tear away.

MR. KAY: Yes . . .

RACHEL: And yet I will not.

MR. KAY: Any others?

RACHEL: Thus will I fold them, one upon another.

MR. KAY: Yes, good, I agree. And did you notice how nearly every one of the moments you just mentioned is either a *decision* or a *realization*?

(A pause while Rachel considers that idea.)

And this is a smart way to orchestrate the speech, because it means that you're *sharing your thinking* with the audience as you attempt to recon-struct the letter, pausing to use the audience as a *sounding board* for your *actions* as you pursue your objective.

Good work, Rachel. Thank you.

(Rachel comes down off the stage.)

Who hasn't worked today?

〰 QUALITIES TO ACTIONS 〰

MADISON: I want to go next!

(Madison goes up onto the stage.)

MR. KAY: Good. And what are you going to show us, Madison?

MADISON: Joan la Pucelle, from *Henry the Sixth, Part One.*

MR. KAY: Good, and place yourself in your scene, please, while I ask you some questions.

(Madison stands center stage and gazes outward.)

Where are you, Joan?

MADISON: On a battlefield in France.

MR. KAY: And who are you talking to?

MADISON: Charles, the Dauphin.

MR. KAY: And what do you want from him?

MADISON: I want to convince him to let me fight for France.

MR. KAY: And what are the obstacles to that?

MADISON: Well, I'm a young woman, and women don't fight; I'm not of noble birth; I'm untrained; I'm poor; I'm uneducated . . .

MR. KAY: Yes, good, then let's see how you convince the Dauphin to let you fight. Begin, please.

PUCELLE: Dauphin, I am by birth a shepherd's daughter,
My wit untrain'd in any kind of art.
Heaven and our Lady gracious hath it pleas'd
To shine on my contemptible estate.
Lo, whilst I waited on my tender lambs
And to sun's parching heat display'd my cheeks,
God's mother deignèd to appear to me,
And in a vision full of majesty
Will'd me to leave my base vocation
And free my country from calamity.
In complete glory she reveal'd herself;
And with those rays which she infus'd on me,
That beauty am I blest with, which you may see.
Her aid she promis'd, and assur'd success.
Ask me what question thou can'st possible,
And I will answer unpremeditated.
My courage try by combat, if thou dar'st,
And thou shalt find that I exceed my sex.
Resolve on this: thou shalt be fortunate
If thou receive me for thy warlike mate.

MR. KAY: Good, Madison. I notice you trimmed that awkward line about her being "black and swart before," which I think is wise.

Let me ask you a few questions about the text before we look at the speech again.

First of all, about your name—what does "la Pucelle" mean?

MADISON: The maiden, or the virgin.

MR. KAY: I see. And what do you mean by "My wit untrain'd in any kind of art"?

MADISON: I've not had any formal schooling.

MR. KAY: What do you mean by "Resolve on this"?

MADISON: You can be sure about one thing.

MR. KAY: What do you mean by "warlike mate"?

MADISON: A military colleague.

MR. KAY: But there's also a sexual meaning there, too, isn't there?

MADISON: Oh, definitely.

(The class laughs.)

MR. KAY: So, let's talk a bit about Joan.

(To the class) For those of you who don't know this play, it's important to know that Shakespeare's Joan was certainly no *saint*. That's how *we* think of Joan of Arc because she was canonized as a saint in 1920. But Shakespeare's Joan, a character written by an Englishman in the 1590s, is not only France's savior, but also a sorceress, and a bit of a slut.

(To Madison) Now, this is the first time the audience sees her in the play, is that right?

MADISON: Yes.

MR. KAY: So, let me ask you this: what do you want the audience to know about Joan right from the start? What *qualities* do you want to reveal?

MADISON: Well . . . she's smart, and devout, and she's fearless . . .

MR. KAY: Wait a minute. Let's make a list—will someone write these down?

TRINITY: I will! *(Writing)* Smart, devout, fearless . . .

MR. KAY: Yes. What else?

MADISON: She's eloquent, and self-confident . . .

MR. KAY: Yes.

MADISON: And she's loyal to the King, and to France.

MR. KAY: So she's . . . patriotic?

MADISON: Yes. Patriotic.

MR. KAY: All right. What else?

MADISON: She's a shepherd's daughter, so she's earthy, but she can also be very blunt.

MR. KAY: Yes.

MADISON: And she's magical, and witchlike . . .

MR. KAY: Yes.

MADISON: And I think she can also be very alluring.

MR. KAY: Yes. *(To Trinity)* How many is that?

TRINITY: Uh . . . *(counting)* . . . twelve.

MR. KAY: Good, that's enough. May I have that list, please?

(Trinity hands Mr. Kay the list.)

(To the class) So, we have a list of twelve qualities that describe Joan la Pucelle. Some of these qualities we've arrived at from studying the text, some from reading what the scholars have to say, some are from a character conference with the director, some are from watching a few movie versions, and some are ideas that came from watching another actress play the role in summer stock. A list of qualities.

So, let me ask you this—how many of these qualities are *playable*?

(A long silence.)

The answer is—*none.* Not one.

(Another silence.)

Why? Because qualities are not playable. *Actions* are playable.

Then how are we going to reveal those twelve qualities which describe Joan to the audience?

By playing actions. *Actions reveal qualities.*

(The students write "actions reveal qualities" in their notebooks.)

So we're going to have to convert those qualities, those twelve descriptive *adjectives,* into *verbs,* into psycho-physical *actions* played in pursuit of the objective.

(The students write "converting qualities into psycho-physical actions" in their notebooks.)

For example, a director might say to you: "Can you be more courageous in that moment?"

So you think to yourself: "*To be courageous* isn't playable. I must play an action which *reveals* courage. I must play *to dare,* or *to challenge.*"

Or, the director might say: "I need you to be a bit sexier."

So you think: "I can't play *to be sexy*. But I *can* play *to seduce, to charm,* or *to entice.* These actions *reveal* sexuality to an audience."

You all understand what I'm saying? You must learn how to *translate,* and *instantly* translate, director-speak into *acting* terms, into playable *verbs.*

(To Madison) So, Madison, let's do this again. I'll be the typical director, and I'll give you the *quality* I want you play. You'll have to quickly come up with an action to *reveal* that quality. You'll say that action aloud, and then play it through the text. Understand?

MADISON: Yes, I think so.

MR. KAY: Good then, restore your scene in your imagination, if you would, please.

(Madison restores the scene in her imagination.)

And, remind us, please, Joan, what's your objective?

MADISON: To convince the Dauphin to let me fight for France.

MR. KAY: All right, then, let's begin.

(Mr. Kay puts on his "well-meaning but misguided director" voice.)

Now, when you kneel to the King, I want to see how *loyal* you are.

MADISON: TO PAY OBEISANCE.

Dauphin,

MR. KAY: *(As the director)* Remember, she's a shepherd's daughter, so I need you to be more *earthy.*

MADISON: TO HUMBLE MYSELF.

I am by birth a shepherd's daughter,
My wit untrain'd in any kind of art.

MR. KAY: *(As the director)* This is the first time we see that she's *devout.*

MADISON: TO INSPIRE.

Heaven and our Lady gracious hath it pleas'd
To shine on my contemptible estate.

MR. KAY: *(As the director)* I'm interested in there being something *magical* about her here.

MADISON: TO SPELLBIND.

Lo, whilst I waited on my tender lambs
And to sun's parching heat display'd my cheeks,

MR. KAY: *(As the director)* And now I think the magic turns into something more, I don't know . . . *witchlike.*

MADISON: TO CONJURE.

God's mother deignèd to appear to me,
And in a vision full of majesty

MR. KAY: *(As the director)* I just love this line . . . because it shows how *patriotic* she is, don't you think?

MADISON: TO ROUSE.

Will'd me to leave my base vocation
And free my country from calamity.

MR. KAY: *(As the director)* Can you feel in this next part how she becomes quite *eloquent?*

MADISON: TO GLORIFY.

In complete glory she reveal'd herself;

MR. KAY: *(As the director)* I'd like you to be more *alluring* here.

MADISON: TO ENTICE.

And with those rays which she infus'd on me,
That beauty am I blest with, which you may see.

MR. KAY: *(As the director)* She's very *self-confident,* isn't she?

MADISON: TO ASSURE.

Her aid she promis'd, and assur'd success.

MR. KAY: *(As the director)* Don't forget that she's *smarter* than the Dauphin.

MADISON: TO MATCH WITS.

Ask me what question thou can'st possible,
And I will answer unpremeditated.

MR. KAY: *(As the director)* Can you be more *fearless* in this moment?

MADISON: TO DARE.

My courage try by combat, if thou dar'st,
And thou shalt find that I exceed my sex.

MR. KAY: *(As the director)* Blunt, blunt, be *blunt* with him.

MADISON: TO CLINCH THE DEAL.

Resolve on this: thou shalt be fortunate
If thou receive me for thy warlike mate.

MR. KAY: *(As himself)* Excellent, Madison, well done. Thank you.

(Madison comes down off the stage.)

What a fascinating character! She's strong, she's smart, she's articulate, she's unintimidated, she's beautiful, she's sexual, she's spiritual, she's a warrior, she's a match for any man, yikes—she's a *witch!* Burn her at the stake!

(The class laughs.)

Seriously, people, you must always remember, when you're building a role, that a character is the sum total of the actions she plays during the course of the show. Actions reveal character. I'll say that again because I want you to write it down. *Actions reveal character.*

(The students write "actions reveal character" in their notebooks.)

Now, it's crucial that you remember that directors will almost *never* speak in acting terms. Directors are trained to speak in qualities, moods, and colors. They offer adjectives and adverbs. They impart metaphors and similes. They discuss rhythm and pace. They share feelings. They relate anecdotes. They demonstrate.

In a word, they speak in *results.*

This is *director-speak*—terms which are essentially unplayable, but give you an idea of the *result* that they would like to see.

You must learn to *translate,* and *instantly* translate, director-speak into *acting* terms, into *verbs.* Translating director-speak into acting terms is a survival skill which you *must* acquire if you hope to earn a weekly paycheck as an artist in the theater.

More importantly, you must stop directing *yourself* in terms of results.

You must train yourself to think of *process* first.

That is the very heart of the art of orchestration.

(Mr. Kay looks up at the clock.)

That's all the time we have for today, folks.

For tomorrow's class, I'd like you to incorporate all the work we did this week on speech measures, focal points, images, spoken subtext, and actions into your orchestrations.

See you all tomorrow.

BLACKOUT.

Complex Orchestration

The Acting Studio. Saturday.

MR. KAY: Good morning, folks.

All week we've been looking at the basic elements of the art of orchestration: speech measures, focal points, images, subtext, and actions.

We've been assembling an *actor's toolkit*—a collection of ways to select, arrange, and heighten your artistic choices for each moment of your time onstage.

Up to now we've been working with only *one* tool at a time. But today, we're going to use *all* of the tools now available to us to create a *complex orchestration.*

(The students write "complex orchestration" in their notebooks.)

So, who wants to go first?

❧ THE ACTOR'S TOOLKIT ☙

SARAH: I will!

(Sarah goes up onto the stage.)

MR. KAY: Thank you, Sarah. What are you going to show us?

SARAH: Imogen, from *Cymbeline.*

MR. KAY: All right. And would you place yourself in your scene, please, so I can ask you a few questions.

(Sarah stands center stage and gazes outward.)

Where are you, Imogen?

SARAH: I'm lost in the woods.

MR. KAY: And where are these woods?

SARAH: In Wales.

MR. KAY: I see. And who are you talking to?

SARAH: Myself.

MR. KAY: Just yourself?

SARAH: And the audience, sometimes.

MR. KAY: I see. And what do you hope to accomplish in the woods? What's your objective?

SARAH: I'm trying to get to Milford Haven.

MR. KAY: Why?

SARAH: To see my husband, Posthumus.

MR. KAY: I see. And why is he in Milford Haven?

SARAH: He was banished from the court by my father, King Cymbeline.

MR. KAY: I see. And what's making it hard for you to get to Milford Haven? What are the obstacles?

SARAH: Well, I'm lost, and I'm hungry, and I'm tired, and I'm scared, and I'm confused, and I'm dressed like a man . . .

MR. KAY: Why are you dressed like a man?

SARAH: Because my husband wants to murder me.

MR. KAY: Why?

SARAH: Because he thinks that I slept with another man.

MR. KAY: And did you sleep with another man?

SARAH: No, of course, not! But I'm heartsick that my husband believes that I could be unfaithful to him.

MR. KAY: I see. All right, then let's see if you can get to Milford Haven. Begin, please.

IMOGEN: I see a man's life is a tedious one.
I've tir'd myself, and for two nights together
Have made the ground my bed. I should be sick,
But that my resolution helps me. Milford,
When from the mountain top Pisanio show'd thee,
Thou wast within a ken. O Jove, I think
Foundations fly the wretched. Two beggars told me

I could not miss my way. Will poor folks lie,
That have afflictions on them, knowing 'tis
A punishment or trial? Yes; no wonder,
When rich ones scarce tell true. To lapse in fullness
Is sorer than to lie for need; and falsehood
Is worse in kings than beggars. My dear lord,
Thou art one o' th' false ones. Now I think on thee
My hunger's gone; but ev'n before I was
At point to sink for food. But what is this?
'Tis some savage hold.
I were best not call; I dare not call. Yet famine
Makes me valiant.
Plenty and peace breeds cowards; hardness ever
Of hardiness is mother. Ho! Who's here?
If any thing that's civil, speak; if savage,
Take or lend. Ho! No answer? Then I'll enter.
Best draw my sword; and if mine enemy
But fear the sword like me, he'll scarcely look on't.
Such a foe, good heavens!

MR. KAY: Good, Sarah. It sounds like you made a few small cuts in the speech?

SARAH: Yes. I cut that one line about the path . . .

MR. KAY: Yes? Why?

SARAH: Because it's too hard to have a path in a small space like this.

MR. KAY: Ah, I see. So you cut it to solve a staging problem?

SARAH: Yes.

MR. KAY: All right, that sounds reasonable to me. What else did you cut?

SARAH: I also changed one line, so it just says "Yet famine makes *me* valiant."
I thought that was clearer.

MR. KAY: Yes. I think that's fine. Now, let's make sure we all understand every
word of the text before we look at this again.
What do you mean by "within a ken"?

SARAH: In sight.

MR. KAY: What do you mean by "I think foundations fly the wretched"?

SARAH: Help seems to elude those who need it most.

MR. KAY: What do you mean by "To lapse in fullness is sorer than to lie for
need"?

SARAH: To lie when you're rich is a greater sin than to lie when you're poor.

MR. KAY: Who do you mean when you say "My dear lord"?

SARAH: My husband, Posthumus.

MR. KAY: What do you mean when you say "'Tis some savage hold"?

SARAH: It's some wild animal's cave.

MR. KAY: What do you mean by "hardness ever of hardiness is mother"?

SARAH: Hardships breed courage.

MR. KAY: What do you mean by "Take or lend"?

SARAH: Take my life and money, or give me help and food.

MR. KAY: Good, Sarah. Now, let's talk a bit before we look at this again.

I think this speech is a great place for us to begin today, because all of the basic elements we've been talking about this past week are built right into Imogen's text.

For example, what are some of the possible *focal points* for the speech, Sarah? Who does Imogen talk to in the text?

SARAH: Well, she talks to Jove, and to Milford Haven, and to the audience, and to herself, and to whoever is in the cave . . .

MR. KAY: Yes. And what are some of the possible *images*? What does Imogen see-hear-taste-touch-smell in the text?

SARAH: Well, she imagines Posthumus, and the King, and the Queen . . .

MR. KAY: Yes. And what about her *subtext*? Does she tell us about any of her *secret fears*?

SARAH: She says she's afraid that savages live in the cave.

MR. KAY: Does she tell us about a *realization* she has?

SARAH: She realizes she's stumbled onto a cave.

MR. KAY: Does she tell us about a *decision* she makes?

SARAH: She decides to go into the cave.

MR. KAY: Does she tell us about any *actions* she plays?

SARAH: She says she draws her sword.

MR. KAY: Good. And besides all these things that are actually *specified* by the text, there are countless more possibilities that we haven't even thought of yet!

So, let's have another look at the speech, Sarah, and orchestrate it from speech measure to speech measure, using all of the tools that are now in our actor's toolkit.

And for the sake of review, let's work with those tools in the same order that we learned them. All right?

SARAH: That sounds great.

MR. KAY: All right, then, let's begin by dividing the text into *speech measures* by honoring the *punctuation.*

Do you remember how this works, Sarah? I'll say the punctuation out loud as you work through the text.

SARAH: Yes, I remember.

MR. KAY: Good. Then would you please restore the scene in your imagination? *(Sarah does so.)*

And remind us, please. What's your objective, Imogen?

SARAH: To get to Milford Haven.

MR. KAY: And begin, please. First measure?

SARAH: I see a man's life is a tedious one.

MR. KAY: PERIOD.

SARAH: I've tir'd myself,

MR. KAY: COMMA.

SARAH: and for two nights together
Have made the ground my bed.

MR. KAY: PERIOD.

Good, and now let's work with *operative words.*

Operative word for the next speech measure, Imogen?

SARAH: SICK.

MR. KAY: And text?

SARAH: I should be *sick,*

MR. KAY: Operative for the next measure?

SARAH: RESOLUTION.

But that my *resolution* helps me.

MR. KAY: Good, and now let's work with *focal points.*

Focal point for the next speech measure, Imogen?

SARAH: *(Focusing the house right "x")* MILFORD.

MR. KAY: Good, and text?

SARAH: Milford,

MR. KAY: Next focal point?

SARAH: *(Focusing on the house left "x")* MOUNTAIN TOP.
When from the mountain top Pisanio show'd thee,

MR. KAY: Focal point?

SARAH: *(Focusing on the house right "x")* MILFORD.
Thou wast within a ken.

MR. KAY: Focal point?

SARAH: *(Focusing on the "x" on the ceiling)* THE GODS.
O Jove, I think
Foundations fly the wretched.

MR. KAY: Focal point?

SARAH: *(Focusing upstage)* THE PATH.
Two beggars told me
I could not miss my way.

MR. KAY: Focal point?

SARAH: AUDIENCE.

MR. KAY: House right, left, or center, Imogen?

SARAH: *(Focusing center)* CENTER.
Will poor folks lie,
That have afflictions on them,

MR. KAY: *(Focusing right)* Good, next focal point?

SARAH: AUDIENCE.

MR. KAY: Yes, but please be specific this time, Imogen. *Describe* who you are talking to.

SARAH: A MAN IN A WHEELCHAIR.
knowing 'tis
A punishment or trial?

MR. KAY: Good! Next focal point?

SARAH: *(Focusing on the house center "x")* SELF.
Yes; no wonder,
When rich ones scarce tell true.

MR. KAY: Good, and now let's work with *images.*

Image for the next speech measure, Imogen? What do you *see-hear-taste-touch-smell*?

SARAH: I SEE THE QUEEN.

> To lapse in fullness
> Is sorer than to lie for need;

MR. KAY: Next image?

SARAH: I SEE THE KING.

> and falsehood
> Is worse in kings than beggars.

MR. KAY: Next image?

SARAH: I SEE POSTHUMUS.

> My dear lord,
> Thou art one o' th' false ones.

MR. KAY: Good, and now let's work with *subtext.*

> *Head, heart, guts or groin* for the next measure, Imogen?

SARAH: HEART.

MR. KAY: Yes, and text?

SARAH: Now I think on thee
My hunger's gone;

MR. KAY: Good. Next speech measure—head, heart, guts or groin?

SARAH: GUTS.

> but ev'n before I was
> At point to sink for food.

MR. KAY: Good. *Realization* for the next measure, Imogen?

SARAH: I REALIZE THAT THERE'S A HOLE IN THE ROCK.

> But what is this?

MR. KAY: Another realization?

SARAH: I REALIZE THAT IT'S A CAVE.

> 'Tis some savage hold.

MR. KAY: Good! Secret fears? *I'm afraid that . . . ?*

SARAH: I'M AFRAID THAT SAVAGES LIVE IN THAT CAVE.

> I were best not call;

MR. KAY: Another secret fear?

SARAH: I'M AFRAID THAT WILD BEASTS WILL TEAR ME APART.

I dare not call.

MR. KAY: Good! Secret hopes and dreams, Imogen? *I wish, I want, I hope, I need, I must?*

SARAH: I NEED FOOD!

Yet famine
Makes me valiant.

MR. KAY: And again—I wish, I want, I hope, I need, I must?

SARAH: I MUST BE BRAVE.

Plenty and peace breeds cowards;

MR. KAY: *Decision*, Imogen?

SARAH: I'M GOING TO APPROACH THE CAVE.

hardness ever
Of hardiness is mother.

MR. KAY: Good, and now let's work with *actions*.

Advance or retreat for the next measure, Imogen?

SARAH: ADVANCE.

Ho!

MR. KAY: And again—*advance or retreat*?

SARAH: RETREAT.

Who's here?

MR. KAY: *Effort action* for the next measure, Imogen—*stroke, wring, flick, or slash*?

SARAH: WRING.

(Wringing on the phrase) If any thing that's civil,

MR. KAY: And again—*stroke, wring, flick, or slash?*

SARAH: SLASH.

(Slashing on the operative word) speak;

MR. KAY: And now—*shake, pull, whip, or shove*?

SARAH: SHAKE.

(Shaking on the phrase) if savage,

MR. KAY: And now—*stir, squeeze, punch, or jerk?*

SARAH: STIR.

(Stirring on the phrase) Take or lend.

MR. KAY: Good! *Psycho-physical action* for the next measure, Imogen?

SARAH: TO SOOTHE.

Ho!

MR. KAY: Action?

SARAH: TO WHISPER.

No answer?

MR. KAY: Action?

SARAH: TO STEEL MYSELF.

Then I'll enter.

MR. KAY: Action?

SARAH: TO DRAW.

Best draw my sword;

MR. KAY: Action?

SARAH: TO CRINGE.

and if mine enemy
But fear the sword like me, he'll scarcely look on't.

MR. KAY: Action?

SARAH: TO TIPTOE.

Such a foe, good heavens!

MR. KAY: Nicely done. Sarah. Thank you.

(Sarah comes down off the stage.)

(To the class) Now, it just so happens that we were able to apply these tools to the speech in the order that we learned them. But of course, that doesn't usually happen.

Most often you'll have to study each speech measure and make an artistic choice about what is the best tool for the moment based on an understanding of the character and the situation.

Sometimes Shakespeare will tell you exactly what tool he wants you to use in the speech measure by giving you strong clues in the text.

Sometimes Shakespeare's intent is less obvious, and you'll only find the right tool for the speech measure after lots of trial and error on your feet.

Either way, you must remember, folks, that the goal of orchestration is to find the tool which most fully illuminates the speech measure, to make an *acting choice* which makes the meaning of the speech measure absolutely clear to the audience.

So, with that in mind, let's look at another speech.

Who's up next?

✑ THE RIGHT TOOL ✑

JESSE: I'm up!

(Jesse goes up onto the stage.)

MR. KAY: Thanks, Jesse. And what are you going to show us today?

JESSE: Macbeth, from *Macbeth.*

MR. KAY: All right. And would you place yourself in you scene, please, so I can ask you a few questions.

(Jesse stands center stage, gazing outward.)

Where are you Macbeth?

JESSE: I'm in my castle, at night.

MR. KAY: Your castle in Scotland?

JESSE: Yes, in Inverness.

MR. KAY: I see. And who are you talking to?

JESSE: Myself, and a dagger.

MR. KAY: A dagger! Why are you talking to a dagger? What do you hope to accomplish?

JESSE: I want to screw up the courage to kill Duncan.

MR. KAY: And who is Duncan?

JESSE: The King of Scotland.

MR. KAY: And what are the obstacles? Why must you screw up your courage?

JESSE: Well, he's a friend of mine. And he's a guest in my house. And he's just honored me with a new title. And he trusts me. And his door is guarded by two men. And his two sons are sleeping down the hall.

MR. KAY: Are you afraid to kill him?

JESSE: Well, I've killed plenty of men in battle. But killing a king is different. So, yes, I'm afraid to kill him.

MR. KAY: All right, then, let's see if you can screw up your courage to kill him. Begin, please.

MACBETH: Is this a dagger which I see before me,

The handle toward my hand? Come, let me clutch thee:
I have thee not, and yet I see thee still.
Art thou not, fatal vision, sensible
To feeling as to sight? or art thou but
A dagger of the mind, a false creation,
Proceeding from the heat-oppressèd brain?
I see thee yet, in form as palpable
As this which now I draw.
Thou marshallst me the way that I was going,
And such an instrument I was to use.
Mine eyes are made the fools o' th' other senses,
Or else worth all the rest. I see thee still;
And on thy blade and dudgeon gouts of blood,
Which was not so before. There's no such thing:
It is the bloody business which informs
Thus to mine eyes. Now, o'er the one half world
Nature seems dead, and wicked dreams abuse
The curtain'd sleep; witchcraft celebrates
Pale Hecate's off'rings; and wither'd murder,
Alarum'd by his sentinel, the wolf,
Whose howl's his watch, thus with his stealthy pace,
With Tarquin's ravishing strides, towards his design
Moves like a ghost. Thou sure and firm-set earth,
Hear not my steps, which way they walk, for fear
The very stones prate of my whereabout,
And take the present horror from the time,
Which now suits with it. Whiles I threat, he lives:
Words to the heat of deeds too cold breath gives.
I go, and it is done; the bell invites me.
Hear it not, Duncan, for it is a knell,
That summons thee to heaven, or to hell.

MR. KAY: Good, Jesse, good. Now, before we look at this again, let's go through the text and make sure we understand everything you say.

What do you mean by "fatal vision"?

JESSE: A deadly apparition.

MR. KAY: What do you mean by "sensible to feeling"?

JESSE: Able to be felt.

MR. KAY: What do you mean by "the heat-oppressèd brain"?

JESSE: A feverish mind.

MR. KAY: What do you mean by "Thou marshall'st me the way that I was going"?

JESSE: You're guiding me towards Duncan's door.

MR. KAY: What do you mean by "or else worth all the rest"?

JESSE: Or perhaps my eyes alone are telling the truth.

MR. KAY: What's a "dudgeon"?

JESSE: The handle of the dagger.

MR. KAY: What are "gouts of blood"?

JESSE: Drops of blood.

MR. KAY: What do you mean by "Now o'er the one-half world nature seems dead"?

JESSE: Everything on the dark side of the earth is still and quiet.

MR. KAY: What are "Pale Hecate's offerings"?

JESSE: Sacrifices made to Hecate, goddess of witchcraft.

MR. KAY: What do you mean by "Alarum'd by his sentinel"?

JESSE: Called to action by his guard.

MR. KAY: What do you mean by "whose howl's his watch"?

JESSE: The wolf's howl is the password.

MR. KAY: Who was "Tarquin"?

JESSE: The Roman prince who raped Lucrece.

MR. KAY: What do you mean by "his design"?

JESSE: His planned victim.

MR. KAY: What do you mean by "take the present horror from the time"?

JESSE: Take away the deadly silence of this moment.

MR. KAY: What do you mean by "Words to the heat of deeds too cold breath gives"?

JESSE: Talking just puts off what needs to be done.

MR. KAY: Good, Jesse. Now remember, even though the speech is famous, the language and the images are extremely dense. So you must take great pains to make acting choices which illuminate the meaning of each speech measure as much as possible.

And in order to do that, you're going to have to look at each speech measure, and select the right tool for the job.

You're going to have to ask yourself: which tool from my actor's toolkit will make this parcel of text absolutely clear to the audience?

So, with that in mind, let's go through the speech again, and orchestrate it, from measure to measure, using all of the tools now available to us.

If you would restore the scene in your imagination, please.

(Jesse focuses intently on the "x" at house center.)

And remind us, please, what's your objective?

JESSE: To work up the courage to kill Duncan.

MR. KAY: Yes, and what tool are you going to use for the first speech measure?

JESSE: Um . . . I'm not sure.

MR. KAY: Well, what's the first speech measure?

JESSE: Is this a dagger which I see before me,

MR. KAY: So what tool is suggested by the *text* inside that measure?

JESSE: Um . . . an image?

MR. KAY: Yes, an image, good. Then be specific—what do you see-hear-taste-touch-smell?

JESSE: I SEE A DAGGER FLOATING IN THE AIR.

MR. KAY: Yes, and text?

JESSE: Is this a dagger which I see before me,

MR. KAY: Good, that's very clear. And the next speech measure? What tool are you going to use next?

JESSE: Um . . . it's another image.

MR. KAY: Yes, and what do you see-hear-taste-touch smell in this speech measure?

JESSE: I SEE THE HANDLE POINTING AT ME.

MR. KAY: Yes, and text?

JESSE: The handle toward my hand?

MR. KAY: Good, Jesse. Now, as we continue, it's important to keep in mind that the dagger is essentially your *scene partner* for the speech. So you not only have to orchestrate your *own* work in the scene, but your have to spend some time directing the *dagger* as well. You must create a "movie in your head" which tells you exactly where the dagger is, and what the dagger does from moment to moment.

So, let's continue, please, from where we left off.

(Jesse sees the dagger in his imagination.)

Tool for the next speech measure?

JESSE: Um . . . I think it's an action.

MR. KAY: Yes—what action?

JESSE: TO REACH.

MR. KAY: And text?

JESSE: Come, let me clutch thee:

MR. KAY: Yes, Jesse, that works just fine.
But what if we divide that measure into two moments? What if we see Macbeth *decide* to reach for the dagger before he actually *reaches* for it?

JESSE: Okay. Let me try that.
(Jesse sees the dagger again.)

MR. KAY: Decision, Macbeth?

JESSE: I'M GOING TO TOUCH IT.
Come,

MR. KAY: Action?

JESSE: TO REACH.
(He reaches out his hand.)
let me clutch thee:

MR. KAY: Excellent! Let's continue, please. Tool for the next measure, Macbeth?

JESSE: Um . . . subtext.

MR. KAY: Yes, what?

JESSE: It's a realization.

MR. KAY: Yes, what do you realize?

JESSE: I REALIZE THAT I CAN'T FEEL THE DAGGER WITH MY HAND.
(He curls his fingers through the air.)
I have thee not,

MR. KAY: Yes, very good, and, tool for the next measure?

JESSE: Image.

MR. KAY: Yes, image—what's the dagger doing now?

JESSE: THE DAGGER IS GLOWING.
(He withdraws his hand.)
and yet I see thee still.

MR. KAY: Good. Tool for the next measure?

JESSE: Action.

MR. KAY: Yes, what action, Macbeth?

JESSE: TO INQUIRE.

Art thou not, fatal vision,

MR. KAY: Yes, that's fine, Jesse, but it seems like you're glossing over the words "fatal vision." I think we need to orchestrate a choice for just that phrase. Let me ask you this—why do you call the dagger a "fatal vision"?

JESSE: Well, I guess I'm calling it that because it's such a creepy thing to see.

MR. KAY: So, it scares you?

JESSE: Yes.

MR. KAY: All right, then—so what tool do you want to use for that moment?

JESSE: Um . . . secret fears?

MR. KAY: Good, then, let's go back and try that.

(Jesse sees the dagger again.)

Action?

JESSE: TO INQUIRE.

Art thou not,

MR. KAY: Secret fears?

JESSE: I'M AFRAID OF THIS DEADLY SIGHT.

fatal vision,

MR. KAY: Excellent. Now we understand the meaning of the phrase "fatal vision" and understand why you say it. The phrase has been illuminated by your acting choice.

And, tool for the next measure?

JESSE: Action.

MR. KAY: Yes, what action?

JESSE: TO INTERROGATE (THE DAGGER).

sensible

To feeling as to sight?

MR. KAY: Good, and tool for the next measure?

JESSE: Another secret fear.

MR. KAY: Yes, what are you afraid of?

jesse: I'M AFRAID THAT I MIGHT BE SEEING THINGS.

or art thou but
A dagger of the mind,

MR. KAY: That's very clear. Tool for the next measure?

JESSE: Action.

MR. KAY: Yes, what action?

JESSE: TO SHUN (THE DAGGER).

(He looks away.)

a false creation,
Proceeding from the heat-oppressèd brain?

MR. KAY: That's fine, Jesse, I think TO SHUN (THE DAGGER) works well there. But I also think you're blazing through a comma that might help you to play this as *two* moments.

Do you have a choice for "proceeding from the heat-oppressèd brain?"

JESSE: Well, I think his head starts to hurt.

MR. KAY: Good, let's look at that. From "to shun," please.

(Jesse sees the dagger again.)

Action?

JESSE: TO SHUN (THE DAGGER).

(He looks away.)

a false creation,

MR. KAY: Head, heart, guts, or groin, Macbeth?

JESSE: HEAD.

(Jesse holds his head in his hands.)

Proceeding from the heat-oppressèd brain?

MR. KAY: Good, the acting choice has illuminated the text, so that now we can really hear and understand the phrase "heat-oppressèd brain."

And continue, please. Tool for the next measure?

JESSE: Subtext.

MR. KAY: Yes, state your subtext aloud.

JESSE: I MUST LOOK AGAIN.

(He looks at the dagger again.)

I see thee yet,

MR. KAY: Good, and, tool for the next measure

JESSE: A decision.

MR. KAY: Yes, let's hear your decision.

JESSE: I'M GOING TO DRAW MY OWN DAGGER.

> in form as palpable
> As this which now I draw.

MR. KAY: Good, that decision is very clear.

> *(To the class)* And now—those of you following along in your *Complete Works*—you'll notice there are four missing syllables in the line.

> *(To Jesse)* Tool for those four missing syllables?

JESSE: TO DRAW.

> *(He draws his dagger in silence.)*

MR. KAY: Yes, that's a very powerful moment of silence. Tool for the next measure?

JESSE: Image.

MR. KAY: Yes, what's the dagger doing now?

JESSE: I SEE THE DAGGER HEADING FOR THE STAIRS.

> Thou marshall'st me the way that I was going,

MR. KAY: Tool for the next measure?

JESSE: Image.

MR. KAY: Yes, what do you see-hear-taste-touch-smell?

JESSE: I SEE THE DAGGER IN MY OWN HANDS.

> And such an instrument I was to use.

MR. KAY: Tool for the next measure?

JESSE: Action.

MR. KAY: Yes, what action, Macbeth?

JESSE: TO SCOLD (MY EYES).

> *(He closes his eyes.)*

> Mine eyes are made the fools o' th' other senses,

MR. KAY: Good! Tool for the next measure?

JESSE: Action.

MR. KAY: Yes, what action?

JESSE: TO RECONSIDER.

> *(He opens his eyes.)*

> Or else worth all the rest.

MR. KAY: Next tool?

JESSE: Operative word.

MR. KAY: Yes? What is it?

JESSE: STILL.

I see thee *still;*

MR. KAY: Good, and, tool for the next measure?

JESSE: Image.

MR. KAY: Yes? What image? What's the dagger doing now?

JESSE: I SEE BLOOD DRIPPING FROM THE DAGGER.

And on thy blade and dudgeon gouts of blood,
Which was not so before.

MR. KAY: Yes! Tool for the next measure?

JESSE: Action.

MR. KAY: Yes, what action?

JESSE: TO DENY.

There's no such thing:

MR. KAY: Good. Tool for the next measure, Macbeth?

JESSE: Um . . . his head hurts again.

MR. KAY: Yes, so—head, heart, guts, or groin?

JESSE: HEAD.

It is the bloody business which informs
Thus to mine eyes.

MR. KAY: Good, and let me stop you there for a moment, Jesse.

(Jesse relaxes.)

Because at this point in the story, Macbeth is a man who still knows right from wrong. And he could still stop the whole thing, here and now. He could ignore the prophecy of the weird sisters. He could stand up to his wife. He could ignore this deadly apparition. He could smother his own ambition, and let Duncan live.

But he doesn't. He chooses to kill the King.

So, this is the decisive moment for Macbeth—the moment when he must overcome his fears and doubts, when he must push himself over the edge to the dark side of his nature. Here and now, he must conjure up his deadliest impulses, not to serve king and country, but to serve *himself,* and his own lust for power.

And this means that to orchestrate this speech, Jesse, you have to do the *same thing*. You have to tap into impulses from the dark side of your nature, to summon up the deadliest images, the most unspeakable thoughts, and the most abominable actions within yourself. Or the speech will ring hollow, and the play will falter.

Are you ready to do that?

JESSE: Yes.

MR. KAY: All right, then, let's proceed.

(Jesse restores the scene in his imagination.)

Tool for the next measure, Macbeth?

JESSE: Image.

MR. KAY: Yes, what do you see-hear-taste-touch-smell?

JESSE: I SEE HALF THE PLANET EARTH, IN DARKNESS.

Now, o'er the one half world
Nature seems dead,

MR. KAY: Good—tool for the next speech measure?

JESSE: Image.

MR. KAY: Yes—what image?

JESSE: I SEE CHILDREN ASLEEP IN THEIR BEDS, HAVING NIGHTMARES.

and wicked dreams abuse
The curtain'd sleep;

MR. KAY: Tool?

JESSE: Image.

MR. KAY: Yes?

JESSE: I SEE DANCING FIRE.

witchcraft celebrates
Pale Hecate's off'rings;

MR. KAY: Tool?

JESSE: Image.

MR. KAY: Yes?

JESSE: I SEE MYSELF, STANDING WITH MY DAGGER DRAWN.

and wither'd murder,

MR. KAY: So *you* are "wither'd murder"?

JESSE: Yes.

MR. KAY: So why are you "wither'd"?

JESSE: Because I'm standing in one place, paralyzed by the thought of the deed.

MR. KAY: Excellent. Next tool?

JESSE: Image.

MR. KAY: Yes?

JESSE: I SEE LADY MACBETH.
Alarum'd by his sentinel, the wolf,

MR. KAY: Lady Macbeth is the wolf?

JESSE: Yes. She's keeping watch while I do the deed.

MR. KAY: I see. Next image?

JESSE: I HEAR MY WIFE, HOWLING.

MR. KAY: What is she howling?

JESSE: SCREW YOUR COURAGE TO THE STICKING PLACE!

MR. KAY: Yes, and text?

JESSE: Whose howl's his watch,

MR. KAY: Good. Tool?

JESSE: Action.

MR. KAY: Yes, what action?

JESSE: TO CREEP.
(He begins to move towards Duncan's door.)
thus with his stealthy pace,

MR. KAY: Tool?

JESSE: Image.

MR. KAY: Yes?

JESSE: I SEE TARQUIN.
With Tarquin's ravishing strides,

MR. KAY: Tool?

JESSE: Image.

MR. KAY: Yes?

JESSE: I SEE DUNCAN.

towards his design
Moves like a ghost.

MR. KAY: Tool?

JESSE: Image.

MR. KAY: Yes?

JESSE: THE EARTH.

Thou sure and firm-set earth,

MR. KAY: Tool?

JESSE: Action.

MR. KAY: Yes, what action?

JESSE: TO CONSPIRE.

MR. KAY: You're *conspiring* with the earth?

JESSE: Yes.

MR. KAY: Good choice! Continue.

(He kneels down.)

JESSE: Hear not my steps, which way they walk,

MR. KAY: Tool?

JESSE: Secret fears.

MR. KAY: Yes? What's your secret fear?

JESSE: I'M AFRAID THAT THE STONES WILL CRY OUT FOR HELP.

for fear
The very stones prate of my whereabout,

MR. KAY: Good. Tool?

JESSE: Subtext.

MR. KAY: Yes, tell us what you're thinking.

JESSE: I HOPE THAT I CAN GO THROUGH WITH THIS.

And take the present horror from the time,
Which now suits with it.

MR. KAY: Tool?

JESSE: Action.

MR. KAY: Yes?

JESSE: TO BERATE MYSELF.

(He rises.)

Whiles I threat, he lives:

MR. KAY: Tool?

JESSE: Action.

MR. KAY: Yes, what action?

JESSE: TO SCREW MY COURAGE TO THE STICKING PLACE.

Words to the heat of deeds too cold breath gives.

MR. KAY: Tool?

JESSE: I make a decision.

MR. KAY: Yes, make it!

JESSE: I'M GOING TO GO THROUGH WITH IT.

I go, and it is done;

MR. KAY: Tool?

JESSE: Image.

MR. KAY: Yes. What do you see-hear-taste-touch-smell?

JESSE: I HEAR THE SOUND OF THE BELL, RINGING.

the bell invites me.

MR. KAY: Tool?

JESSE: Image.

MR. KAY: Yes, what is it?

JESSE: I SEE THE SLEEPING DUNCAN.

Hear it not, Duncan,

MR. KAY: Tool?

JESSE: Action.

MR. KAY: Yes, what action?

JESSE: TO CONDEMN TO DEATH.

for it is a knell,
That summons thee to heaven,

MR. KAY: Tool?

JESSE: Subtext.

MR. KAY: Yes?

JESSE: I HOPE HE SAID HIS PRAYERS TONIGHT.

or to hell.

MR. KAY: Well done, Jesse.

(To the class) Keep in mind, folks, that this is just *one* possible way to orchestrate this speech using all the tools we've been exploring. It's just a step in the process, like a first rough draft, or a sketch, or a study.

Jesse should continue to reshape and restructure his orchestration in the same way any artist grapples with any work of art—through extensive trial and error, and constant questioning.

Should I split that speech measure into two? Is that the best operative word? Should I change my focal point here? Is there a more specific image I can use here? Is this where I make my decision? Do I need a stronger action here? Is this the right tool for this moment?

There are an infinite number of artistic choices to be made, and every artistic choice affects all the others.

Ultimately, you're limited only by the depth of your talent, and the strength of your commitment to achieve something artistically unique.

And, of course, the amount of *time* you have to rehearse.

Thank you, Jesse.

(Jesse comes down off the stage.)

Who wants to work?

❦ SPONTANEITY ❦

NOAH: I do.

(Noah goes up onto the stage and places a coat on the floor.)

MR. KAY: Good. What are you going to show us today, Noah?

NOAH: Trinculo, from *The Tempest*.

MR. KAY: All right. If you would place yourself in your scene, please, so I can ask you a few questions.

(Noah stands upstage right and gazes outward.)

Where are you, Trinculo?

NOAH: On a deserted island.

MR. KAY: What are you doing there?

NOAH: I was shipwrecked by a storm on my way home to Naples.

MR. KAY: Who are you talking to?

NOAH: Myself, mostly. And the audience, too.

MR. KAY: And what's the objective? What do you hope to accomplish?

NOAH: I need to find shelter.

MR. KAY: And what's the obstacle to that? What's making it hard to find shelter?

NOAH: I'm on the beach, so there are no bushes or shrubs or trees to hide under. And there's another storm coming.

MR. KAY: Good, then let's see if you can manage to find some shelter. Begin, please.

TRINCULO: Here's neither bush nor shrub to bear off any weather at all. And another storm brewing, I hear it sing i' th' wind. Yond same black cloud, yond huge one, looks like a foul bombard that would shed his liquor. If it should thunder as it did before, I know not where to hide my head. Yond same cloud cannot choose but fall by pailfuls. What have we here? a man or a fish? dead or alive? A fish, he smells like a fish; a very ancient and fish-like smell. A strange fish! Were I in England now, (as once I was) and had but this fish painted, not a holiday fool there but would give a piece of silver. There would this monster make a man. When they will not give a doit to relieve a lame beggar, they will lay out ten to see a dead Indian. Legg'd like a man; and his fins like arms! Warm, o' my troth! I do now let loose my opinion, hold it no longer: this is no fish, but an islander, that hath lately suffered by a thunder-bolt. Alas, the storm is come again! My best way is to creep under his gaberdine; there is no other shelter hereabout. Misery acquaints a man with strange bedfellows. I will here shroud till the dregs of the storm be past.

MR. KAY: Good, Noah, good. Now, let's be sure we understand every word of the text before we look at this again.

What's a "bombard"?

NOAH: A leather jug for drinking liquor.

MR. KAY: What do you mean by "and had but this fish painted"?

NOAH: If I had this fish painted on a sign to attract customers.

MR. KAY: What do you mean by "a holiday fool"?

NOAH: Someone on vacation, with spending money in his pocket.

MR. KAY: What do you mean by "make a man"?

NOAH: Make a fortune for a man.

MR. KAY: What's a "doit"?

NOAH: A coin worth next to nothing.

MR. KAY: What do you mean by "o' my troth"?

NOAH: By my faith.

MR. KAY: What do you mean by "suffered by a thunder-bolt"?

NOAH: Killed by lightening.

MR. KAY: What's a "gaberdine"?

NOAH: A long cloak.

MR. KAY: What do you mean by "the dregs of the storm"?

NOAH: The very last drop of rain.

MR. KAY: Good, Noah. Let's talk about Trinculo for a minute before we look at this again.

(To the class) The thing to remember about Shakespeare's clowns, folks, is that they require ferocious *commitment* and enormous *specificity.*

Commitment, because pursuing your objective in a way that consumes your entire being is what gets the laughs. Just look at any Charlie Chaplin film if you have any doubts about that.

Specificity, because comedy must be orchestrated with great precision, even greater precision than drama. Again, just look at any Charlie Chaplin film if you have any doubts about that.

Noah, as we all know, has the ferocious commitment of a U.S. Navy SEAL. But *specificity* is another story.

(To Noah) You have a wonderful gift for improvisation, Noah, which, for Shakespeare, can be both a blessing and a curse. It's a *blessing* because you never seem to run out of ideas. But it's also a *curse,* because it sometimes means you cannot *repeat* your ideas, cannot *shape* them into a performance.

If this were a film, the ability to repeat your choices wouldn't be a factor at all. The director would shoot twelve takes, you'd give him twelve different ideas, and the editor would pick the best choices for you later and string them together in a linear sequence.

But in the theater, improvising a scene in rehearsal twelve different ways has to *lead* to something. Improvisation must be a *tool* to find the best way to play each moment through trial and error. And the goal must be to build an orchestration which is *repeatable* in performance.

So, let's have another look at this, Noah, and I'm going to ask you which *tool* you intend to use from measure to measure. And I want to encourage you to be even more rigorous about orchestrating specific, repeatable choices for the speech. All right?

NOAH: *(As a Navy SEAL)* Sir, yes, sir!

MR. KAY: At ease.
   (The class laughs.)
   And would you place yourself in your scene again, please.
   (Noah does so.)
   And remind us, please, Trinculo—what's your objective?

NOAH: To find shelter.

MR. KAY: And what tool are you going to use for this first speech measure?

NOAH: Um . . . an image.

MR. KAY: Yes, then be specific—what do you see-hear-taste-touch-smell?

NOAH: I SEE A SAND DUNE.

MR. KAY: And text?

NOAH: Here's neither bush nor shrub to bear off any weather at all.

MR. KAY: Good! Tool for the next speech measure?

NOAH: Um . . . I guess I'm shifting my focal point.

MR. KAY: Yes, where's your focus now?

NOAH: *(Focusing on the house right "x")* THE AUDIENCE.

MR. KAY: And text?

NOAH: And another storm brewing,

MR. KAY: Good. Tool for the next speech measure?

NOAH: Image.

MR. KAY: Yes, what do you see-hear-taste-touch-smell?

NOAH: I HEAR THE WIND HOWLING.
   I hear it sing i' th' wind.

MR. KAY: Yes, tool for the next measure?

NOAH: Image.

MR. KAY: Yes, what is it?

NOAH: I SEE A BLACK CLOUD.
   Yond same black cloud,

MR. KAY: Tool for the next measure?

NOAH: Focal point.

MR. KAY: Yes, and where's your focus now?

NOAH: *(Focusing on the house left "x")* THE AUDIENCE.
yond huge one,

MR. KAY: Good. Next tool?

NOAH: Action.

MR. KAY: Yes, what action?

NOAH: TO MOCK THE CLOUD.
looks like a foul bombard that would shed his liquor.

MR. KAY: Next tool?

NOAH: Focal point.

MR. KAY: Yes, and where's your focus now?

NOAH: *(Focusing on the house center "x")* THE AUDIENCE.
If it should thunder as it did before,

MR. KAY: Next tool?

NOAH: Subtext.

MR. KAY: Yes, what is it?

NOAH: I'M AFRAID THAT I'LL BE HIT BY LIGHTNING.
I know not where to hide my head.

MR. KAY: Next tool, Trinculo?

NOAH: Action.

MR. KAY: Yes, what action?

NOAH: TO BACK AWAY.
Yond same cloud cannot choose but fall by pailfuls.

MR. KAY: Next tool?

NOAH: Image.

MR. KAY: Yes? What do you see-hear-taste-touch-smell?

NOAH: I SEE A CARCASS.
What have we here?

MR. KAY: Next tool?

NOAH: Subtext.

MR. KAY: Yes, what are you thinking?

NOAH: I'M AFRAID THAT IT MIGHT BE A MAN.
   a man or a fish?

MR. KAY: Next tool?

NOAH: Subtext.

MR. KAY: Yes, what?

NOAH: I'M HOPING THE THING IS DEAD.
   dead or alive?

MR. KAY: Next tool?

NOAH: Action.

MR. KAY: Yes, what action?

NOAH: TO INVESTIGATE.

MR. KAY: Good. Next tool?

NOAH: Image.

MR. KAY: Yes, what image?

NOAH: I SMELL A DEAD FISH!
   A fish, he smells like a fish;

MR. KAY: Good. Next tool?

NOAH: I'm shifting my focal point back to the audience.

MR. KAY: Yes, and now be specific—*describe* who you are talking to.

NOAH: Um . . . A FISHERMAN.

MR. KAY: And text?

NOAH: a very ancient and fish-like smell.

MR. KAY: Very good. Next tool?

NOAH: Image.

MR. KAY: What image?

NOAH: I SEE TWO HEADS!
   A strange fish!

MR. KAY: Next tool?

NOAH: I'm shifting my focus back to THE AUDIENCE.

MR. KAY: Good, and describe who you're talking to.

NOAH: AN ENGLISHMAN.

Were I in England now,

MR. KAY: Next tool?

NOAH: I'm shifting my focus to AN UGLY AMERICAN.

(as once I was)

MR. KAY: Next tool?

NOAH: Image.

MR. KAY: Yes, what image?

NOAH: I SEE A HUGE FISH SIGN ON A TALL POLE.

and had but this fish painted,

MR. KAY: Next tool?

NOAH: I'm shifting my focus to A TOURIST

not a holiday fool there but would give a piece of silver.

MR. KAY: Next tool?

NOAH: Subtext.

MR. KAY: Yes?

NOAH: I HOPE THIS MONSTER WILL MAKE ME RICH.

There would this monster make a man.

MR. KAY: Very good. Next tool?

NOAH: I'm shifting to A BANKER.

When they will not give a doit to relieve a lame beggar,

MR. KAY: Next tool?

NOAH: I'm shifting to A NATIVE AMERICAN.

they will lay out ten to see a dead Indian.

MR. KAY: Next tool?

NOAH: Action.

MR. KAY: Yes, what action?

NOAH: TO AUTOPSY.

Legg'd like a man; and his fins like arms!

MR. KAY: Good, next tool?

NOAH: Image.

MR. KAY: Yes? What do you see-hear-taste-touch-smell?

NOAH: IT'S WARM TO THE TOUCH!

Warm, o' my troth!

MR. KAY: Next tool?

NOAH: Subtext?

MR. KAY: Yes, what?

NOAH: A REALIZATION.

MR. KAY: Yes, what do you realize?

NOAH: I REALIZE THAT THIS IS NOT A FISH.

I do now let loose my opinion, hold it no longer:

MR. KAY: Next tool?

NOAH: I'm shifting to A HAWAIIAN GIRL.

this is no fish, but an islander,

MR. KAY: Next tool?

NOAH: I'm shifting to A DOCTOR.

that hath lately suffered by a thunder-bolt.

MR. KAY: Next tool?

NOAH: Image.

MR. KAY: Yes? What do you see-hear-taste-touch-smell?

NOAH: I SEE A LIGHTNING FLASH!

Alas, the storm is come again!

MR. KAY: Next tool, Trinculo?

NOAH: Subtext.

MR. KAY: Yes, what?

NOAH: A DECISION.

MR. KAY: What's your decision?

NOAH: I'M GOING TO KEEP HIS GABERDINE.

My best way is to creep under his gaberdine;

MR. KAY: Next tool?

NOAH: I'm shifting my focus to A LITTLE BOY.

there is no other shelter hereabout.

MR. KAY: Next tool?

NOAH: Action.

MR. KAY: Yes, what action?

NOAH: TO TAKE THE PLUNGE.

> *(Noah dives under the coat.)*

MR. KAY: So there's no text for that measure. Next tool?

NOAH: Subtext.

MR. KAY: Yes, what?

NOAH: A REALIZATION.

MR. KAY: Yes, what do you realize, Trinculo?

NOAH: I REALIZE THAT MISERY ACQUAINTS A MAN WITH STRANGE BEDFELLOWS.
Misery acquaints a man with strange bedfellows.

MR. KAY: Yes, next tool?

NOAH: Subtext.

MR. KAY: Yes, what?

NOAH: I MUST MAKE THE BEST OF IT.
I will here shroud till the dregs of the storm be past.

MR. KAY: Excellent, Noah. Now you have an orchestration which is *repeatable,* but allows for *spontaneity* from moment to moment.

You might think of it like downhill skiing—the gates are fixed, but you'll never go down the hill the same way twice.

Thank you, Noah. Well done.

(Noah comes down off the stage.)

(To the class) Just for the record, I want to make it clear that this is a challenge that you *all* will face in your careers in the theater—the challenge of achieving this seemingly impossible balance—how to make it *repeatable,* so everyone else can do their jobs, and how to make it *spontaneous,* even after 153 performances.

Who hasn't had a chance to work today?

〜 EMOTION 〜

TAYO: I'm up!

(Tayo goes up onto the stage.)

MR. KAY: What are you going to be showing us, Tayo?

TAYO: Lady Percy, from *Henry the Fourth, Part Two.*

MR. KAY: All right. And if you would place yourself in your scene, please, so I can ask you a few questions.

(Tayo stands center stage and gazes outward.)

Where are you, Lady Percy?

TAYO: I'm in a castle in Northumberland.

MR. KAY: And who are you talking to?

TAYO: The Earl of Northumberland.

MR. KAY: And what's your relationship to him?

TAYO: He's my husband's father.

MR. KAY: I see. And who is your husband?

TAYO: My husband was Harry Percy, but he was known as Hotspur.

MR. KAY: And where is he now?

TAYO: He's dead.

MR. KAY: I'm sorry. How did he die?

TAYO: He was killed in the last battle against the King.

MR. KAY: Who killed him?

TAYO: Prince Hal, the King's son, killed him.

MR. KAY: And did the rebels lose that battle?

TAYO: Yes.

MR. KAY: Why?

TAYO: Because Northumberland didn't send the soldiers he promised to my husband.

MR. KAY: I see. So what did Northumberland do when he heard his son had been killed?

TAYO: When he heard the news, he made an oath to rejoin the fight against King Henry.

MR. KAY: Yes. So why are you talking to Northumberland? What do you want from your father-in-law?

TAYO: I want to convince him to break that oath.

MR. KAY: Why? Why don't you want him to fight?

TAYO: I don't want to see any more of my family killed.

MR. KAY: Yes, and what are the obstacles? What makes it hard to convince him to break his oath?

TAYO: His sense of honor.

MR. KAY: Yes. Anything else?

TAYO: Well, the fact that I'm a woman, and have no power, and am not taken seriously in matters of war.

MR. KAY: Anything else?

TAYO: Um . . . I don't think so.

MR. KAY: All right, then, let's see if you can get him to break his oath. Begin, please.

LADY PERCY: O, yet, for God's sake, go not to these wars;
 The time was, father, that your broke your word
 When you were more endear'd to it than now,
 When your own Percy, when my heart's dear Harry,
 Threw many a northward look to see his father
 Bring up his powers; but he did long in vain.
 Who then persuaded you to stay at home?
 There were two honors lost, yours and your son's.
 For yours, the God of heaven brighten it;
 For his, it stuck upon him as the sun
 In the gray vault of heaven, and by his light
 Did all the chivalry of England move
 To do brave acts. He was indeed the glass
 Wherein the noble youth did dress themselves,
 So that in speech, in gait,
 In military rules, humors of blood,
 He was the mark and glass, copy and book,
 That fashion'd others. And him—O wondrous him!
 O miracle of men! him did you leave,
 Second to none, unseconded by you,
 To look upon the hideous god of war
 In disadvantage, to abide a field
 Where nothing but the sound of Hotspur's name
 Did seem defensible: so you left him.
 Never, O never do his ghost the wrong
 To hold your honor more precise and nice
 With others than with him. Let them alone.
 Lord Mowbray and the Archbishop are strong.
 Had my sweet Harry had but half their numbers

Today might I, hanging on Hotspur's neck,
Have talk'd of Monmouth's grave.

MR. KAY: Good, Tayo, good. I noticed you've made a few nips and tucks in the speech, which I think work well.

Now, let's make sure we understand every word of the speech before we look at it again.

What do you mean by "When you were more endear'd to it than now"?

TAYO: You once made an oath even more solemn than this one.

MR. KAY: What do you mean by "all the chivalry of England"?

TAYO: Every English soldier.

MR. KAY: What do you mean by "He was indeed the glass wherein the noble youth did dress themselves"?

TAYO: Every young nobleman wanted to be exactly like Harry Percy.

MR. KAY: What do you mean by "humors of blood"?

TAYO: His temperament.

MR. KAY: What do you mean by "He was the mark and glass, copy and book"?

TAYO: He was the target, the mirror, the model, and the manual for other men.

MR. KAY: What do you mean by "to abide a field"?

TAYO: To face a battle.

MR. KAY: What do you mean by "more precise and nice"?

TAYO: More meticulously kept.

MR. KAY: Who is "Monmouth"?

TAYO: Prince Hal, the son of King Henry the Fourth.

MR. KAY: Good. Now, I was trying to give you a hint, Tayo, before you started, because I think there's an *obstacle* in this scene that you may have forgotten. Can you think of what it is?

TAYO: Um, no, I don't know—what did I forget?

MR. KAY: Lady Percy's *emotions*.

TAYO: Her emotions?

MR. KAY: Yes. You've got to remember that the speech is not about what *you* feel, it's about making *him* feel something so he will change his mind, and stay.

Your tears, your anger, and your bitterness cannot be used as *tactics* to convince Northumberland to break his oath. If anything, your emotions are getting in the way. Because the more emotional you get, the easier it is for him to dismiss you as an irrational woman.

So remember, when we go through the scene again, you must choose strong actions and evocative images that make *him* feel something. You must convince him to stay *despite* your emotions. All right?

TAYO: Yes. I see that.

MR. KAY: Good, so let's try this again, please. And this time through, I'm not going to ask you which tool you intend to use. I'm simply going to ask you to make your own acting choices from measure to measure, then tell us that choice aloud before you speak. All right?

TAYO: I'll do my best.

MR. KAY: I'm sure you will. Then if you'd restore the scene in your imagination, please.

(Tayo does so.)

And remind us, please, Lady Percy—what's your objective?

TAYO: To convince Northumberland to break his oath to fight against the King.

MR. KAY: Yes, and acting choice for your first measure?

TAYO: I MUST STOP HIM FROM GOING.

MR. KAY: And text?

TAYO: O, yet, for God's sake, go not to these wars;

MR. KAY: Acting choice for your second measure?

TAYO: I WANT TO MAKE HIM FEEL HYPOCRITICAL.

The time was, father, that your broke your word
When you were more endear'd to it than now,

MR. KAY: Acting choice for the third measure?

TAYO: I WANT TO MAKE HIM FEEL REMORSEFUL.

When your own Percy, when my heart's dear Harry,

MR. KAY: Acting choice for the fourth measure?

TAYO: I SEE HOTSPUR, LOOKING NORTHWARD.

Threw many a northward look to see his father
Bring up his powers;

MR. KAY: Choice for the fifth measure?

TAYO: I WANT TO MAKE HIM FEEL GUILTY.

but he did long in vain.

MR. KAY: Choice for the sixth measure?

TAYO: TO ADMONISH.

Who then persuaded you to stay at home?

MR. KAY: Choice for the next measure?

TAYO: HONORS.

There were two *honors* lost,

MR. KAY: Choice for the next measure?

TAYO: TO SPELL OUT.

yours and your son's.

MR. KAY: Choice for the next measure?

TAYO: YOURS.

For *yours,*

MR. KAY: Next choice?

TAYO: TO BLESS.

the God of heaven brighten it;

MR. KAY: Next choice?

TAYO: HIS.

For *his,*

MR. KAY: Next choice?

TAYO: I SEE THE SUN.

it stuck upon him as the sun
In the gray vault of heaven,

MR. KAY: Next choice?

TAYO: I SEE SOLDIERS, DRENCHED IN SUNLIGHT.

and by his light
Did all the chivalry of England move
To do brave acts.

MR. KAY: Choice?

TAYO: I SEE A MIRROR.

He was indeed the glass

MR. KAY: Choice?

TAYO: I SEE A YOUNG BOY, PLAYING SOLDIER.

Wherein the noble youth did dress themselves,

MR. KAY: Choice?

TAYO: I HEAR MY HUSBAND'S VOICE.

So that in speech

MR. KAY: Choice?

TAYO: I SEE HIS WALK.

in gait,

MR. KAY: Choice?

TAYO: I SEE MY HUSBAND, IN ARMS.

In military rules,

MR. KAY: Next choice?

TAYO: I SEE MY HUSBAND, ANGRY.

humors of blood,

MR. KAY: Next choice?

TAYO: I WANT TO MAKE HIM FEEL PROUD.

He was the mark and glass, copy and book,
That fashion'd others.

MR. KAY: Next choice?

TAYO: I FEEL MY HUSBAND'S ROUGH FACE.

And him—

MR. KAY: Next choice?

TAYO: I SEE MY HUSBAND, ON HORSEBACK.

O wondrous him!

(Tayo is on the verge of tears.)

MR. KAY: Keep control of it now, Lady Percy! Obstacle?

(She suppresses her tears.)

TAYO: MY EMOTIONS.

O miracle of men!

MR. KAY: Good! Acting choice for the next measure?

TAYO: TO BLAME.

him did you leave,

MR. KAY: Choice for the next measure?

TAYO: TO GLORIFY.

Second to none,

MR. KAY: Next measure?

TAYO: I WANT TO MAKE HIM FEEL RESPONSIBLE.
unseconded by you,

MR. KAY: Next measure?

TAYO: I SEE THE GOD OF WAR.
To look upon the hideous god of war
In disadvantage,

MR. KAY: Next measure?

TAYO: I SEE THE BATTLEFIELD.
to abide a field

MR. KAY: Choice for the next measure?

TAYO: I HEAR SOLDIERS SHOUTING!
Where nothing but the sound of Hotspur's name
Did seem defensible:

MR. KAY: Next choice?

TAYO: I WANT TO MAKE HIM FEEL ASHAMED.
so you left him.

THE MASTER: Choice?

TAYO: TO INSIST.
Never,

MR. KAY: Choice?

TAYO: TO DEMAND.
O never do his ghost the wrong

MR. KAY: Choice?

TAYO: TO REPRIMAND.
To hold your honor more precise and nice
With others than with him.

MR. KAY: Choice?

TAYO: TO IMPLORE.
Let them alone.

MR. KAY: Choice?

TAYO: TO PROTEST.

Lord Mowbray and the Archbishop are strong.

MR. KAY: Choice?

TAYO: I WANT TO MAKE HIM FEEL CONTRITE.

Had my sweet Harry had but half their numbers,

MR. KAY: Choice?

TAYO: I WISH MY HUSBAND WERE ALIVE TODAY.

Today might I,

MR. KAY: Choice?

TAYO: I FEEL MY HUSBAND'S NECK.

hanging on Hotspur's neck,

MR. KAY: Choice?

TAYO: I SEE PRINCE HARRY, DEAD.

Have talk'd of Monmouth's grave.

MR. KAY: Very good, Tayo. You made some great acting choices, *specific* choices using a *variety* of tools inspired by the text that made every moment of the speech absolutely clear. Well done.

You also showed us that by using emotion as an *obstacle* to the speech, you won't have to struggle to dredge up those feelings each and every time you do the scene. If strong emotions arise as a *result* of playing your orchestration, that's great. But if those emotions elude you, that's fine, too.

Thank you, Tayo.

(Tayo comes down off the stage.)

(To the class) Remember, folks, emotion is undependable, it's fickle, it's treacherous. Don't trust it, don't count on it, don't rely on it.

You must never attempt to build a role upon the shifting sands of emotion. Instead, build your performance upon the bedrock of a carefully orchestrated score. It will be there for you when you need it.

(Mr. Kay looks at the clock.)

We're just about out of time, folks.

For tomorrow, please keep working on these speeches, using all of your tools to create a complex orchestration. After you've done that work on your feet through trial and error, I'd like you to create a written *score* which specifies your choices for each speech measure in your text.

I want to emphasize that the written score is a way of *recording* the work you've already done on your feet through trial and error. You should not attempt to create a score from your head while sitting in a comfy chair, sipping a Mocha Frappuccino.

(The class laughs.)

Tomorrow, please bring those scores with you to the acting studio.

See you tomorrow.

BLACKOUT.

SCENE 7

Towards Performance

The Acting Studio. Sunday.

MR. KAY: Good morning, folks.

Yesterday we looked at how to create complex orchestrations using all of the acting tools now available to us.

Today we're going to start looking at how your orchestration becomes part of a larger artistic endeavor—the performance of a play.

We're going to take a closer look at *objectives,* and how they serve as a foundation upon which you can build a role, moment by moment, into a performance.

PREVISUALIZATION

But before we begin that work, I'd like to take a few moments to try what Einstein used to call a "thought-experiment."

I'd like to ask you to sit quietly, as if you were waiting for your turn at an audition. You can do this with eyes shut if you like, but open is better.

First, I'd like you ask yourself, silently, the four basic questions:

"Where am I? Who am I talking to? What do I hope to accomplish? What obstacles are preventing me from accomplishing that?"

Then, I'd like you to run through your speeches—not by muttering your lines under your breath, as many actors do, but *silently,* in your *mind,* by recalling your *orchestration* from moment to moment.

Go through your orchestration—measure to measure, focal point to focal point, image to image, subtext to subtext, action to action.

Visualize the sequence of things which *inspire* your text, rather than going through the text itself.

Don't skip steps. Be specific! If you can't remember what comes next, check your written score.

You *know* the words. Don't worry about the words. What *inspires* the words? That's the thing to take into that audition with you.

Your orchestration is what harnesses the power of your imagination.

Your orchestration is what keeps the speech spontaneous and alive.

Your orchestration is what reveals your unique qualities as an actor.

They've seen a hundred actors today! What distinguishes you from the two other Juliets, the five other Violas, the seven other Benedicks?

Your orchestration.

Ready? And begin.

(A two-minute silence as the students sit quietly and previsualize their orchestrations.)

And when you're finished, just relax, please.

(Slowly, one by one, the students relax.)

Very good. And I hope the point of that experiment is clear to you now— that if you have a detailed and specific orchestration, you can prepare for an audition virtually *anywhere*—on the subway, in a booth at a coffee shop, and yes, even while sitting in the casting agent's office waiting for your turn. Make sense?

(The students nod affirmatively.)

Good. Now would you all please hand me the written *scores* that I asked you to prepare for today.

(The students dig into their bags and backpacks.)

Today I'm going to ask you to perform your orchestrations just as you've rehearsed them and recorded them in your written scores.

You'll be flying solo, without side-coaching or prompting from me.

I've asked you to do this because that's ultimately what you're going to have to do in the profession—take responsibility for your own work. You're going to have to be able to work independently, without my help, or even, at times, the help of a director.

In other words, you're going to have to learn how to "pack your own parachute."

(The students laugh as they pass their scores back to Mr. Kay.)

Thank you.

Who wants to go first?

✑ SCENE OBJECTIVES ✑

TIM: I will!

(Tim goes up onto the stage.)

MR. KAY: Thanks, Tim. What are you going to show us today?

TIM: Coriolanus, from *Coriolanus*.

MR. KAY: All right. If you would place yourself in your scene, please, while I ask you a few questions.

(Tim stands center stage and gazes outward.)

Where are you, Coriolanus?

TIM: In the city of Antium.

MR. KAY: What are you doing in Antium? Aren't you a Roman?

TIM: Yes, but I've just been banished from Rome. So I've come to Antium to find my arch enemy, Aufidius.

MR. KAY: Who is Aufidius?

TIM: The general of the Volsces.

MR. KAY: I see. So who are you talking to now?

TIM: To myself, and to the city.

MR. KAY: I see. And what do you hope to accomplish by talking to yourself and to the city? What's the *speech* objective?

TIM: To decide whether to approach Aufidius.

MR. KAY: I see. So you're not entirely sure whether you should approach him?

TIM: No, not yet.

MR. KAY: Are there any other obstacles?

TIM: Well, I'm not armed, and I'm in disguise, but someone might recognize me, and I could be caught at any moment. Besides that, Aufidius hates me and might kill me when I show up at his door.

MR. KAY: Good, and what's your *scene* objective?

TIM: My scene objective?

MR. KAY: Yes. What do you hope to accomplish before the *scene* is over?

TIM: Um . . . I hope to make an alliance with Aufidius to destroy Rome.

MR. KAY: Good, then let's hear how you convince yourself to approach Aufidius in order to make an alliance with him. Begin, please.

CORIOLANUS: A goodly city is this Antium. City,
    'Tis I that made thy widows. Many an heir
    Of these fair edifices 'fore my wars
    Have I heard groan and drop. Then know me not,
    Lest that thy wives with spits and boys with stones
    In puny battle slay me.
    O world, thy slipp'ry turns! Friends now fast sworn,
    Whose double bosoms seem to wear one heart,
    Whose hours, whose bed, whose meal and exercise
    Are still together, who twin as 'twere in love
    Unseparable, shall within this hour,
    On dissension of a doit, break out
    To bitt'rest enmity. So fellest foes,
    Whose passions and whose plots have broke their sleep
    To take the one the other, by some chance,
    Some trick not worth an egg, shall grow dear friends,
    And interjoin their issues. So with me.
    My birthplace hate I, and my love's upon
    This en'my town. I'll enter. If Aufidius slay me,
    He does fair justice; if he give me way,
    I'll do his country service.

MR. KAY: Thank you, Tim. That's a good speech you've put together from two smaller speeches. Well done.

Now, before we look this it again, let's make sure we understand every word of the text.

What do you mean by "fair edifices"?

TIM: Handsome buildings.

MR. KAY: What do you mean by "'fore my wars"?

TIM: During my assaults.

MR. KAY: What do you mean by "puny battle"?

TIM: A petty brawl.

MR. KAY: What are "wives with spits"?

TIM: Women with iron rods used for roasting meat.

MR. KAY: What do you mean by "slipp'ry turns"?

TIM: Unpredictable changes.

MR. KAY: What do you mean by "still together"?

TIM: Always together.

MR. KAY: What do you mean by "dissension of a doit"?

TIM: A fight over next to nothing.

MR. KAY: What do you mean by "fellest foes"?

TIM: Deadliest enemies.

MR. KAY: What do you mean by "whose plots have broke their sleep to take the one the other"?

TIM: Who are kept awake nights plotting how to kill each other.

MR. KAY: What do you mean by "some trick not worth an egg"?

TIM: For petty reasons.

MR. KAY: What do you mean by "interjoin their issues"?

TIM: Make an alliance.

MR. KAY: What do you mean by "If he give me way"?

TIM: If he grants my request.

MR. KAY: Good, Tim. Now, one of the things I want you to keep in mind when we do this again is that this speech is not at all typical for the character.

Coriolanus is not a circumspect man, like Hamlet, but a man of action, a warrior. In fact, this is the *only* moment in the play when we see him alone, thinking about how his life has suddenly led him to an unexpected place. And it does not come naturally to him.

So when we orchestrate this speech, I want you to keep in mind that the images, the actions, the realizations, and the decisions of the speech are not those of a philosopher/poet. These are the reflections of a warrior trying to decide whether to destroy his own birthplace, Rome, with the help of his bitterest enemy.

So the images you choose should be concrete, not abstract; the actions direct, not oblique; the realizations visceral, not intellectual; and his decision to act definitive, not doubtful.

So let's look at this again, Tim, and this time through, I'd like you to say your orchestrated choices aloud before you speak each speech measure.

And as I said before, I won't be side-coaching you today. I may stop you occasionally to make a comment, or ask a question, but I'll try to do that as little as possible. All right?

TIM: Yes, that's fine.

MR. KAY: Good. Then if you would restore your scene in your imagination, please.

(Tim does so.)

And please remind us—what's your speech objective, Coriolanus?

TIM: To decide whether to approach Aufidius.

MR. KAY: And begin, please.

TIM: I REALIZE THAT MY ENEMIES HAVE BUILT A BEAUTIFUL CITY.

A goodly city is this Antium.

TO INTRODUCE MYSELF (TO THE CITY).

City,
'Tis I that made thy widows

I SEE BEDROOM WINDOWS.

Many an heir
Of these fair edifices

I HEAR VOLSCIAN SOLDIERS, DYING.

'fore my wars
Have I heard groan and drop.

TO HUSH (THE CITY).

Then know me not,

I SEE WOMEN WITH PIKES.

Lest that thy wives with spits

I SEE BOYS WITH STONES.

and boys with stones

I SEE MYSELF, BEING KILLED BY THE RABBLE.

In puny battle slay me.

I REALIZE THAT MY WORLD HAS BEEN TURNED UPSIDE DOWN.

O world, thy slipp'ry turns!

I SEE MENENIUS.

MR. KAY: And who is Menenius?

TIM: My most trusted friend.

MR. KAY: Good. Continue, please.

TIM: Friends now fast sworn,

I SEE A PURPLE HEART.

Whose double bosoms seem to wear one heart,

I HEAR A MILITARY DRUM.

Whose hours,

I FEEL MYSELF SLEEPING ON THE GROUND.

whose bed,

I SEE A MILITARY CAMP.

whose meal and exercise
Are still together,

I SEE MY YOUNG SON, MARTIUS.

who twin as 'twere in love
Unseparable,

I SEE A CLOCK TOWER.

shall within this hour,

I SEE A SMALL COIN.

On dissension of a doit,

I SEE MYSELF, SHUNNING MENENIUS.

break out
To bitt'rest enmity.

I SEE AUFIDIUS IN ARMS.

So fellest foes,

I SEE MYSELF PACING IN THE DARK.

Whose passions and whose plots have broke their sleep

I SEE MYSELF KILLING AUFIDIUS.

To take the one the other,

I SEE ROLLING DICE.

by some chance,

I SEE AN EGG.

Some trick not worth an egg,

I SEE MYSELF EMBRADING AUFIDIUS.

shall grow dear friends,

I SEE ROME IN RUINS.

And interjoin their issues.

I REALIZE THERE'S NO CONSTANCY IN FRIENDS NOR FOES.

So with me.

I SEE THE TRIBUNES OF ROME.

My birthplace hate I,

I SEE A STATUE OF A VOLSCIAN WARRIOR.

and my love's upon
This en'my town.

I'M GOING TO GO THROUGH WITH MY PLAN.

I'll enter.

TO STEEL MYSELF.

If Aufidius slay me,
He does fair justice;

TO VOW.

if he give me way,
I'll do his country service.

MR. KAY: So, does Coriolanus achieve his *speech* objective? Does he make a decision?

TIM: Yes, he decides to approach Aufidius.

MR. KAY: And does he achieve his *scene* objective? Does Aufidius agree to form an alliance to destroy Rome?

TIM: Yes, he does.

MR. KAY: *(To Tim)* Thank you, Tim. Well done.

(Tim comes down off the stage.)

(To the class) For those of you who don't know the play, this decision is a tragic mistake for Coriolanus. Because his decision to help Aufidius to destroy Rome leads directly to his own downfall and death. It's the fatally flawed decision of a warrior unable to cope with the politics of peace.

But I think you'll find that nearly *all* of the tragic characters in Shakespeare make *fatally flawed decisions* similar to this one.

Can you think of other examples of what I mean?

(The class thinks for a moment.)

JAKE: Othello decides to kill his wife.

GABRIELLA: Hamlet decides to fence with Laertes.

MADISON: Romeo decides to poison himself in Juliet's tomb.

DANTE: Brutus decides to let Antony speak at Caesar's funeral.

JESSE: Macbeth decides to kill Macduff's wife and children.

ELENA: Hector decides to ignore his family's pleas and fight Achilles.

MR. KAY: Excellent. So my advice to you, when you have the opportunity to play one of these great roles—and I hope you will—is to find the flawed decision, and work backwards from it, orchestrating each moment so that it leads you relentlessly to the fatal mistake.

So who's up next?

ᘒᘐ Act Objectives ᘒᘐ

TRINITY: I am!

(Trinity goes up onto the stage.)

MR. KAY: What are you going to show us today, Trinity?

TRINITY: Tamora, from *Titus Andronicus.*

MR. KAY: All right. Would place yourself in your scene, please, so I can ask you a few questions.

(Trinity stands center stage and gazes outward.)

Where are you, Tamora?

TAMORA: In Rome.

MR. KAY: Where in Rome?

TRINITY: On the steps of the Pantheon.

MR. KAY: And who are you talking to?

TRINITY: To the emperor, Saturninus, and to my enemy, Titus Andronicus.

MR. KAY: Why? What do you hope to accomplish by talking to the emperor and to Titus? What's your *speech* objective?

TRINITY: I want to reconcile them.

MR. KAY: Why? Why do you want to reconcile them?

TRINITY: I want to reconcile them now in *public,* so I can destroy the Andronicus family later without being suspected.

MR. KAY: And what's preventing you from reconciling them now? What's the obstacle?

TRINITY: The emperor is stubborn and impetuous, and Titus hates and distrusts me.

MR. KAY: And what's your *scene* objective?

TRINITY: To win Titus' trust.

MR. KAY: And you must conceal your true intentions in order to win his trust?

TRINITY: Yes.

MR. KAY: So what's your *act* objective?

TRINITY: My act objective?

MR. KAY: Yes—what's the one thing you hope to accomplish before the act is over?

TRINITY: I hope to destroy the Andronicus family.

MR. KAY: Good, then let's see how you reconcile the emperor and Titus in order to win Titus' trust in order to destroy the Andronicus family.

Begin, please.

TAMORA: My worthy lord, if ever Tamora
Were gracious in those princely eyes of thine,
Then hear me speak indiff'rently for all,
And at my suit, sweet, pardon what is past.
The gods of Rome forfend
I should be author to dishonor you,
But on mine honor dare I undertake
For good Lord Titus' innocence in all,
Whose fury not dissembl'd speaks his griefs:
Then at my suit, look graciously on him.
(Aside to Saturninus)
My lord, by rul'd by me, be won at last,
Dissemble all your griefs and discontents.
You are but newly planted in your throne;
Lest, then, the people, and patricians too,
Upon a just survey take Titus' part,
Yield at entreats; and then let me alone.
I'll find a day to massacre them all,
And raze their faction and their family,
The cruel father, and his trait'rous sons,
To whom I suèd for my dear son's life,
And make them know what 'tis to let a queen
Kneel in the streets and beg for grace in vain.
(Aloud)
Come, come, sweet emperor; come, Andronicus,
This day all quarrels die,
And let it be mine honor, good my lord,
That I have reconcil'd your friends and you.

MR. KAY: Good, Trinity. I like the way you've cut and pasted this speech together, and I'll tell you why in just a moment. But first, let's make sure we understand the text completely.

What do you mean when you say "Then hear me speak indiff'rently for all"?

TRINITY: I'll speak impartially for the good of everyone here.

MR. KAY: What do you mean by "The gods of Rome forfend"?

TRINITY: Heaven forbid.

MR. KAY: What do you mean by "Whose fury not dissembl'd speaks his griefs"?

TRINITY: Whose raw anger proves his grief is genuine.

MR. KAY: What do you mean by "a just survey"?

TRINITY: A good, honest look.

MR. KAY: Yes. And what do you mean by "Yield at entreats"?

TRINITY: Do what I ask you to do.

MR. KAY: What do you mean by "And raze their faction and their family"?

TRINITY: And destroy the Andronicus family and their supporters.

MR. KAY: What do you mean by "I suèd for my dear son's life"?

TRINITY: I begged in the street for mercy for my first born son, Alarbus.

MR. KAY: What do you mean by "your friends"?

TRINITY: Titus' family.

MR. KAY: Good, good, Trinity. Now, as I said, I think you've done fine job of editing this speech, and the reason is that it allows you to show Tamora deftly handling the situation in both *public* and *private* moments.

(To the class) The thing to remember here, folks, is that Tamora may be called a barbarian by the Romans, but she's no fool. She's been the ruler of the Goths for many years, and her political experience far exceeds that of Saturninus, who's been emperor of Rome for only a few *hours*.

In this speech, we get a chance to see her cool political savvy in action as she pursues her act objective—to destroy the Andronicus family. She manages to disguise her grief for her son's slaughter—appearing to be the compassionate peacemaker with Titus in public, while advising Saturninus on how to get revenge on the Andronicus family in private. A perfectly executed political juggling act.

(To Trinity) So let's look at this again, Trinity, and with this in mind, I'm going to ask you to tell us *aloud* when you're speaking in public, and when in private, so we can really see the two faces of Tamora.

Also, let's concentrate in particular on the *actions* Tamora plays, because it's these verbs which will reveal her true nature to the audience, who can hear both the public and the private.

So, if you would restore your scene in your imagination, please.

(Trinity does so.)

And remind us, please—what's your speech objective, Tamora?

TRINITY: TO RECONCILE TITUS AND SATURNINUS.

MR. KAY: And is this first moment *public* or *private*?

TRINITY: PUBLIC.

MR. KAY: Good, and begin, please.

TRINITY: SATURNINUS.

My worthy lord,

TO INGRATIATE.

if ever Tamora
Were gracious in those princely eyes of thine,

TO REQUEST.

Then hear me speak indiff'rently for all,
And at my suit,

TO SWEET-TALK.

sweet,

PARDON.

pardon what is past.

TO SWEAR.

The gods of Rome forfend
I should be author to dishonor you,

TO DEFEND.

But on mine honor dare I undertake
For good Lord Titus' innocence in all,

TITUS.

Whose fury not dissembl'd speaks his griefs:

TO ENTREAT.

Then at my suit, look graciously on him.

I NEED TO PULL SATURNINUS ASIDE.

MR. KAY: Is this *public* or *private*?

TRINITY: PRIVATE.

(She pulls Saturninus aside.)

My lord,

TO OVERRULE.

by rul'd by me,

TO INSIST.

be won at last,

TO COUNSEL.

Dissemble all your griefs and discontents.

TO JOG HIS MEMORY.

You are but newly planted in your throne;

TO CAUTION.

Lest, then, the people, and patricians too,
Upon a just survey take Titus' part,

TO DEMAND.

Yield at entreats;

TO TAKE CHARGE.

and then let me alone.

TO VOW.

I'll find a day to massacre them all,

I SEE A BLOODBATH.

And raze their faction and their family,

I SEE TITUS AND HIS SONS, DISMEMBERED.

The cruel father, and his trait'rous sons,

I SEE MY SON ALARBUS, DRAGGED AWAY IN CHAINS.

To whom I suèd for my dear son's life,

I SEE MYSELF, KNEELING IN THE STREET.

And make them know what 'tis to let a queen
Kneel in the streets and beg for grace in vain.

MR. KAY: Good! And is this next speech measure *public* or *private*?

TRINITY: PUBLIC.

MR. KAY: So this is now *public* again?

TRINITY: Yes.

MR. KAY: So you want everyone present to hear this?

TRINITY: Oh, yes! I want to be seen as the peacemaker.

MR. KAY: Good—continue, please.

TRINITY: TO COAX.

Come, come, sweet emperor;

TO BEFRIEND.

come, Andronicus,

TO DECLARE PEACE.

This day all quarrels die,

TO TAKE CREDIT.

And let it be mine honor, good my lord,

TO RECONCILE.

That I have reconcil'd your friends and you.

MR. KAY: Excellent, Trinity. Now we can really see, through Tamora's *actions,* the public and private machinations of one of Shakespeare's most Machiavellian characters.

By the way, does Tamora get her *speech* objective? Does she publicly reconcile these two men?

TRINITY: Yes, she does.

MR. KAY: And does she get her *scene* objective? Does she win Titus' trust?

TRINITY: Yes, for the moment.

MR. KAY: And does she get her *act* objective? Does she destroy the Andronicus family?

TRINITY: Yes, very nearly.

MR. KAY: How?

TRINITY: Well, let's see. First, she tells her two sons to rape Titus' daughter Lavinia. So they both rape her, and cut off her hands, and slice out her tongue. Then Tamora accuses Titus' two sons, Martius and Quintus, of murdering the emperor's brother. So the emperor cuts off the two boys' heads and banishes Titus' eldest son, Lucius, from Rome. Then Tamora's lover, Aaron, tricks Titus into cutting off his own right hand.

MR. KAY: Wow! And she accomplishes all that before the intermission?

TRINITY: Yes! That's just the first half of the play!

MR. KAY: I see. So, what happens to Tamora in the *second* half of the play?

TRINITY: Well, then Titus gets his revenge. He kills Tamora's two sons, bakes them in a pie, and serves them to her at a feast. Then he stabs her to death.

MR. KAY: I see.

(To the class) So Tamora *achieves* her act objective in the first half of the play—but just look at the consequences in the second half! The violence she unleashes comes back upon her own head, causing the destruction of her own family, and her death.

Which is, after all, the point of Shakespeare's bloodiest play—that violence begets more violence, and revenge breeds more revenge.

(To Trinity) Thank you, Trinity.

(Trinity comes down off the stage.)

MR. KAY: Who's next?

ᯤ Play Objectives ᯤ

JAKE: I'm ready!

(Jake goes up onto the stage.)

MR. KAY: And what are you going to show us today, Jake?

JAKE: Arcite, from *The Two Noble Kinsmen.*

MR. KAY: All right. If you would place yourself in your scene, please, so I can ask you a few questions.

(Jake stands center stage, gazing outward.)

Where are you, Arcite?

JAKE: I'm on the road, just outside Athens.

MR. KAY: And where are you going?

JAKE: I'm on my way home to Thebes.

MR. KAY: Why?

JAKE: I was a prisoner of war, but I've just been released from prison, and banished forever from Athens.

MR. KAY: I see. And who are you talking to?

JAKE: Myself.

MR. KAY: Why are you talking to yourself? What do you hope to accomplish?

JAKE: Well, I'm trying to talk myself into staying in Athens.

MR. KAY: Why? Why would you risk staying in Athens after you've been banished?

JAKE: To see my love, Emilia.

MR. KAY: I see. Then what's making it hard to talk yourself into staying? What are the obstacles?

JAKE: If I'm caught in Athens, I'll be put to death. But if I go home to Thebes, my cousin Palamon is sure to win Emilia.

MR. KAY: I see. So what happens once you decide to stay? What's your *scene* objective?

JAKE: To figure out how to avoid being caught.

MR. KAY: Yes, and your *act* objective?

JAKE: To win Emilia.

MR. KAY: Good, and your *play* objective?

JAKE: My play objective?

MR. KAY: Yes, what's the one thing you're pursuing throughout the entire play?

JAKE: Um . . . I guess . . . I want to prove that I'm more noble than my cousin.

MR. KAY: Yes, that's an excellent choice.

(To the class) Do you see how all these objectives fit together, by the way? All of your choices, no matter how small, must add up in such a way as to make it possible to achieve your larger objectives.

You're choosing a tool inside each measure in order to win your *speech* objective. You're pursuing your speech objective in order to win your *scene* objective. You're pursuing your scene objective in order to win your *act* objective. You're pursuing your act objective in order to win your *play* objective.

Make sense?

(Many nods of sudden enlightenment.)

MR. KAY: *(To Jake)* All right, then, let's see how you talk yourself into staying in Athens in order to figure out how to avoid being caught in order to win Emilia in order to prove you're more noble than your cousin Palamon.

Begin, please.

ARCITE: Banish'd the kingdom? 'Tis a benefit,
A mercy I must thank 'em for; but banish'd
The free enjoying of that face I die for,
O, 'twas a studied punishment, a death
Beyond imagination; such a vengeance
That, were I old and wicked, all my sins
Could never pluck upon me. Palamon,
Thou hast the start now; thou shalt stay and see
Her bright eyes break each morning 'gainst thy window,
And let in life into thee; thou shalt feed
Upon the sweetness of a noble beauty
That nature ne'er exceeded, nor ne'er shall.
Good gods, what happiness has Palamon!
Twenty to one, he'll come to speak to her,
And if she be as gentle as she's fair,
I know she's his; he has a tongue will tame
Tempests, and make the wild rocks wanton.
Come what can come,
The worst is death. I will not leave the kingdom.
I know mine own is but a heap of ruins,

And no redress there. If I go, he has her.
I am resolv'd another shape shall make me,
Or end my fortunes. Either way I'm happy:
I'll see her, and be near her, or no more.

MR. KAY: Good, good, Jake. Now, before we look at this again, let's make sure we understand the text completely.

What do you mean by "that face I die for?"

JAKE: Emilia's face.

MR. KAY: What do you mean by "a studied punishment"?

JAKE: A carefully thought-out punishment.

MR. KAY: What do you mean by "A death beyond imagination"?

JAKE: Dying in a way too horrible to be imagined.

MR. KAY: What do you mean by "Thou hast the start now"?

JAKE: You have the advantage, Palamon.

MR. KAY: What do you mean by "see her bright eyes break each morning 'gainst thy window"?

JAKE: Emilia's eyes will rise like the sun in Palamon's window every morning.

MR. KAY: What do you mean by "he'll come to speak to her"?

JAKE: Palamon will find some way to talk with her.

MR. KAY: What do you mean by "mine own is but a heap of ruins"?

JAKE: My own city, Thebes, has been destroyed by the war.

MR. KAY: What do you mean by "another shape shall make me"?

JAKE: A disguise will bring me success in Athens.

MR. KAY: What do you mean by "Or end my fortunes"?

JAKE: Or else I'll die trying.

MR. KAY: Good, Jake.

(To the class) I'm curious, folks—how many of you know this play? Has anybody ever actually seen it performed?

(No one raises a hand.)

Not surprising. It's actually a *collaboration* with another playwright of the time, John Fletcher.

(To Jake) In fact, you might be surprised to know, Jake, that this speech was probably written by Mr. Fletcher, and not by Mr. Shakespeare.

JAKE: *(Shocked)* Fletcher! I'm doing a speech by Fletcher?

(The class laughs.)

MR. KAY: Not to worry, though, it's still a good speech.

JAKE: I think it's a great speech.

MR. KAY: Yes. *(A new topic)* Now, let me ask you this, Jake—do you ever say Emilia's *name* in this speech?

JAKE: *(Pondering)* Um . . . no, I guess not. Hmm. I hadn't noticed that.

MR. KAY: That's an important clue, don't you think? Does he even *know* her name at this point?

JAKE: Um . . . no, I don't think he does.

MR. KAY: No, in fact, he doesn't. He doesn't find it out until later in the play.

So, he's willing to risk *death* to win a woman he's only glimpsed once, and whose name he doesn't even *know*?

JAKE: Yes. But she's the perfect woman!

(The class laughs.)

MR. KAY: Yes. Well, for those of you who don't know the play—which is *all* of you, evidently—Arcite and his cousin Palamon see this "perfect" woman in the garden, picking flowers underneath their prison window, and instantly start squabbling over who is the more worthy man to have her.

And how does this "noble" competition between cousins end? Let's wait and see.

But for now, you need to understand that the play is about *honor* and *chivalry*—tough things for an actor to play these days because they're so misunderstood and devalued and even ridiculed in our world.

And it would be very tempting to take a cynical approach to this material and "send it up." Or to mock it somehow in the playing of it. But that would be a grave mistake.

If anything, Jake, you have to take the *opposite* approach. You have play the chivalry in the speech with absolute conviction.

Because as an actor, it's your job to make choices which illuminate the play. It's your job to immerse yourself in the world of the playwright— whether it be Fletcher, or Molière, or Shaw, or Miller—and pursue the character's play objective with total abandon.

Which means you have to play Arcite's decision to stay in Athens, and his *reasons* for doing so—the pursuit of the perfect woman in order to prove himself more noble—with every fiber of your being.

You must pursue that play objective, even when the playwright seems to frown upon it. You must pursue that play objective, even when the play seems to condemn your character's code of conduct. You must pursue that play objective, even when the reviews are bad and theater is half-empty.

(The class laughs.)

So let's look at this speech again, Jake, and orchestrate it from speech measure to speech measure with all this in mind.

If you would restore your scene, please.

(Jake does so.)

And remind us, please, what's your speech objective?

JAKE: To talk myself into staying in Athens.

MR. KAY: Good, and begin, please.

JAKE: I REALIZE THAT I CAN NEVER RETURN TO ATHENS.

Banish'd the kingdom?

I SEE THESEUS.

'Tis a benefit,

I SEE THE ATHENIANS.

A mercy I must thank 'em for;

HEART.

but banish'd
The free enjoying of that face I die for,

I FEEL MY BODY STRETCHED OUT ON THE RACK.

O,

MR. KAY: Excellent! *(To the class)* There's a good example of a *one-sound speech measure*—a random vocalization on an "o" vowel!

(To Jake) Continue, please, Arcite.

JAKE: STUDIED.

'twas a *studied* punishment,

I FEEL MYSELF BURNING IN HOT OIL.

a death
Beyond imagination;

THE GODS.

such a vengeance
That,

I SEE MYSELF, AS AN OLD MAN.

were I old and wicked,

TO GRIEVE.

all my sins
Could never pluck upon me.

I SEE PALAMON.

Palamon,
Thou hast the start now;

I SEE EMILIA'S EYES, RISING LIKE THE SUN.

thou shalt stay and see
Her bright eyes break each morning 'gainst thy window,
And let in life into thee;

I SEE EMILIA IN THE GARDEN BELOW OUR WINDOW, PICKING FLOWERS.

thou shalt feed
Upon the sweetness of a noble beauty
That nature ne'er exceeded,

I SEE EMILIA SMELL A FLOWER.

nor ne'er shall.

TO COVET.

Good gods, what happiness has Palamon!

I'M AFRAID THAT PALAMON WILL WIN HER LOVE.

Twenty to one, he'll come to speak to her,
And if she be as gentle as she's fair,
I know she's his;

TO SPIT UPON.

he has a tongue will tame
Tempests,

MR. KAY: *(To the class)* And do you see how effective it is when he chooses an action that allows him to play that triple "t" sound built into the language?

(To Jake) Next speech measure, please, Arcite.

JAKE: GROIN.

and make the wild rocks wanton.

I REALIZE THAT I'D RATHER DIE THAN LOSE HER.

Come what can come,
The worst is death.

I'M NOT GOING TO LEAVE.

MR. KAY: Please phrase that decision positively!

(To the class) You understand, folks, that even if the *text* phrases a decision in the negative, you must convert it into positive action. What you're *not* going to do isn't playable! There are an infinite number of things

you're *not* going to do. You're not going to make a cheese sandwich. You're not going to have your teeth cleaned. But there is one thing, and *only* one thing you plan on doing next.

(To Jake) What is it? Tell us what you've decided to do—what action you will take next?

JAKE: I'M GOING TO STAY IN ATHENS.

I will not leave the kingdom.

MR. KAY: Excellent! Continue, please.

JAKE: HEAD.

I know mine own is but a heap of ruins,
And no redress there.

I SEE EMILIA, IN PALAMON'S ARMS, KISSING HIM.

If I go, he has her.

I'M GOING TO DISGUISE MYSELF.

I am resolv'd another shape shall make me,

I'M GOING TO RISK CAPTURE, AND DEATH.

Or end my fortunes.

I MUST WIN HER.

Either way I'm happy:

I NEED TO SEE HER AGAIN.

I'll see her,

I WANT TO BE NEAR HER.

and be near her,

I MUST PUT AN END TO MY MISERY.

or no more.

MR. KAY: Good, Jake. So, let me ask you this—does Arcite achieve his *speech* objective?

JAKE: Yes, he decides to stay in Athens.

MR. KAY: And does he achieve his *scene* objective? Does he figure out how to stay in Athens without being caught?

JAKE: Yes, he decides to wear a disguise and to compete in the Athenian games.

MR. KAY: And does he achieve his *act* objective? Does he win Emilia?

JAKE: Yes, he defeats Palamon in a tournament of knights set up by Theseus to decide who will have her.

MR. KAY: And does he achieve his *play* objective? Does he prove that he's more noble than his cousin?

JAKE: Well . . . no, actually . . .

MR. KAY: No? Why not?

JAKE: Well, he's killed in the end when his horse falls on him and crushes him. And so Palamon gets to marry Emilia.

MR. KAY: And they all live miserably ever after.

(The class laughs.)

Well done, Jake. Thank you.

(Jake comes down off the stage.)

(To the class) This kind of unexpected reversal of fortune, which happens several times during this play, is a good reminder that in the theater, as in life, fate has a way of intervening in human affairs. Sometimes on our behalf. And sometimes to destroy everything we hold dear.

Which reminds me—there are three things, and *only* three things, that can happen to you while you pursue your objective. Can anybody tell me what they are?

RACHEL: You can *win* your objective.

MR. KAY: Yes, Rachel, sometimes you win.

AVI: You can *fail* to win your objective,

MR. KAY: Yes, Avi, sometimes you lose. And the third?

GABRIELLA: Um . . . you can *change* to a different objective?

MR. KAY: Yes, you can get *sidetracked* to a new objective. Very good, Gabriella.

And it's important to keep those three things in mind when you orchestrate a role. So as you're rehearsing, keep asking yourself: "When do I win? When do I lose? When do I change my mind?" And remember to use the answers to those questions as signposts in the journey of the character.

Let's look at another speech. Who wants to work?

ᯅ SUPER-OBJECTIVES ᯊ

SAM: Me!

(Sam goes up onto the stage.)

MR. KAY: And what are you going to show us today, Sam?

SAM: Pericles, from *Pericles*.

MR. KAY: All right. If you would place yourself in your scene, please, so I can ask you a few questions.

(Sam stands center stage, gazing outward.)

Where are you, King Pericles?

SAM: I'm on the beach at Pentapolis.

MR. KAY: How did you get there?

SAM: Well, I've just been shipwrecked by a storm, and I've lost absolutely everything.

MR. KAY: I see. So who are you talking to?

SAM: I'm talking to two fishermen.

MR. KAY: Can you describe them?

SAM: Yes. One is old, and one is young.

MR. KAY: And why are you talking to these two fishermen? What do you hope to accomplish? What's your *speech* objective?

SAM: I want to convince them to let me have the armor they just found in their nets.

MR. KAY: Why do you want it?

SAM: Well, it was mine.

MR. KAY: Why can't you to convince them to give it to you? What are the obstacles?

SAM: Well, I'm a total stranger to these men. And I can't prove that I'm a king or a king's son. I'm wet, I'm cold, I'm practically naked, I'm exhausted . . .

MR. KAY: Good, and what's your *scene* objective?

SAM: I want the fishermen to take me to Pentapolis so I can joust in the King's tournament.

MR. KAY: And what's your *act* objective?

SAM: To win Thaisa, the princess of Pentapolis.

MR. KAY: And what's your *play* objective?

SAM: To secure the future of the Kingdom of Tyre.

MR. KAY: And what's your *super-objective*?

SAM: My super-objective?

MR. KAY: Yes, your super-objective.

(To the class) Do you all know what I mean by a super-objective?

(Blank stares abound.)

The *super-objective* is a single concept, or idea, or goal, that encompasses all of the character's objectives.

(The students write "super-objectives" in their notebooks.)

The super-objective must be phrased as *one word*—like Respect, or Happiness, or Knowledge, or Freedom.

And everything the character says and does during the play should point to that super-objective. Every speech measure, every speech, every scene, every act, every moment of the play, every moment of the character's *life*, must be driven by the relentless pursuit of the super-objective.

The challenge for the actor is to find that word—the one word that illuminates the motivation of the character from start to finish—and to orchestrate every moment of your performance to point to that word.

NOAH: Kind of like "Rosebud?"

(The class laughs.)

MR. KAY: Yes, Noah, kind of like "Rosebud."

(To Sam) So what is your super-objective, Pericles?

SAM: Um . . . I'm not sure.

MR. KAY: All right, then, listen to the speech, and maybe we can figure it out later.

SAM: Okay.

MR. KAY: Good, then let's see if you can convince the fishermen to give you the armor and take you Pentapolis so you can joust in the King's tournament in order to win the love of Princess Thaisa in order to secure the future of the Kingdom of Tyre.

Begin, please.

PERICLES: An armor, friends? I pray you let me see it.
Thanks, Fortune, yet that after all thy crosses
Thou giv'st me something to repair myself.
It was mine own, part of my heritage,
Which my dead father did bequeath to me,
With this strict charge, even as he left his life:
"Keep it, my Pericles; it hath been a shield
'Twixt me and death. For that it sav'd me, keep it.
In like necessity, (the which the gods
Protect thee from), may it defend thee."
It kept where I kept, I so dearly lov'd it,
Till the rough seas, that spare not any man,
Took it in rage, though, calm'd, have giv'n it again.

I thank thee for't. My shipwreck now's no ill,
Since I have what my father gave me in his will.
I beg of you, kind friends, this coat of worth,
For it was sometime target to a king.
I know it by this mark: In hac spe vivo:
In this hope I live. He lov'd me dearly,
And for his sake I wish the having of it,
And that you'd guide me to your sov'reign's court,
Where with it I may appear a gentleman.
And if ever my low fortune's better,
I'll pay your bounties; till then rest your debtor.

MR. KAY: Good, good, Sam. I notice you've made a few changes in the text, but I think they work quite well. I especially like how you've added the Latin motto about hope from the tournament scene. That's a nice touch.

(To the class) Of course, you all know that this speech was probably not written by Shakespeare at all, but by a unknown collaborator, whom scholars have dubbed "Playwright X." And the work of Playwright X is considered to be inferior.

That's why it's actually very common for directors to tinker with the text of this play to make it more accessible. So, there's no reason in my mind why Sam shouldn't do the same. As long as he does it well. And I think he has.

SAM: Thank you.

MR. KAY: Now, let me ask you a few questions about the text, Sam, just to make sure we understand everything.

What exactly do you mean by "An armor"?

SAM: A shield.

MR. KAY: And what do you mean by "after all thy crosses"?

SAM: After all the misfortune you've thrown my way.

MR. KAY: What do you mean by "it kept where I kept"?

SAM: I've kept the shield with me since my father died.

MR. KAY: What do you mean by "I'll pay your bounties"?

SAM: I'll repay you for your generosity.

MR. KAY: Good. Now let's talk about this speech for a few minutes before we look at it again.

One of the wonderful things about playing Pericles, Sam, when you do the entire play—and I hope you will some day—is how the man's fortunes ebb and flow as he goes through his life. He loses his kingdom, and he gets it back; he loses his wife, and he gets her back; he loses his daughter, and gets her back; he loses his health, and gets it back; he loses his hope, and gets it back. You get the picture. This is great stuff for an actor to play, and a rewarding role to orchestrate, even if the text does feel clunky on occasion.

But I want to draw your attention now to the most vulnerable and exposed moments in this speech. Because these moments—when he talks to fortune, when he talks to the sea, when he sees his father in his mind's eye, when he realizes what's happened to him, when he decides what he must do next—are not throwaway lines, Sam. They must not be glossed over, because they reveal the very essence of the character. They reveal how the man grows over time, how he learns to face adversity and loss, and how he finds a way to go on.

So let's have another look at this speech, Sam, and let's pay special attention to these things—to fortune, to the sea, to your father, to your realizations, to your decisions. Let's be very specific about how you select, heighten, and arrange your choices for each of them. All right?

SAM: Yes.

MR. KAY: Good. So, please restore to the beginning of the scene, Sam.

(Sam does so.)

And remind us, please—what's your speech objective, Pericles?

SAM: To convince the fishermen to let me have the armor they found in the sea.

MR. KAY: Good, and begin, please.

SAM: I REALIZE THAT THE ARMOR MIGHT ME MINE.

An armor, friends?

THE FISHERMAN.

MR. KAY: Which one?

SAM: Um . . . THE YOUNG FISHERMAN.

MR. KAY: Good, and text?

SAM: I pray you let me see it.

I SEE THE LATIN MOTTO ON THE SHIELD.

I FEEL THE LETTERS WITH MY FINGERS.

I REALIZE THAT THE ARMOR IS MINE.

MR. KAY: *(To the class)* And did you notice how there was no *text* for those three orchestrated moments—seeing the motto, feeling the letters, and realizing that the armor is his? That sequence makes this a very personal moment for the character, and tells us something about who he is, and what he's learned.

(To Sam) Continue, Pericles.

SAM: FORTUNE.

MR. KAY: Is FORTUNE your operative word, or your focal point?

SAM: It's an image. I'm talking to the Goddess of Fortune.

MR. KAY: I see, good—and, continue.

SAM: Thanks, Fortune, yet that after all thy crosses
Thou giv'st me something to repair myself.

THE YOUNG FISHERMAN.

It was mine own,

THE OLD FISHERMAN.

part of my heritage,

THE YOUNG FISHERMAN.

Which my dead father did bequeath to me,
With this strict charge,

THE OLD FISHERMAN.

even as he left his life:

MY FATHER.

MR. KAY: Can you be more specific, please?

SAM: I SEE MY FATHER, ON HIS DEATHBED.

"Keep it, my Pericles; it hath been a shield
'Twixt me and death.

I HEAR MY FATHER'S VOICE, WHISPERING.

For that it sav'd me, keep it.

I FEEL MY FATHER'S HAND, QUIVERING.

In like necessity, (the which the gods
Protect thee from), may it defend thee."

THE OLD FISHERMAN.

It kept where I kept, I so dearly lov'd it,

THE SEA.

Till the rough seas, that spare not any man,
Took it in rage,

I REALIZE THAT THE SEAS HAVE SPARED MY LIFE.

though, calm'd, have giv'n it again.

TO GIVE THANKS.

I thank thee for't.

I REALIZE THAT THE SEA HAS SPARED MY MOST CHERISHED POSSESSION.

My shipwreck now's no ill,
Since I have what my father gave in his will.

I HOPE I CAN CONVINCE THEM TO HELP ME.

I beg of you, kind friends, this coat of worth,
For it was sometime target to a king.

TO IDENTIFY.

I know it by this mark:

THE ARMOR.

In hac spe vivo:

HOPE.

In this *hope* I live.

THE OLD FISHERMAN.

He lov'd me dearly,
And for his sake I wish the having of it,

I'M GOING TO ENTER THE TOURNAMENT IN PENTAPOLIS.

And that you'd guide me to your sov'reign's court,
Where with it I may appear a gentleman.

TO STRIKE A BARGAIN.

And if ever my low fortune's better,
I'll pay your bounties; till then rest your debtor.

MR. KAY: Very well done. Thank you, Sam.

(Sam comes down off the stage.)

(To the class) What I like about Sam's approach to this role now is that he's making choices that are simple and direct and personal, choices that allow him to be *vulnerable,* that reveal his heart to the audience.

Remember, folks, that *Pericles* is one of Shakespeare's *romances,* like *Cymbeline, The Tempest,* and *The Winter's Tale.* It's the work of a mature playwright who's no longer content with the pat formulas of comedy and tragedy.

The romances are, for lack of a better word, *spiritual* plays—full of reconciliation and reunion, of the forces of nature and the supernatural, of the dead coming back to life, of old wounds healed by love, and the power of forgiveness.

So, as an actor, in order to make a play like *Pericles* work, you have to be willing to do what Sam has just done, that is, check your cynicism at the door, and bring your heart, and a sense of wonder, into rehearsal room.

In other words: "It is required you do awake your faith."

(To Sam) Oh, yes, I almost forgot, Sam—what's Pericles' super-objective? Did you figure it out?

SAM: Um . . . Love?

MR. KAY: Love. Yes, Sam, I agree. Love.

And, while we're on the subject of super-objectives . . .

(To Jake) Jake, what about *Arcite*? What's Arcite's super-objective?

JAKE: Oh, that's easy! Nobility.

MR. KAY: Yes, of course. Nobility. It's in the title of the play, isn't it?

(To Trinity) And Trinity—what about *Tamora*? What's Tamora's super-objective?

TRINITY: Um . . . Revenge?

MR. KAY: I think that's what she hopes to achieve before the *play* is over. But what about her *super-objective*? Can you sum up her *life's* pursuit in a single word?

TRINITY: Um . . . Power?

MR. KAY: Yes, that's good. Power.

(To Tim) And Tim—what about Coriolanus? What's his super-objective?

TIM: Um, I guess . . . Honor.

MR. KAY: Honor. Yes, excellent.

(Elena raises her hand.)

MR. KAY: Yes, Elena?

ELENA: Well, I'm confused . . . when do you *do* all this? I mean, *when* do you decide all of your character's objectives?

MR. KAY: As soon as possible.

Remember, Elena, your objective is what you *want,* and your orchestration is how you go about *getting it.* So you always need to know your objectives before you can begin to orchestrate. It's that simple.

Luckily, Shakespeare isn't coy about objectives. He almost always tells you exactly what they are, right up front. Think about it. All week long, we've been hearing his characters tell us, right in the text, *exactly* what they're pursuing, and sometimes even *how* they intend to go about getting it.

Which means a well-trained actor can, by studying the text, determine the speech, scene, act, play, and super-objectives of the character early in the rehearsal process.

Which means you can make a *sketch* of the role before you begin to detail it, a kind of *blueprint* that you can refer to again and again as you work to build the role in rehearsal.

And, of course, once you've built that role, once you've orchestrated every moment of your performance, the objectives become the driving force, the *engine* behind everything the character says and does in the play.

In other words, the objectives make the orchestration *go.*

(Claire raises her hand.)

MR. KAY: Yes, Claire?

CLAIRE: Well, I get that, but when you're working on a role, you know, and you're, like, sweating over the *small* stuff, like a sword fight, or a comic bit, or a kiss, how do you keep from losing track of the *big* stuff, like your play objective and your super-objective?

MR. KAY: I'm glad you brought that up, Claire, because it's a real danger, not just for actors, but for *any* artist working over time on a large-scale project.

It might help you to think of each moment of your orchestration as one of the small dots of color in one of Georges Seurat's master paintings. When you stand up close to one of Seurat's paintings you see only the individual points of color and lose sight of the whole image. But if you step back, the dots blend together, and you begin to see flowers and hats and parasols. Step back again, and you begin to see figures. Step back again, and those figures inhabit a landscape. Step back again, and you can see the glory of the whole picture.

The process of orchestrating a major Shakespearean role is the same process Seurat used to make a painting. You're applying small dots of color to a huge canvas. The dots are your acting choices for each moment, and the canvas is Shakespeare's play.

So when you're orchestrating a role, like Seurat, you must keep stepping back, to see how the moment affects the speech. You must keep stepping back, to see how the speech fits into the scene. You must keep stepping back, to see how the scene drives the act. You must keep stepping back, to see how the act serves the entire play.

In other words, knowing the objectives of the character makes it possible to orchestrate the minute details of your performance without losing sight of the big picture: the play itself.

(Mr. Kay looks up at the clock.)

ᕬᕬ QUESTIONS AND ANSWERS ᕬᕬ

MR. KAY: We have just a few minutes left before we have to stop. Are there any other questions you'd like to ask about what we've been doing this week?

(Avi raises his hand.)

MR. KAY: Yes, Avi?

AVI: So, after you've done all this—broken the text down into speech measures, and chosen operative words, focal points, images, subtext, and actions for every measure in the sequence—what's the best way to put the speech back together again?

MR. KAY: Once you've made acting choices for every measure in your text, there are precisely *three* things you need to do in order to put the speech back together again.

(To the class) Does anybody know what those three things are?

(The class is silent.)

The three things you need to do in order to put these speeches back together are—*(holding up three fingers)*—be sure to write these down, folks . . .

(The students are poised over their notebooks.)

practice . . . practice . . . and practice.

(The class laughs.)

So you've created a brilliant orchestration through lots and lots of painstaking trial and error. *Mazel tov!*

But now is not the time to rehearse the acceptance speech for your Tony Award.

(The class laughs.)

Now is the time to rehearse your orchestration until you've *mastered* it. Now is the time to run through the sequence again and again until it flows *seamlessly* from start to finish. Now is the time to go over your score moment by moment until the individual choices blend together to become a perfectly polished performance.

Remember, folks, that the whole point of breaking a role down into its smallest parts like this is to put it back together again so that it cascades smoothly, like a row of meticulously aligned dominoes, from your first choice to your last choice.

And the only way to make that happen is to practice, practice, practice.

(Sarah raises her hand.)

MR. KAY: Yes, Sarah?

SARAH: So when you work this way, when should you memorize your lines?

MR. KAY: Never.

SARAH: *(A bit stunned)* Never?

MR. KAY: That's right—never. You should never set out to "learn your lines."

That's because when most actors try to "learn their lines," they usually do so through mindless repetition—by *rote*. And memorizing a text by rote is counterproductive, because it puts the words in the wrong side of your brain—the intellectual, analytical side of your brain, which *thinks*, but doesn't *act*.

Have you ever tried to remember your lines, and seen them in your mind as black ink on white paper?

That's because you've memorized the *words*, but not the *impulse* for the words. And that's unfortunate, because now you have to go back and fill in the blanks, search *backwards* for the reason you say the language that you've already committed to memory. Which can be an agonizing process.

Instead of *memorizing* text, you should be up on your feet, working, through trial and error, to create a sequence which *inspires* text. You should be *selecting, arranging,* and *heightening* your acting choices from speech measure to speech measure, rather than attempting to "learn your lines."

And if you spend enough time doing that—orchestrating every moment of your performance—you'll never have to memorize a text by rote. You'll simply remember your text as a result of playing your orchestration.

In other words, if you're working well, you should never have to "learn your lines."

(Sam raises his hand.)

MR. KAY: Yes, Sam?

SAM: How does this work when you have a scene partner?

MR. KAY: Working with other actors onstage is *exactly* the same as working alone. Except for the fact that it's completely *different*.

(The class laughs.)

Because working with other actors means *sharing* an orchestration. Which is much more challenging, and much more complicated than working alone.

It means you must be truly *talking* and *listening* to the other people onstage, as well as executing your own orchestration; not only *acting*, but *reacting* to what your scene partners are doing from moment to moment.

Take the "wooing scene" in *The Taming of the Shrew,* for instance. To make that scene work, the two actors playing Kate and Petruchio must weave their orchestrations together so tightly that they become one thing—like a duet.

Or look at the last scene of *As You Like It.* To make that scene work, an entire *company* must agree on an orchestration to keep the action moving swiftly forward to the grand finale, like a symphony.

Working onstage with other actors is like playing an instrument in an orchestra—it demands that you completely immerse yourself in your individual *part,* while always being mindful of the *whole.*

It demands that you negotiate, through the process of rehearsal, a *shared* orchestration, in which each character's *individual* orchestration blends together to make a meaningful *whole* which tells a story.

(Gabriella raises her hand.)

MR. KAY: Yes, Gabriella.

GABRIELLA: What happens when your director doesn't like the way you've orchestrated a speech?

MR. KAY: You should call your agent and renegotiate your contract.

(The class laughs.)

Seriously, though, if the director doesn't like what you're doing, you should change your orchestration.

Since you can't see your own work, you have no choice but to trust an outside eye to give you feedback, to tell you whether your orchestration is working. And that person, sometimes for better, and sometimes for worse, is the director.

But I suspect there's a bigger question behind your question, Gabriella, which is: how do I work this way when someone else in the room has all the power?

In my experience, most directors simply don't have the time to think about your acting process. They'll just be so grateful that you're bringing new ideas to rehearsal every day, that most of the time you'll get to keep your choices for a role.

But yes, there will also be times when you and a director will disagree about how to orchestrate a role. And that's when it's extremely important to take a *collaborative,* rather than an *adversarial,* approach.

In my opinion, the actors who can walk this tightrope, who can remain open and flexible and cooperative with a director while maintaining a sense of what *they* want to accomplish in a role, are the ones who manage to survive, and thrive, in this crazy business.

(Claire raises her hand.)

MR. KAY: Yes, Claire.

CLAIRE: Yuh, I've been wondering—like, does this only work for Shakespeare? I mean, can you do the same thing with, you know, contemporary roles?

MR. KAY: Yes, Claire, these same tools can, like, totally be used for contemporary roles.

For example: can you divide your text into speech measures when you're working on an Ibsen? Why, yes! I can assure you that people will do such things.

Can you connect with focal points when you're playing a role in an Odets? You're goddamn right, you can, baby!

Can you work with images when you're staging a Williams? Why, of course—especially when you're ridin' on that hot tin streetcar named *Iguana*.

Can you play actions when you're acting in a Mamet? Abso-fuckin'-lutely!

Can you use subtext when you're performing in a Chekhov? Someday, we will know. But until then, we must work. We must work.

(The class laughs.)

On the other hand, folks, having said all that, it's important to keep in mind that these tools cannot always be used for contemporary roles. Because playing contemporary roles means imitating modern behavior. And imitating modern behavior often means breaking the rules of orchestration.

How? By slurring speech measures together, ignoring punctuation, taking illogical pauses, neglecting operative words, stressing pronouns, negatives, conjunctions, and prepositions, failing to connect with focal points, panning and scanning through many focal points, disregarding images in the text, blurring images together, playing the same action repeatedly, switching actions at illogical pauses, on so on and so forth . . .

In other words, all the habits I've been trying to break you of for the past two years!

(The class laughs.)

MADISON: *(Raising her hand)* What about TV?

MR. KAY: Yes, Madison, what about TV?

MADISON: Can you work this way in front of a TV camera?

MR. KAY: Sure you can! For example: what tools can you use to get a confession out of a suspect on a cop show?

MADISON: Um . . . actions?

MR. KAY: Yes, of course—you use a variety of actions in order to make the suspect confess.

And what tools can you use to play a wife secretly fantasizing about sleeping with her husband's best friend on a soap opera?

TRINITY: Subtext?

MR. KAY: Yes, Trinity—you fill yourself up with secret hopes and dreams while the camera moves in for your close-up.

And what tools can you use to testify in a rape trial in a courtroom drama?

GABRIELLA: Images?

MR. KAY: Yes, Gabriella. You replay images of the rape in your mind—what you see-hear-taste-touch-smell—as you testify.

And what tools can you use to talk to your friends on a TV sitcom?

JESSEE: Focal points!

MR. KAY: You bet, Jesse. You aim specific punch lines at specific friends.

And what tools can you use to divide up your copy for a laxative ad?

AVI: Speech measures.

MR. KAY: Of course, Avi. You divide your copy into speech measures.

NOAH: *Easily digestible* speech measures!

(The class laughs.)

DANTE: *(Raising his hand)* So, what about film? Can you work this way in front of a movie camera?

MR. KAY: Absolutely, Dante! For example, when might you use *speech measures* in shooting a film?

DANTE: Um . . . how about . . . delivering a eulogy for fishermen lost at sea?

MR. KAY: Yes, a eulogy, Dante, good.

And when might you use *focal points* in a film?

JAKE: When you're surrounded by bloodsucking aliens!

MR. KAY: Yes! Especially when the aliens are actually tennis balls on sticks, and the effects department will use a computer to fill in the aliens later.

When might you use *images* in a film?

SAM: When you're standing on the bow of a sinking ship.

MR. KAY: Yes, especially when you're actually standing on a box in front of a blue screen.

And when might you use *subtext* in a film?

TAYO: When you see dead people in your house.

MR. KAY: Yes, Tayo, you fill yourself up with secret fears as you creep down the hall to find out why the lights suddenly went out.

And when might you use *actions* in a film?

AVI: When you're rousing the team at halftime in the locker room.

MR. KAY: Yes, excellent! You orchestrate a variety of actions in order to spur the team on to victory.

You see folks, it doesn't matter whether you're working in the theater, or in television, or in film. The basic principles and tools of orchestration can help you to meet all of these acting challenges, and more, in all of these mediums, provided that you know how to use them *masterfully,* and use them *invisibly.*

In other words, my friends, if you can master the art of orchestrating *Shakespeare* as an actor, you can do *anything.*

(Jake raises his hand.)

MR. KAY: Yes, Jake?

JAKE: How long does it take before this way of working becomes second nature?

MR. KAY: That depends entirely upon your talent, and experience.

I think we've already seen that some of these tools will suit your talents perfectly, and will come easily and naturally to you right away. Some of these tools will be more difficult for you to manage, and will require a lot of hard work and discipline before you can master their use. And some of these tools will always seem to elude you entirely.

The main thing to remember is that it takes decades of experience in the theater to master *all* of the tools you've been acquiring. And that your work is just beginning. So be patient with yourselves.

(Rachel raises her hand.)

MR. KAY: Yes, Rachel?

RACHEL: How do you know when your orchestration is finished?

MR. KAY: The process of orchestration is *never* finished. An actor who is truly an artist and is open to new ideas will always be making subtle changes in his orchestration, adjusting for audience responses, reacting to nuances in a partner's performance, or allowing for sudden divine inspiration. An orchestration must be constantly fine-tuned, adjusted, and readjusted. It is never finished.

That is, not until the play closes.

(Mr. Kay looks up at the clock.)

Well, I'm sorry to say that we're out of time, folks. Thank you very much for your efforts this week. You've done some great work.

You're beginning to understand how to make artistic choices based on an understanding of a play. How to shape these choices, moment by moment, into a performance. How to create a role.

You're beginning to understand the art of orchestration.

Which means you're becoming not just actors, but *artists.*

(Pause. A moment of grace.)

Next week, we'll begin looking at those Shakespearean *scenes* I assigned, using these same tools to orchestrate them from moment to moment.

See you tomorrow.

BLACKOUT.

Index

A

actions
  as a familiar term, xiv
  bleeding together, 166, 168
  converted from qualities,
    177–181
  defined, 139
  differences between, 165–168
  from decisions, 137
  from secret intentions, 124
  in complex orchestration, 186,
    190–191, 195–205, 208–213,
    218, 221, 228, 230, 233–235,
    241–243, 248–250
  in stillness, 154, 160
  Laban effort actions, 154–160,
    190
  on film, 258
  on television, 256
  opposing physical movements,
    141–145
  progressions, 156, 160, 165,
    166, 167,
  psycho-physical actions,
    163–168, 191, 196–204,
    209–213, 218–221, 228–230,
    234–235, 241–243, 248–250
  stated as metaphor, 164
  stated as an idiomatic

  expression, 164
  sudden, 155, 156, 158, 159
  sustained, 155, 156, 158, 159
  revealing qualities, 178
  translating director-speak, 178,
    181
  two opposing actions, 147–151,
    190
  unplayable, 163–164, 178, 181
  using a thesaurus, 151
  variety, 151, 154, 160
  with multiple focal points,
    171–175
Actor's Studio, The, xiii
actor's toolkit, the, 183, 186, 194
Adler, Stella, xii
All's Well that Ends Well
  Bertram, 105, 107, 109, 110,
  Countess of Rousillion, The,
    105–111
  Helena, 105–111
American Laboratory Theater, The,
    xiii
Antony and Cleopatra
  Antony, 118–124
  Charmian, 118–124
  Cleopatra, 117–124
  Enobarbus, 124
  Fulvia, 118, 123
As You Like It

final scene, 255
Phoebe, 145–151
Rosalind (Ganymede), 146–148
Silvius, 145–151

Imogen, 183–191
King Cymbeline, 184, 186, 189
Pisanio, 184, 188
Posthumus, 184, 186, 189
Queen, The, 186, 189

B

Barton, John, xi, xiii
Berry, Cicely, xi, xiii
Boleslavsky, Richard, xiii–xiv
   Acting: The First Six Lessons,
      xiii, xiv
Branagh, Kenneth, xi
Brando, Marlon, xii, xiii
Brookfield Center, xii

D

Damon, Matt, xii
Danes, Claire, xi
decisions (*see* spoken subtext)
decisions, fatally flawed, 230
Dench, Judi, xi
DiCaprio, Leonardo, xi
discipline, 81, 258

C

Character
   revealed through actions, 180
   complexity and contradiction in,
      100–101
chasing the text, 18
Chekhov, Anton, 256
chivalry, 240
Cliff's Notes, 107
Clurman, Harold, xii
comedy, 51, 128, 174, 207
commitment, 111, 207, 124, 148,
   205, 207
complex orchestration (*see* orchestration)
Condell, Henry, 20
contemporizing (*see* speech measures)
Coriolanus
   Aufidius, 225–230
   Coriolanus, 225–230, 251
courage, 104, 108, 110, 111,
   200–201
Crawford, Cheryl, xii
Cymbeline

E

Einstein's "thought-experiment,"
   223
emotions, 18, 69, 81, 100, 213–222

F

figures of speech
   anaphora, 167
   antithesis, 29, 123
film acting, 257–258
Fletcher, John, 239–240
focal points
   alternating between audience and
      self, 51–55
   availability to the audience, 47,
      52
   consistency, 92
   defined, 33
   describe the person in the audi-
      ence, 53–55, 188, 210, 211,
      212
   direct address, 44–48, 174–175
   imagined scene partners, 36

in complex orchestration,
    186–191, 195–205, 208–213,
    217–221, 228–230, 233–235,
    241–243, 248–250
  initiating and terminating, 86
  in the balcony, 48
  multiple focal points, 58
  multitasking, 58
  on film, 257
  on television, 257
  panning and scanning, 45, 47,
    256
  reviewing a sequence without
    text, 63
Folio, the first, 20, 75
Fonda, Jane, xii
fourth wall, the, 174

G

given circumstances, xiv
Greeks, The, xiv
Group Theatre, The, xii, xiii

H

Hamlet
  Claudius, 67
  film version, xi
  Gertrude, 66–72
  Hamlet, 137, 230
  King Hamlet, 69
  Laertes, 67, 230
  Ophelia, 67–72
  Polonius, 69
Hanks, Tom, xii
Harris, Julie, xii
Heminge, John, 20
Henry the Fifth
  Chorus, 88–96
  King Henry the Fifth, 88–96
Henry the Fourth, Part Two

Falstaff, 131
  Harry Percy (Hotspur), 214–222
  King Henry the Fourth, 216
  Lady Percy, 214–222
  Northumberland, 214–222
  Prince Hal (Monmouth), 131,
    138, 214, 216, 221
  Rumor, 90
Henry the Sixth, Part One
  Charles the Dauphin, 175–181
  Joan la Pucelle, 175–181
Henry the Sixth, Part Three
  King Henry the Sixth, 2–10, 13,
    56
  Prince Edward, 56
  Queen Margaret, 3
  Warwick, 3, 56
honor, 240, 251
Hopkins, Anthony, xi

I

Ibsen, Henrik, 256
illogical pauses (*see* speech meas-
    ures)
images
  defined, 65
  in complex orchestration, 186,
    188–189, 195–205, 208–213,
    217–221, 228–230, 234–235,
    241–243, 248–250
  movie in your head, 72, 195
  on film, 257
  on television, 257
  personal, 8, 65–66, 76, 81, 101
  see-hear-taste-touch-smell,
    defined, 66
  using multiple focal points,
    76–81
  using single focal points, 69–72
  while talking to scene partners,
    84–88
  while talking to the audience, 91

J

Jacobi, Derek, xi
Joan of Arc, 177
Julius Caesar
  Antony, 230
  Brutus, 21–32, 230
  Caesar, 21–31, 230

K

Kazan, Elia, xii
Keaton, Michael, xi
Kennedy, John F., 8
King John
  Arthur, 162
  Blanche, 162
  Cardinal Pandulph, 161–168, 171
  King John, 161
  Lewis, 161–168, 171
King, Jr., Martin Luther, 8, 167
King Lear
  Edgar, 131–137
  Edmund, 44, 133
  Gloucester, 133
Kline, Kevin, xii

L

Laban, Rudolf, 154–155
Laban effort actions (*see* actions)
Lange, Jessica, xi
Lemmon, Jack, xi
Lincoln, Abraham, 167
logical pauses (*see* speech measures)
Love's Labors Lost
  Berowne, 33–41
  Dumaine, 34–40
  film version, xi
  King of Navarre, The, 34–40
  Longaville, 34–40
  Princess of France, The, 34

M

Macbeth
  Duncan, 192
  Lady Macbeth, 202
  Macbeth, 131, 192–205
  Macduff, his wife and children, 230
Mamet, David, 256
Measure for Measure
  Angelo, 97–104, 131
  Claudio, 98, 100, 103
  Isabella, 98–104, 131, 138
memorizing, 18, 64, 76, 107, 254
Merchant of Venice, The
  Bassanio, 111–117
  Portia, 111–117
  Shylock, 131
Midsummer Night's Dream, A
  Bottom, 84
  Oberon, 82–88
  Puck, 82–88
  Titania, 131
Miller, Arthur, 240
Molière, 240
Moscow Art Company, xiii
Movement
  dance, 1, 10, 49
  fencing, 1, 49
  focusing physical energies, 36, 40, 49, 157
  juggling, 1
  Laban effort actions (*see* actions)
  opposing physical movements (*see* actions)
  physicalizing decisions, 134
  physicalizing realizations, 128
  physical response to subtext, 102, 117
  physical transformation, 134–137
  physical variety, 63
  psycho-physical actions (*see* actions)

tai chi, 49
training, 88
yoga, 49
Much Ado about Nothing
  Beatrice, 49–54
  Benedick, 49–55
  Film version, xi
  Leonato, 49
mythology (see Shakespeare's texts)

N

Newman, Paul, xii
Nicholson, Jack, xii

O

objectives
  act objectives, 231, 233, 236,
    237, 238, 243, 245
  added up, 238, 252
  as a familiar term, xiv
  determined from the text, 251
  play objectives, 88, 238,
    240–241, 244, 245,
  scene objectives, 225, 231, 237,
    243, 245
  speech objectives, 3, 11, 13, 21,
    34, 42, 50, 56, 67, 73, 82,
    88, 98, 105, 112, 118, 125,
    127, 131, 140, 146, 161, 196,
    175, 184, 192, 206, 214, 223,
    225, 231, 237, 243, 245
  super-objectives, 245–246, 251
  win, lose, or change, 244
obstacles
  as a familiar term, xiv
  in speeches, 3, 11, 21, 34, 42,
    50, 56, 67, 73, 82, 89, 98,
    105, 112, 118, 125, 131, 140,
    141, 146, 152, 161, 169, 176,
    184, 192, 206, 215, 221, 223,
    225, 231, 237, 245

Odets, Clifford, 256
operative words
  choosing, 23–32
  defined, 23
  in complex orchestration, 187,
    200, 218
  listing, 31
  primary stress, 23
  secondary stress, 23, 28, 30
  tertiary stress, 23
  testing, 25
  using parts of speech, 27
orchestration
  adjusting, 258
  breaking the rules, 256
  complex orchestration, defined,
    183
  contemporary roles, 256
  creating a score, 94–96, 151,
    221–222, 224
  defined, 2
  directors, collaborating with,
    178–180, 255
  finishing, 258
  mastering, 253
  practicing, 253
  process, 107, 144, 151, 181,
    205, 252, 258
  reliability, 88, 96
  repeatability, 88, 96, 154, 168,
    207, 213
  select, arrange, and heighten, 2,
    20, 63, 72, 103, 139, 151,
    160, 183, 248, 254
  sharing with a company, 255
  sharing with scene partners,
    254–255
  speaking the score aloud, 95–96
  specificity, 151, 207
  textual repetitions, 62, 103
  through improvisation, 207
  trial and error, 9, 62, 103, 107,
    191, 205, 207, 221
  without text, 199, 248,

variety, 58, 120, 124, 221
Othello
  Cassio, 42–49
  Desdemona, 42–49, 230
  Iago, 42–49, 130
  Othello, 42–49, 130, 230

P

Page, Geraldine, xii
Paltrow, Gwyeth, xii
Pericles
  Gower, 90
  Pericles, 90, 244–251
  Thaisa, 245
  two fishermen, 244–251
playwright x, 247
previsualization, 223–224
psychological realism, xii, xiii
public and private, 112, 233–236
punctuation
  differences in various editions,
    19–20
  honoring, 14–18, 187
  in complex orchestration, 187

Q

Quartos, 20, 75
questions, the four basic, 223

R

realizations (*see* spoken subtext)
rehearsal, 62, 154, 244, 251, 255
Richard the Second
  Henry Bolingbroke, 152–160
  King Richard, 152–160
  Northumberland, 152–160
Richard the Third
  Lady Anne, 55–64

Richard, 44, 55–64
Roberts, Julia, xii
Rodenburg, Patsy, xi, xiii
Romances, Shakespeare's, 250
Romeo and Juliet
  Chorus, 90
  film version, xi
  Juliet, 73–81, 130, 138, 230
  Romeo, 73–81, 130, 230
Roosevelt, Franklin D., 8

S

scansion
  analyzing the meter, 4, 25
  contractions, 26
  iambic pentameter, 25
  missing syllables, 199
  pyrrhic, 1
  spondee, 1
  stressed syllables, 25, 26
Schmidt's Lexicon, 4
Scofield, Paul, xi
Seurat's master paintings, 252
Shakespeare scholars, 12, 19–20,
    41, 75, 145,
Shakespeare's texts
  changing words, 12, 185, 247
  conflating, 41
  cutting, 35, 106–107, 144–145,
    176, 185, 216
  cutting and pasting, 119, 232
  directorial emendations, 12, 41,
    106, 247
  editions of, 19
  mythology, 106–107
  paraphrasing, 107
Shaw, George Bernard, 240
Silverstone, Alicia, xi
speech measures
  choosing the right tool for, 187
  contemporizing, 9
  defined, 5

illogical pauses, 9, 256
in complex orchestration, 187,
   191, 208
lengths, 5
logical pauses, 9
on film, 257
on television, 257
parcel of text, 5
units of sense, 5, 6
spoken subtext
decisions, 134–138, 175, 186,
   190, 196, 198, 199, 204, 212,
   227, 229, 243, 248, 250
defined, 97
head, heart, guts, and groin,
   100–104, 189, 198, 200, 241,
   243
in complex orchestration, 186,
   189–190, 195–205, 208–213,
   217–221, 228–230, 233–235,
   241–243, 248–250
on film, 257–258
on television, 257
personalizing, 111
phrasing positive intentions, 116
realizations, 127–131, 175, 186,
   189, 196, 212, 213, 227, 228,
   229, 241, 242, 248, 249
rephrasing negative decisions,
   242
secret fears, 108–111, 189, 190,
   197, 203, 209, 210
secret hopes and dreams,
   113–117, 190, 198, 203, 205,
   210, 213, 217, 219, 243, 250
secret intentions, 120–124, 217,
   221
spontaneity, 64, 207, 213
Stanislavsky, Constantin
Actor Prepares, An, xii, xiii,
Building a Character, xiii
Stanislavsky-based training,
   xii–xiii
Stanislavsky System, The, xiii

Strasberg, Lee, xii, xiii
Streep, Meryl, xii
strip of terror, the, 19

T

talking and listening, 9, 254
Taming of the Shrew, The
Kate, 255
Petruchio, 255
technique, 81
television, 160, 256–257
Tempest, The
Caliban, 205–213
Prospero, 137
Trinculo, 205–213
Thompson, Emma, xi
Titus Andronicus
Aaron, 44, 236
film version, xi
Saturninus, 231–236
Tamora, 231–236, 251
Titus Andronicus, 231–236
Troilus and Cressida
Achilles, 230
Cressida, 131, 139–145
Hector, 230
Pandarus, 139–145
Troilus, 131, 139–145
Thatcher, Margaret, xi
Twelfth Night
Malvolio, 125–130, 137
Olivia, 125–130
Orsino, 125–130
Viola, 124–131
Two Gentlemen of Verona, The
Julia, 169–175
Lucetta, 169–171
Proteus, 130, 169–175
Sylvia, 130
Two Noble Kinsmen, The
Arcite, 237–244, 251
Emilia, 237–244

Palamon, 237–244
Theseus, 241

V

Voice and Speech
    articulation, 83, 84, 88
    breath capacity, 10
    breath support, 36, 47, 84
    breathy tone, 84
    consonants, 135, 242
    duration, 23
    dynamic variety, 48
    hearing and understanding, 10,
        47, 84
    inhalations, 18, 33, 46–48, 59,
        69, 84, 85, 86, 88, 148, 164,
        165, 168
    pitch, 23, 167
    random vocalization, 241

resonance, 36, 40, 47, 48
response to images, 79
response to subtext, 101, 117,
    129
tonal quality, 47, 88
vocal builds, 166–167
vocal variety, 40, 63, 157
volume, 23, 48, 167
vulnerability, 104, 111, 248, 250

W

Webster's Dictionary, 4
Williams, Tennessee, 256
    Streetcar Named Desire, A, xiii
Winter's Tale, The
    King Leontes, 10–20
    Queen Hermione, 10–20
    Time, 90

Books from Allworth Press

Allworth Press is an imprint of Allworth Communications, Inc. Selected titles are listed below.

Clues to Acting Shakespeare
by Wesley Van Tassel (paperback, 6 × 9, 208 pages, $16.95)

Movement for Actors
edited by Nicole Potter (paperback, 6 × 9, 288 pages, $19.95)

Acting for Film
by Cathy Haase (paperback, 6 × 9, 224 pages, $19.95)

Creating Your Own Monologue
by Glenn Alterman (paperback, 6 × 9, 192 pages, $14.95)

Promoting Your Acting Career
by Glenn Alterman (paperback, 6 × 9, 224 pages, $18.95)

An Actor's Guide—Making It in New York City
by Glenn Alterman (paperback, 6 × 9, 288 pages, $19.95)

Career Solutions for Creative People
by Dr. Rhonda Ormont (paperback, 6 × 9, 320 pages, $19.95)

Building the Successful Theater Company
by Lisa Mulcahy (paperback, 6 × 9, 240 pages, $19.95)

Technical Theater for Nontechnical People
by Drew Campbell (paperback, 6 × 9, 256 pages, $18.95)

The Health and Safety Guide for Film, TV and Theater
by Monona Rossol (paperback, 6 × 9, 256 pages, $19.95)

The Perfect Stage Crew: The Compleat Technical Guide for High School, College, and Community Theater
by John Kaluta (paperback, 6 × 9, 256 pages, $19.95)

Producing Your Own Showcase
by Paul Harris (paperback, 6 × 9, 240 pages, $18.95)

Please write to request our free catalog. To order by credit card, call 1-800-491-2808 or send a check or money order to Allworth Press, 10 East 23rd Street, Suite 510, New York, NY 10010. Include $5 for shipping and handling for the first book ordered and $1 for each additional book. Ten dollars plus $1 for each additional book if ordering from Canada. New York State residents must add sales tax.

To see our complete catalog on the World Wide Web, or to order online, you can find us at ***www.allworth.com***.